FAMILIES
VALUED

FAMILIES VALUED

Parenting and Politics
for the Good of All Children

JACK NELSON - PALLMEYER

Friendship Press · New York

Library of Congress Cataloging-in-Publication Data

Nelson-Pallmeyer, Jack.
    Families valued : parenting and politics for the good of all
children / Jack Nelson-Pallmeyer.
      p. cm.
    ISBN 0-377-00309-3
    1. Parenting – United States. 2. Children – United States –
Attitudes. 3. Social values. Title.
HQ755.8.N458 1996
649'.1 – dc20   96-24592
                                                      CIP

To Sara, Hannah, Audrey, and Naomi,
who fill my life with hope and love

"I cried out to God, 'Show me your face,'
and God sent me a child."

—Susan Marie Doyle

Contents

Preface

Shortly before her third birthday our youngest daughter, Naomi, established a pattern of waking up in the middle of the night and calling for Mom or Dad. One evening, as I walked her to the room she shares with her two older sisters, I reminded her that we loved her deeply but that moms and dads appreciate and need uninterrupted sleep. "Dad," she explained matter-of-factly, "my dreams are full of troubles."

"Full of troubles" seems an apt description of how many parents and children experience the present and a fair characterization of our dreams for the future. Evidence abounds of troubled children's lives, of families in disarray, and of a deepening crisis of values and priorities within the broader society and world of which we are a part. How many families in our society live a nightmare and how many of us, more privileged perhaps, are reasonably comfortable and yet look at the future with a measure of fear and trembling? It seems many of us — parents, grandparents, teachers, and others whose lives intersect with children — live somewhere between honesty and hope.

"Dreams full of troubles" is suggestive in another way as well. Not only are our hopes for children sometimes undermined by harsh realities of poverty and crime, violence and neglect, inequality and deprivation, drugs and abuse, but our dreams themselves may fall victim to our lack of imagination. Children of affluence abandoned to Nintendo have much in common with those abandoned to mean streets. Even our dreams of the good life, it seems, are often short-sighted, even harmful to children. Family values, by way of example, undoubtedly vital and important, have been so desecrated in present public debate that they may be killing us. The unspoken and unfortunate truth is that troubled children's lives are rooted in dysfunctional adult behaviors, both personal and political. It follows, therefore, that if we are to move beyond the rhetoric of family values to homes and a society in which all families and children are valued, then quite simply we must be willing to change the direction of our lives and our society.

Families Valued: Parenting and Politics for the Good of all Children is a father's reflection on how the needs of children could change personal and social priorities. My hope is rooted in the belief that love for children and troubled dreams can prompt us to change course. Taking the needs of children and families seriously, in other words, offers the possibility for personal and social transformation, hope, and renewal.

Introduction

It's a sunny afternoon in the summer of 1993. My three-year-old daughter, Audrey, and her nine-month-old sister, Naomi, have set out with me to pick up their oldest sister, Hannah, from an afternoon program at the local park and school. Audrey and I are excited as she climbs on her red tricycle, a hand-me-down of a hand-me-down that is so old it is made of metal. She positions herself carefully on the seat as I strap Naomi into another hand-me-down, an old stroller that like a cat has nine lives.

Hand-me-downs are important to our family. They reflect choices we make and symbolize the family value system we strive for in which time is valued more than money, an alternative lifestyle over unfettered consumption, durable goods over disposables, coparenting and part-time employment more than lofty careers and traditional roles, community more than isolated affluence. Hand-me-downs not only save us money that is made available for other purposes; they give our children a sense of belonging to an extended family and community, of being connected to cousins, friends, and family, to the joys and needs of others who came before us. Hand-me-downs demonstrate that things are most valuable when they are cared for. A gift received is a future gift to be given. A possession well cared for can be passed on to younger siblings or friends or given to the poor. Hand-me-downs provide us with an opportunity to talk to our children about the environment, land and landfills, garbage and possessions. Because our children are comfortable with used clothes, tricycles, and other items, it isn't such a big leap for them or ourselves to see that when we forego purchase of unnecessary items we are being considerate of future generations. Our children are learning that although we may be rich enough to have options when it

1

comes to our family's lifestyle, we cannot afford to be wasteful nor can the world afford our waste.

Audrey is setting out on the longest tricycle journey of her life, a straight block-and-a-half shot down level sidewalks to the school. Her smile, wide as a canyon, will soon become a tear-soaked frown.

Audrey pedals flawlessly and beams radiantly as each harmonious movement of her legs fills her with pride. Naomi, her legs extended from the stroller, kicks in rhythm with the wheels on the sidewalk. She rides in joyful expectation of seeing Hannah and marks our arrival with a squeal. It is then that Audrey asks a simple question. It is a question that shatters the distance of nearly forty years separating my childhood from hers. "Daddy," she says, climbing down from her trike, "don't you think we should bring the tricycle inside?"

The question seems so natural to her that she could be asking me if I like popcorn. Audrey is concerned, but in retrospect it is the casual nature of her question that disturbs me most. My initial response has no retrospective knowledge in it. I dismiss her concern as easily as I brush away an unwelcome fly. "No, Audrey," I say. "The tricycle will be fine."

Now, forgive me some parental license as I tell you that Audrey, like each child in Garrison Keillor's Lake Wobegon, is above average. She is our resident philosopher, always grasping connections, reasoning in ways that astound me. By way of example, let me recount an incident that occurred sometime before her fourth birthday.

I'm sitting in the kitchen looking at the paper and drinking a soda. For a number of reasons I'm trying to drink less soda, and I don't like my small children to have it very often. It's not a big issue, and somewhat irrationally as Audrey approaches an image of my father smoking after he'd promised to quit flashes into my mind. Drinking soda doesn't cause lung cancer, and I've never promised not to drink it. However, I am troubled because children learn by seeing, and I am modeling a behavior that I dislike. I would feel the same way if I were to watch a lot of television while restricting my children's viewing. "Monkey see, monkey do," as the saying goes. Or, as my daughter Hannah, who never quite got the saying right, used to say, "Monkey do, monkey don't."

Audrey looks around, sees her cup sitting on a nearby counter, re-trieves it, and walks over to me cup in hand. I share a little soda with her. "Is that a lot?" she asks. "Yes," I say, thinking that any amount will pacify her. However, Audrey looks at the can and the amount of soda in her cup and doesn't like what she sees. She isn't fussing, cry-ing, whining, or any such thing, but she is unhappy with a situation that seems unfair. She illustrates her point with an analogy.

On the table along with the soda is a pitcher of apple juice, which proves to be my undoing. "Dad," Audrey says, looking at the apple juice. "Would you say that is a lot?" Oblivious to a three-year-old's strategy of entrapment, I glance at the pitcher and answer affirma-tively. "Yes, Audrey, that is a lot." Audrey then takes her cup, looks into it and lifts it in my direction. "Then how can you say this is a lot?"

I feel awe for her ability to reason and her sense of fairness. Her reasoning then and now warrants respect. So too does her concern about her tricycle.

The school entrance before us, her tricycle behind, Audrey senses my dismissal of her question. "Dad," she repeats, in a voice that makes it clear that my first assurance has failed to reassure her, "don't you think we should bring the tricycle inside?" She then verbalizes the reason for her fear. "Somebody might take it."

Audrey has given me a second chance to take her and her imme-diate concern seriously, and I blow it. "It's okay," I say. "No one will take your tricycle. We'll be inside only a few minutes." Audrey casts one last glance back and then follows me inside. We find Hannah and depart quickly, as I knew we would. Leaving the school, how-ever, we discover, as you may have guessed, that Audrey's tricycle is gone.

We look up and down the street and spot a neighbor standing in the alley holding a deformed piece of metal, the remains of Audrey's tricycle. Three young boys, she tells us, carried the trike from the school. They took turns smashing it against the pavement until she chased them away.

As Audrey looks at her tricycle, her eyes fill with tears. I apol-ogize. I am amazed she isn't angry with me. She is sad. And perplexed. "Daddy," she says, a hand on her demolished trike and a look on her face that I will never forget, "why would anyone do this?"

You might want to take a moment and think about how you would answer her question: Why would anyone take the tricycle of an innocent three-year-old, not to steal it for their own use, but to pound it against unforgiving pavement?

Audrey spoke clearly to me about her fear. I didn't listen very well, and my failure to do so resulted in both a wrecked tricycle and emotional trauma. There are similar consequences to our failure as parents and as a society to digest the full weight of judgment that troubled children's lives bring against adults concerning personal and social priorities. *Families Valued: Parenting and Politics for the Good of All Children* explores what we would do differently as parents and as a society if we cared about children. It is one parent's attempt to allow children's lives to judge our own, to let their stories help us reassess personal choices and the economic and social priorities of our country.

"Why would anyone do this?" There may be no good answer to Audrey's question, perhaps no right one, but how we answer it matters. The innocent query of a three-year-old can, if we are open to an honest assessment of our lives and our society, lead us on a journey where personal and social responsibility meet, and where issues of race, parenting, poverty, and politics clash or converge. How we answer Audrey's question may determine the future, not only of our children, but of our society in which troubled kids are a disturbing symbol of a deeper crisis.

Part I

Chapter 1

A Loss of Innocence

We have to face the fact that we have the highest murder rate in the world, and that our children are more at risk here than they would be in most other countries and in all other advanced countries.
—President Bill Clinton

A smashed tricycle isn't a catastrophic event, even for a three-year-old. We came home, got out the hammer, and pounded, straightened, and improvised as best we could. Miraculously, the trike "worked," but a block-and-a-half trip was out of the question: the pedals turned with great difficulty, and when Audrey sat on the seat she leaned so far to the right that it made for uncomfortable travel. She didn't complain, but she spent less time on her tricycle in the weeks that followed.

Perhaps it is a testimony to the resiliency of children, but the smashed tricycle seemed more disturbing to me than to Audrey. On the positive side I relearned the valuable lesson that children, even small children, need to be heard and taken seriously. Generally speaking, children are wiser, more perceptive, and more forgiving than adults give them credit for.

A deep wave of sadness engulfed me following the incident. Searching for its source, I realized that rightly or wrongly I was troubled by how much the world had changed since I was a child. Audrey had asked me a question that seemed as foreign to my childhood as Einstein's theory of relativity. The working-class neighborhood of my earliest memories is one in which we locked neither bicycles nor houses. Even if Audrey's trike had not been stolen and trashed, the very fact that *my three-year-old had internalized and expressed fear that her trike might be stolen* seemed alarming. I resented her early loss of innocence.

This reaction on my part may seem naive, remarkably so, to many. The world, after all, is not and perhaps never has been a place of innocence for most children. I know that. Nearly twenty years before Audrey's tricycle was trashed I taught at a poor school in Chicago where a fourth-grader informed me that she would be unable to attend an after-school program because she had to clean the blood off her steps from the previous night's murder. One of my students, whose brother died when gang members slit his throat, walked me home each night after basketball practice. I know that young girls in Washington, D.C., plan their funerals because so many of their friends die in the street violence that pervades their neighborhoods.

I don't think of myself as sheltered. Although I was too young for direct memories of the Holocaust, I visited memorials in Israel that graphically detailed the tragedy. As a college student on a train to Hiroshima I picked up a discarded newspaper whose headline indicated that U.S. Secretary of State Henry Kissinger had threatened to use nuclear weapons against North Vietnam. Several hours later I saw devastating footage and photographs of Hiroshima after the United States dropped an atomic bomb on civilian populations. Still etched in my memory is the image of a child covered with burns, sitting in a fetal position, shivering uncontrollably.

I witnessed children starving to death or seriously malnourished in India. I wrote about my encounter with one child as a young college student in *Hunger for Justice:*

> One day as I walked through the streets of Calcutta feeling guilty and powerless, I decided to buy bananas and distribute them to children. One child whose arms had been cut off above the elbow ran up to me. He looked at me intensely, and I put a banana under his arm pit. His face grew more stern, and his brown eyes cut to the center of my conscience and my heart. So I took another banana and put it under his other stumplike arm. At that moment his face broke into a smile, and he ran away into the street and disappeared.

I felt better about myself for just a moment as the child's smile radiated hope to this guilt-ridden American. But I continued walking, and there were many children in need and my money was limited. After a while my heart that had been opened by the suffering of children began to harden. I could not deal with their suffering or with the inadequacy of my response. So I stopped feeling or caring or at least I tried to. As I emotionally distanced myself from those who suffered, I began blaming the poor for their poverty.[1]

When I lived in Nicaragua in the mid-1980s, I saw children brutalized by violence. Mines placed indiscriminately on roads by U.S.-backed contra forces ripped through the flesh of children and adults alike. I watched schoolchildren crawl on their stomachs from their classrooms to the nearby bomb shelters with pencils in their mouths (biting down on something would keep their mouths closed and prevent their eardrums from bursting in the event of bombs blasting nearby). And although I was too young and too removed to have been an active participant in the civil rights movement, I remember television images of vicious dogs and fire hoses being turned on women and children and other demonstrators.

In short, I am not unfamiliar with injustice and evil and their consequences for children. And I understand that in the context of the events and issues described above, a trashed tricycle is, relatively speaking, a minor offense. But it serves as a powerful symbol of children being unsafe, of kids being victimized by other kids, and of a society in crisis.

There is a debate raging in our country about whether crime is in fact a growing problem. Even government statistics can't agree. Using data compiled by the Federal Bureau of Investigation (FBI) suggests a *rising* crime rate, especially for violent crime. Violent crime, according to FBI statistics, has risen by 81 percent since 1973 and more than quadrupled since 1960. However, according to National Crime Victimization Surveys carried out by the Bureau of

Justice Statistics, which like the FBI is a branch of the Department of Justice, violent crimes have actually *decreased* slightly since 1973.[2]

Statistics may cloud the issue, but several things seem clear. First, in daily papers and nightly newscasts, in television shows, movies, and music, in our cities and in our homes, in Bosnia and in our cartoons, in our nation's foreign policy and in our glorification of war, violence and crime, actual and described, permeate our lives. New Testament scholar Walter Wink calls violence "the ethos of our times," "the spirituality of the modern world," and "the real religion of America."[3] Violence, in one way or another, is the predominant story line in present U.S. culture.

Second, media coverage of crime and violence has increased dramatically in recent years. According to one study, time devoted to crime on the three nightly network news shows in the three years ending with January 1992 averaged 67 minutes a month. From October 1993 until January 1994, however, crime coverage averaged 157 minutes a month.[4] Increased media attention given to crime has impacted public perceptions. In a *Washington Post*/ABC national poll conducted in June 1993, only 5 percent of those polled named crime the most important issue facing the country. In February 1994, after increased media coverage of crime, 31 percent of those polled said crime was the most important issue, far surpassing any other concern. A month later 65 percent of those polled by the *Los Angeles Times* said they got their information about crime from the media.[5] Heightened coverage of crime, our actual experiences of "trashed tricycles," and the general culture of violence that pervades television, films, and the popular culture undoubtedly affect our perceptions and contribute to our fears.

Third, fear of crime, violence, and other such threats contribute to the exhaustion of parents. Occasionally my wife, Sara, and I look at each other with mutual weariness and wonder out loud how our parents did it. How is it that they raised families larger than ours and yet we feel overwhelmed, at least some of the time, with the demands of three children? We have come to understand that our parents "did it" by spending less quality time with each of us and that they had the advantage of sending their children outside alone without fear of crime, abduction, and violence.

Whether or not increased crime is statistically verifiable, I am angry that Audrey is worried about her tricycle being stolen and that I have to worry about my children's safety when they go out to play. I am not alone. The number of people, especially parents, giving voice to such concerns convinces me that there is something deeper going on than simply the media's ability to saturate us with crime coverage.

Concerns extend beyond the safety of children. Similar frustrations are voiced frequently. In "Take Back the Night" marches in Minneapolis and other cities around the country, women (and some men) express outrage that fear of crime and rape robs us of simple pleasures and rights such as walks at night. Tracy Chapman in one of her songs captures something of the discord that I and others feel when she asks why babies starve when there's enough food to feed the world and why a woman isn't safe in her own home.[6]

Fourth, although various branches of the Justice Department can't agree on whether or not violent crime is a growing problem, nearly everyone agrees that deadly violence among young people has increased dramatically in recent years. The murder rate among white male teenagers has doubled in the past decade, and the rate among black male teens has tripled.[7] Criminologists gathered at the annual meeting of the American Association for the Advancement of Science cited a variety of reasons for growing teen homicide and violence, including lack of gun control, deteriorating family structure, the introduction of crack cocaine, the breakdown of the social structure in low-income neighborhoods, and the absence of hope for a decent economic future felt by many young people.[8] James Fox, dean of Northeastern University's College of Criminal Justice, notes that not only are teenagers "becoming more ruthless, but they are increasing in numbers. We now have forty million kids under the age of ten," Fox said, "and 50 percent of those kids live in single-parent or dual-earner homes. Unless we act today," he warns, "we may have a bloodbath in ten years when all of those kids grow up."[9]

Rising violent crime among teenagers should not deflect attention from adult violence. For example, according to a California Department of Justice report, 83 percent of murdered children, half of murdered teens, and 85 percent of murdered adults are slain by adults over twenty, not by kids.[10] However, such violence is both problematic in itself and symptomatic of a deepening crisis with dire personal and social consequences.

Fifth, fear of crime and violence that grows out of our domestic experience is also fed by our perceptions of international crises. The visual images accompanying the brutality, violence, and social breakdown of Somalia, Rwanda, Haiti, and Bosnia, for example, add to a feeling that our world, far and near, is spinning out of control. The cover of the *Atlantic Monthly*, February 1994 issue, reads:

> The coming anarchy: nations break up under the tidal flow of refugees from environmental and social disaster. As borders crumble, another type of boundary is erected — a wall of disease. Wars are fought over scarce resources, especially water, and war itself becomes continuous with crime, as armed bands of stateless marauders clash with the private security forces of the elites. A preview of the twenty-first century.[11]

The article, according to its author Robert Kaplan, uses "crime in West Africa" as "a natural point of departure" for his "report on what the political character of our planet is likely to be in the twenty-first century." He quotes an African diplomat who speaks of "the revenge of the poor, of the social failures, of the people least able to bring up children in a modern society."

The social breakdown, Kaplan tells us, is not disconnected from our domestic reality. The "gun-wielding guards who walk you the fifteen feet or so between your car and the entrance" to the restaurants in the capital of the Ivory Coast, he says, give you "an eerie taste of what American cities might be like in the future."

> West Africa is becoming *the* symbol of worldwide demographic, environmental, and societal stress, in which criminal anarchy emerges as the real "strategic" danger. Disease, overpopulation, unprovoked crime, scarcity of resources, refugee migrations, the increasing erosion of nation-states and international borders, and the empowerment of private armies, security firms, and international drug cartels are now most tellingly demonstrated through a West African prism.

If this isn't devastating enough, Kaplan adds that "West Africa's future, eventually, will also be that of most of the rest of the world."

I confess that after reading this article my feelings jumped around like popcorn in a popper. I felt like hugging my children. Then I felt guilty for having children and wondered how I could have been irresponsible enough to bring them into the world. This was followed by additional feelings of guilt because I thought maybe I spent too much time with my children and not enough time trying to make the world a better place. This feeling gave way quickly to its opposite as I wondered if my preoccupation with broader justice issues was robbing my children of the parental presence they need to live in a world that seems to be unraveling. Then I felt like yelling at Kaplan, not because the world he portrays is so out of touch with reality as to be unthinkable (in fact we may end up where Kaplan thinks we are going or already are), but because he provides a devastating critique, with limited and in my view often faulty analysis, and then offers not one shred of hope, not one suggestion for redress, not one alternative action, not one possibility for a different future. Thank you very much, Mr. Kaplan.

The rough parallel between fear of domestic crime and international breakdown can be seen in two quotations from President Clinton. The first, presented at the beginning of this chapter, is from a speech in which he defended a $30 billion crime bill, which was heavy on punishment, prisons, and more police but which also provided modest funding for programs that address the social causes of criminal behavior. The crime bill was subsequently approved by Congress but with significant funds *cut* from crime prevention efforts such as drug treatment, jobs, and anti-violence education programs. "We have to face the fact," the president said, "that we have the highest murder rate in the world, and that our children are more at risk here than they would be in most other countries and in all other advanced countries."

The second quotation is from a speech given by President Clinton in France in June 1994:

Militant nationalism is on the rise, transforming the healthy pride of nations, tribes, religious and ethnic groups into cancerous prejudice, eating away at states and leaving their people addicted to the political painkillers of violence and demagoguery. We see the dark future of these trends in mass slaughter, unbridled terrorism, devastating poverty and total environmental and social disintegration.[12]

I believe that real, imagined, or somewhere in between, fears about crime and international breakdown are becoming our own because they are repeated many times and because they touch insecurities that reside deep within us. Listening to our fears about present realities or about the future — whether those of a three-year-old concerned that her tricycle might be stolen or fears about losing a job or crime in the neighborhood or the implications of chaos in Rwanda — and verbalizing them is important, because doing so can shatter a silence or place of numbness or detachment we sometimes find comforting. How we express ourselves, however, can be problematic, because our diagnosis of a problem in many ways determines our response: indifference or action, denial or honest assessment, hope or cynicism.

Not surprisingly, whether or not we perceive or define a problem correctly will facilitate or undermine our capacity for finding effective solutions. Imagine me walking downstairs to retrieve a jar of homemade applesauce only to discover that my basement is flooded. It's been a wet spring, and waterlogged basements are a common problem throughout the city. I waste no time and jump into action. I race to the garage and gather shovel and pick. After several difficult days I manage to slope the land adjacent to the foundation away from my house, lay gravel to help filter water, and install a sump pump.

I'm tired, but upon completing these tasks I feel uplifted by a sense of accomplishment. I reenter the basement and notice for the first time that water is leaking from a rusted pipe extending from the laundry tub. I have responded splendidly to the problem of water seeping into the basement from the outside, only to discover that the source of my problem is something internal and altogether different.

My faulty diagnosis leaves me frustrated, tired, despondent, angry, and broke.

A similar danger applies when we assess our tasks as parents, the needs of children, the causes of family and social crises, the implications of trashed tricycles, or the deeper personal and social challenges posed by a society in which many kids and those responsible for them are failing. A faulty diagnosis in any of these areas can lead to frustration and failure.

This leads to a final point in my preliminary assessment of what lies behind trashed tricycles, namely, that our fear of crime, like crime itself, can be dangerous. Fear is a useful instinct. It can save us from injury or death. Anger at injustice, a response much preferable to cynicism or indifference, is essential for constructing a better world for our children, for all children. Gone awry, however, fear and anger can debilitate us and lead us to places we'd rather not go.

When Robert Kaplan tells a story of social disintegration as a parable of the future without exploring the reasons why or possible ways out, he invites cynicism. When he or President Clinton describes an almost unthinkable social breakdown, we have the responsibility to ask why it is happening. Why are societies unraveling? Is the process irreversible? Are there lessons to be learned? Things to do? Are we involved or merely bystanders? Do solutions entail personal changes? Societal ones? Both?

When President Clinton tells us that crime and insecurity are terrible realities for our children and that these problems are worse here than elsewhere, we have the responsibility to ask why. Why are children safer elsewhere? Is youth violence, or adult violence for that matter, genetic? Or is violence linked to poverty? What does it mean, in Clinton's words, to "face the fact"? Build more prisons? Legislate gun control? Affirm family values? Hire more police? Impose longer prison sentences? Address issues such as racism, joblessness, poverty, inequality, and despair? Both the questions we ask and the answers we provide are critical to the well-being of children.

So where do we go with our anger and our fears? What inferences do we draw from a three-year-old's tricycle being unsafe outside her sister's school for even a few minutes? Or from the fact that children plan their own funerals? Or that babies die of hunger in a world with sufficient food? Or that women aren't safe in their own homes? Or that fear of crime and international lawlessness might distort our understanding, overtake our capacity for compassion, and feed a mean politics? What sense can we make of children's lives as a parable spoken to parents and a troubled society?

Chapter 2

An Honest Assessment

In 1968, Dr. King asked our nation a prescient, urgent, and timely question: Where do we go from here? Chaos or community? In this post-Cold War era of unbearable dissonance between promise and performance, between good politics and good policy, between America's racial creed and America's racial deed, between professed and practiced family values, between calls for community and rampant individualism and greed, and between our capacity to prevent and alleviate child deprivation and disease and our political will to do so, his question demands our...answer with more urgency than ever.

—MARIAN WRIGHT EDELMAN, "AN UNFINISHED SYMPHONY"

There are undoubtedly many heroic parents doing the best they can to hold families together in the context of a dysfunctional society and shattered homes. Some struggle against enormous odds and succeed in raising healthy children. Others struggle equally hard and fail. Some give up before they start, abandoning children at birth or condemning them to a precarious existence by abusing drugs or alcohol while their babies are still in the womb. Too many of our children are abandoned to mean streets; others to shopping malls and Nintendo.

Children in our country today contend with problems of poverty and neglect, hunger and the absence of nurture. One in four is born into actual poverty. Our children deal with violence in the home, on the street, at school, in music and videos, on television and movie screens. With the notable exceptions of the children who endured slavery, who worked in factories prior to child-labor laws, and who lived and died during a period of near genocide against indigenous peoples, children today confront more violence than any prior generation. They also face serious problems of drugs and crime. Many others suffer from "the poverty of affluence" in which an overabundance of material things serves as a poor substitute for relationships that nurture, challenge, and offer reasons for hope. Our children's most decent sensibilities are under attack from failed social policies that lock them into poverty and from market values that define them as consumers rather than as people and provide them daily with images of violence and sex in order to feed fantasies, inadequacies, and profits.

A discouraging number of children make their way through a dangerous and confusing world without the benefit of a nurturing parental presence. In many cases where two parents are in the picture, both are working and overextended. In single-parent households in which children of divorce are abandoned by fathers or in which fathers have never been part of the family, mothers and children are more likely to be victimized by time and financial pressures. It is a sad sign of the times that the principal parent, teacher, role model, and care-giver in most American homes is the television set.

According to a report by the Carnegie Council on Adolescent Development, nearly half of American adolescents are at high or moderate risk of seriously damaging their life chances due to profound societal changes that have left young Americans with less adult supervision while subjecting them to growing pressure to experiment with drugs, engage in sex, and turn to violence to resolve conflicts. The percentage of families headed by a single parent or in which both parents are working, the report noted, increased from 40 percent in 1970 to 70 percent in 1990.[1]

Raising healthy children is hard work. It requires parental guidance, wisdom and humility, the strength of communities, and the resources and commitments of the nation. Children need our personal time and our public resources. Unfortunately, both are in short supply within the present configuration of our personal lives and social priorities. The crisis of our children is symptomatic of an even greater menace that has its deadly tentacles wrapped around our children's lives like an octopus squeezing the life out of its prey. As one group of progressive Christians notes:

> Some see our urban unraveling as a problem to be solved; we see it as a sign to be heeded. It is not only an urban problem, but a crisis that extends to the places where we all live. Kids killing kids is not just a crime problem; it is a parable of pain which points to an illness in our cultural soul. Our children have become our poorest citizens; our most at-risk population; the recipients of our worst values, drugs, illnesses, and environmental practices; our most armed and dangerous criminals; the chief victims and perpetrators of escalating violence; an object of our fears more than our hopes. Their "problems" have become the signs of our times. When children plan their funerals instead of their futures, it a sign we can no longer ignore.[2]

It is easy to feel overwhelmed as a parent. Whether it be through the informational grapevine of our children's lives, our neighborhoods, and our schools, or through newspapers and television, we are surrounded by too much bad news. The number of stories about child abuse or abandonment, guns in schools, teen pregnancies, robbery and murder, children as perpetrators or victims of violence, or court cases in which prosecutors promise to try kids as adults seems endless. They chip away at our hope like persistent termites and carry away pieces of our faith in the future like a colony of ants. A glance at my local paper this morning provides a particularly graphic example: "Boy Stabbed Girl 'to See What It Felt Like,'" the headline screams.[3] A beautiful four-year-old is dead. A fourteen-year-old runaway boy confessed the murder and says the girl had neither provoked him nor fought back. I read this story and shudder, wondering how anyone could murder an innocent child, wondering also about ill health within families and our broader society. What is happening? Where are we headed? How can I offer a lifeline to my own children in such a turbulent, violent, and unpredictable world? Do I share any responsibility for the actions of this fourteen-year-old boy and others like him?

❖

One need not be a careful listener to hear within private and public discourse widespread concern about children, crime, economic insecurity, violence, welfare, taxes, and, above all, families in crisis. As media attention on children and crime has increased, so too has rhetoric from politicians and others about family values. The real and pressing problem of family breakdown is now cited as a major cause of social decline. Within the clamor of dissatisfaction surrounding concerns about family values, there are important issues of personal and social responsibility. However, I believe there is also an eerie silence of meaning that echoes within the corridors of Republicans and Democrats, conservatives and progressives alike.

If there is anything that might push us beyond old, often destructive categories of left and right, conservative and liberal, Republican and Democrat, gay and straight, black and white, it just might be a common concern for children, our own and others. For what seems as clear as the water in a pristine lake is that as parents and as a society we are failing our children, and our children are failing us. Unfortunately, and however ironic it may be, as more coverage is devoted to children's problems and more politicians and others claim the moral high ground of family values, the further we seem from real understanding and real solutions. Part of what obscures clear vision, it seems to me, is the deep alienation felt by many citizens. Fruitful efforts that might uncover the roots of profound disaffection are unfortunately deflected by a politics of deception.

The mid-term elections of 1994 offer a compelling example. In this election Republicans made significant gains at the polls by cultivating and then harvesting a politics of resentment that grows in the fertile ground of insecurity felt by many. The poor, once viewed with sympathy, were blamed for the breakdown of families, their own poverty, and the decline of the nation. Predictably and not for the first time, as we will see in subsequent chapters, efforts to isolate or punish the poor took attention away from strategies to further consolidate wealth among the rich. Transfers of wealth to a relatively narrow segment of U.S. society have numerous, interconnected, and disastrous consequences. They add to poverty and inequality, thus creating social conditions conducive to crime and other dysfunctional behavior among the poor. This in turn triggers

angry responses among the middle class: squeezed financially by political and economic priorities determined by the rich, but fearful of
the chaos brewing in many poor communities and resentful of welfare and other programs utilized by the poor but paid for from their
taxes. Add to this the reality of racism, which becomes more visible during periods of economic and social dislocation, and we have
a potent mix for disaster.

Elections in which more than 60 percent of eligible voters did
not vote would be discredited in many countries of the world. However, when Republicans retook control of the U.S. House and Senate
in 1994 with about 19 percent of the eligible vote, the media and
politicians spoke of "landslides," "mandates," and "political revolu-
tions." Buoyed by such rhetoric, Republican leaders are repeating
and building upon the mistakes of the 1980s, which put enormous
strain on families and which gave rise to insecurity in the 1990s.
At the same time, many Democrats are either retreating and adopt-
ing a strategy of accommodation or defending policy options that
have clearly failed. The electorate grows restless, many refuse to
vote, others embrace a mean politics, some cling to failed policies,
and others more out of desperation than hope look for a fresh "centrist" candidate such as Colin Powell or Ross Perot to save us. In my
view, a view focused through the lens of children's lives and needs,
none of the key players or parties in our present political life as a
nation offers hope to families and children. David C. Korten, in
his groundbreaking book *When Corporations Rule the World,* notes
how the ideas and policy options being offered fail to address critical
issues:

> Although politicians and the press play to the public's frus-
> trations over governmental failure, they display little under-
> standing of the root causes of the conditions of rising poverty
> and unemployment, inequality, violent crime, failing families,
> and environmental deterioration which lead so many people to
> foresee a dark future. Our leaders seem to be unable to move
> beyond blaming their political opponents and promoting the
> same old ineffectual solutions — accelerating economic growth
> through deregulation, cutting taxes, removing trade barriers,

giving industry more incentives and subsidies, forcing welfare recipients to work, hiring more police, and building more jails.[4]

Avoidance of root causes and a politics rooted in fear, failed policies, and false hope add up to a precarious time for children and families. Particularly vulnerable are the poor who in this mean-spirited time are convenient scapegoats, targets of understandable yet in many cases misplaced fears. Nearly as vulnerable, however, are middle-class families with modest incomes whose hostility toward the poor obscures deeper political and economic contradictions that are at the root of their real and often heart-felt insecurities.

Children in our society, through words but more often through the situations and longings in their lives, speak to us from places of physical or emotional poverty, loneliness, rebellion, or despair. Their clear "voices," which express desperate yearnings for meaning, relationship, acceptance, community, intimacy, and hope, have become for us quiet, unintelligible screams. If we can be careful listeners, then our concern for children will offer us opportunities to channel our own deep frustrations into creative action. Meeting the emotional and physical needs of children will require getting past the stale politics of the past and the mean politics of the present. In the future, both our politics and our personal choices will need to be child-friendly.

Beneath the surface of the difficult and visible plight of children is a parable spoken to adults about a troubled people, corrosive values, a dysfunctional culture, a seething racism, a distorted political landscape, a destructive economy, and a bankrupt spirituality. The parable speaks of both pain and possibility as our children's lives call us as individuals, as families, and as a nation to new values, to new life. We need to regain a capacity to listen, to hear, to discern the full implications of children's stories for our personal and social choices. Unraveling the mystery of a parable, like nurturing children, requires time. Allotting sufficient time to both children and discernment is a pressing need in both our homes and our society. It is time to turn off hate radio and turn on our common sense and decency. It is imperative that we move beyond old political categories of left and right, liberal and conservative and focus our attention on how the personal decisions we make and the political and economic landscape we create impact the lives of children.

An honest assessment of children's needs forces a reexamination of our values. We need to take a candid look at our use of time and money, our prejudices, our definitions of life's meaning, our understandings of both personal and social responsibility, our fears about crime, our visions of economics and community, our relationships to the earth itself and to present and future generations, and our capacities for hope.

Chapter 3

A Trial by Children

I love humanity. It's people I can't stand.
— SNOOPY

Snoopy's words remind us that it is relatively easy to love in the abstract. A variation on this wisdom applies to how we view children. In our society it is easier to talk about family values than it is to value families, easier to love children as a generic, faceless category than to demonstrate evidence of specific love. To test the authenticity of our professed love for our children, let us imagine a trial in which children are the judge, witnesses, and prosecuting attorneys. Picture, if you will, the many adult witnesses called to the stand, who if pressed would offer testimony such as the following:

- "I love babies, until they make too much noise during church or wake me up at three o'clock in the morning."

- "I love kids; that's why I prey on the insecurities of teenage girls when it comes to proving my manhood and fulfilling my sexual cravings."

- "I love children, but not those who have difficulty learning and therefore cause trouble in school."

- "I love kids, but not the boys that trash tricycles, create problems at the playground, or deliver drugs on the streets."

- "I love children so much I'm a child molester."

- "I love kids and think it's important to teach them right from wrong. That's why I smack them around when they get out of line."

As parents, and particularly as fathers, we must unfortunately conclude that our love for children doesn't extend to spending much time with them.

- "I love sexual conquest and 'making babies,' but don't expect me to raise the children I sire."
- "I love my kids, at least I did until the divorce. Now I've cut my ties."
- "I love my children almost as much as my job, my promotion, my boat, my football game, my favorite TV program, my alcohol or crack, my multiple sexual partners, my two-week vacation in France."
- "I love my kids, but I've never visited their school."
- "I love my children, but I don't have time to read to them, play with them, hold them, nurture them, or offer them consistent, loving guidance."
- "I love my kids; that's why I work sixty-hour weeks so I can provide them with the best things money can buy."
- "I love my children, and that's why I'm working to save the world. After I get this environmental thing taken care of, I'll make time for them."
- "I love my kids enough to baby-sit but not enough to share fully in parenting. Besides, caring for children is part of a woman's God-given role."

If love of children doesn't translate into parental commitments of time and guidance, it is equally problematic that love doesn't translate into *public* investment of resources to enhance their opportunities and well-being. Hear the testimony of these citizens:

- "I love children, but taxes are way out of line. Don't expect me to support adequate funding for day care or decent schools. And don't hold your breath when it comes to money for WIC or Head Start or health care. Oh, by the way, have you considered reducing the tax rate on capital gains or the rate at which we tax personal income?"

- "I love babies in the womb, but once born they're on their own. Actually, I love *my* baby in the womb, but don't expect me to support adequate funding for someone else's prenatal care."

- "I love kids, but welfare moms drag the country down. Kick them off AFDC and they'll start working and stop having babies. Call it tough love. Oh, but we've got to hold down the minimum wage, promote free trade, and offer tax breaks to corporations that set up shop overseas. Do you like the Cadillac I financed with a home equity loan?"

- "I love my child. That's why I've abandoned the public schools and enrolled her in the best private school money can buy."

- "I love kids, but keeping them safe from communists, nationalists, barbarians, refugees, recent immigrants, and others requires massive military expenditures. Children can get a good education if they join the military or have enough bake sales."

- "I love my children. That's why I'm willing to pay whatever it takes to build more prisons and why I led the fight against the local bond issue that would have pumped more money into the failed public school system."

Beyond parental and societal neglect, our children are also victims of the market economy, legal and illegal:

- "I love kids enough to give them jobs: running drugs. The income is better than McDonald's, and I don't go to jail when they're caught or killed."

- "I love children, at least their profit potential. That's why I target them with messages that fuel their sense of inadequacy, feed on their sexual insecurities, and promise fulfillment through consumption."

- "I love kids, but I can't afford to pay their parents decent wages. I couldn't compete in the age of the global economy. Besides, I'd be crazy not to open a factory in El Salvador where people work for 33 cents an hour. We've got to think about children there too, you know."

Love of children also fails to match our deeds when it comes to passing on prejudices and teaching intolerance:

- "I love my kids. That's why we moved to the suburbs, you know, to avoid the problem peoples of the inner city."

- "I love my children. That's why I won't let them be perverted by homosexuals and other social deviants."

- "I love babies. That's why I kill people at abortion clinics."

- "I love my sons. That's why I teach them to be tough and force them to play football."

- "I loved my daughter until I found out she was a lesbian."

- "I loved my son until he came out of the closet."

As children put us on trial, we are rightfully fearful of a guilty verdict on numerous personal and social counts. One hope we have is that pretrial issues among kids themselves will be divisive enough to disrupt the proceedings. First among them is consideration of where to hold the trial. Children of poverty argue for the vacant lot down the street. It is close to the crack houses and the dilapidated public school where drive-by shootings are more common than good grades. An empty lot surrounded by evidence of social decay serves as a powerful visual reminder of the polluted lake in which children of poverty are forced to swim.

Children of affluence argue for an alternative site, perhaps at a mall or the mall of all malls, the Megamall. In the end these groups, so different and yet so similar, choose a compromise in which the venue of the trial alternates between vacant lot and suburban shopping center. The vivid contrast between mall and mean streets reflects the divergent realities of children, their different yet common experience of neglect, and their desperate struggle for identity in the absence of meaning.

Another contentious pretrial issue is that of jury selection. Some say that a jury charged with judging the personal conduct of parents and parental values reflected in social policies should consist only of children. This is logical enough. "Why not let those of us without voices be heard?" some of the children argue. Others, in the interest of fairness, insist that the jury consist of a mixture of adults and children. This too sounds reasonable. However, in the end an all-adult jury is selected. "Who are we kidding?" a child advocate of this position asks. "With a jury of children we won't need to call a witness. Conviction is guaranteed. On all counts. But what will a conviction by children mean? In the real world we have no power. Our only hope is to convince a jury not of our peers but of adults."

Once the decision is made for an all-adult jury, there is still the question of which adults to seat from a potentially vast jury pool. In the end, it is decided in favor of diversity. Members of the religious right and religious progressives, feminists and traditionalists, parents and adults without children, men and women, black, white, brown, and yellow, young adults and seniors, gay and straight are all represented. The goal of the trial, after all, is persuasion, to make a case for conversion, and not merely to gain a guilty verdict.

In the courtroom at the mall, children of relative affluence testify to their need for love and attention from both mothers and fathers. They speak of empty times in front of televisions, of false advertising, of wasted lives spent in stores in a fruitless pursuit of acceptance, love, and meaning. They tell of parental neglect and emotional longings. Those coming from families with an over-abundance of material resources testify that relationship is more important than ownership; that things are a poor substitute for investments of time and caring; that spiritual needs are real and deep and that they cannot be filled easily, painlessly, without sufficient time and a web of relationships and institutions that weave healthy families and neighborhoods together. They remind absent fathers that men are parents too and that fathers model important behaviors, whether positive or negative. They tell the jury that divorce, though sometimes necessary, is almost always painful.

At the vacant lot within a stone's throw of the crack houses, children of poverty voice similar concerns, but they have much more to add. These children, who experience fundamental deficits of resources as well as time, are doubly angry at parents and society. They too bring charges of relational neglect; the prospect of having healthy families is a dream, given the poverty and economic deprivation that frame their lives. Many who see no future testify to the senseless violence that grows in soil devoid of hope. Children of poverty remind absent fathers that they don't appreciate being regarded merely as the consequences of sexual conquest rather than a gift born out of love and commitment. They tell their teenage mothers that they both understand and resent their mothers' search for intimacy, status, and respect through early sexual encounters and motherhood. These children add that the fact of their birth, whether a consequence of ignorance or desire, has a predictable outcome. If violence, deprivation, hopelessness, fractured homes, and crumbling neighborhoods destroyed intimacy for their parents throughout childhood, if the stigma of being labeled a problem people crushed their spirits, then how could these child-parents have realistically imagined that it would be different for their kids? Children of child-mothers, whose fathers are often adult and absent, offer evidence from their own tragic lives that when young people unprepared emotionally and financially for parenthood have children, they are more likely to repeat cycles of violence, poverty, and abuse than to break them. Children of poverty note that their neighborhoods offer ample testimony to the failure of both a welfare system that fails to break the cycles of poverty and a market economy in which low-paying, service sector jobs and illegal drugs mark the extent of their options.

The trial, of course, has other dimensions. Our children point to ways in which we allow our racial, gender, and sexual prejudices to stand in the way of their needs. Teaching family values, they tell us, too often involves instilling attitudes of intolerance toward others, passing on prejudices, and undermining respect for diversity. "Family values," it seems, corresponds only rarely to personal and social agendas that value *all* children and families.

Children at our mythical trial lift up the African proverb that says "It takes a community to raise a child." This is the basis of a devastating critique of a society dominated by inadequate government programs, market values, and a market morality that undermines community at every turn. Our children ask pointedly:

- "If it takes a community to raise a child, then why do our economic and social policies neglect neighborhoods, rob them of meaningful jobs and hope, and erode the social and economic web of relationships so vital to healthy families and communities?"
- "Why is one of four children born into poverty?"
- "Why are less than half of our small children vaccinated against polio?"
- "Why is it that the United States performs so poorly in measurements of child welfare compared to other countries?"
- "Why, if our bumper stickers and political discourse claim we are the number-one nation, does our country not show up in the top ten on any significant indicator of child welfare?"
- "Why does our country lead all other industrial nations in murders and rapes, in per capita prison population, child poverty, military spending and weapons sales, international indebtedness, use of illicit drugs and tranquilizers, and economic inequality?"
- "Why are nine out of ten young people who are murdered in the twenty largest Western nations U.S. citizens?"
- "Why do we cast so much blame in the direction of welfare mothers while turning a blind eye to the forces that lock families into poverty and that make U.S. income distribution the most unequal and child poverty the most pronounced of any industrialized nation?"

Our children are not impressed when adults answer that we are doing the best we can, that we can't afford to do better, or that, using the words of former President Ronald Reagan, "government is not the answer to our problems; government is the problem." They counter such wisdom by allowing children from Sweden, Germany, France, Canada, and other countries to tell stories of how with the support of their governments they moved out of poverty. They call U.S. sociologist Paul Miller as a witness. He bases his expert testimony on statistics from the U.S. House of Representatives *Green*

Book, telling the jury that while all advanced societies start out with children in poverty, it is in the U.S. where child poverty is most pronounced. The difference, Miller says, is that governments elsewhere intervene effectively to lift children out of poverty. For every one hundred children living in poverty in Sweden, fewer than ten remain poor after government tax breaks and benefits; about twenty-five remain poor in France; and fewer than thirty-four do in West Germany. Children fare somewhat worse in Canada, where fifty-six children live in poverty after government initiatives, but there the pains of child poverty are mitigated by the availability of universal health care.

In the United States, by way of contrast, for every one hundred children living in poverty, more than ninety-two remain stuck there, even after government intervention. The abysmal U.S. record in helping poor children is not only an embarrassment, Miller says. It contrasts sharply with Social Security, which has significantly reduced poverty among elderly Americans.[1] Our children would also challenge myths promoted by popular TV and radio talk-show host Rush Limbaugh, who minimizes the severity of poverty in the United States. "The poorest people in America," Limbaugh told a radio audience, "are better off than the mainstream families of Europe."[2] Countering this perspective, our children call on Penelope Leach, internationally renowned author who writes about infants, children, and society. "Complex though comparisons are," she indicates, "it is clear that individuals who live below the United States poverty line, even in the more generous states, are likely to be, in European terms, not just poor but extremely cold-and-hungry poor. By 1990," she adds, "that was about 34 million people, over 14 percent of the population of the United States, and the percentage is still rising."[3] Other witnesses bolster the testimonies of Miller and Leach. According to one:

> As reported in *Selective Prosperity,* the Luxembourg Income Study — a comprehensive comparison of income levels, poverty rates, and government policies in the United States, Australia, Canada, Germany, Israel, the Netherlands, Norway, Sweden, Switzerland, and the UK — showed that American income is

the most unevenly distributed and found "that the child poverty rate in the U.S., after taxes and benefits are considered, was more than twice that in Canada and four times the average child poverty rate in the other nations in the study. It also showed that the poverty rate, just among white children in the U.S., was higher than the poverty rate among all children in all other countries except Australia. *In short, the private economy in the United States generates more relative poverty among children than the private economies of many other western, industrialized nations — and the U.S. then does far less than the other nations to address this problem.*"[4]

Witness after witness comes forth to testify to the adult jury about how other countries not nearly as rich as the United States distribute wealth more equitably through the private economy and do a better job of lifting children out of poverty through government programs. Voice after voice hammers home that our nation's professed concern for its children is undermined by contradictory practices and priorities.

- Jurors hear how spending on prisons is nearly double that for welfare; that the same ratio applies to welfare and government expenditures for military pensions; and that *the federal government spends nearly three times as much each year on the Central Intelligence Agency* (CIA) *as it does on AFDC* (Aid to Families with Dependent Children).

- A representative of the Government Accounting Office (GAO) describes our nation's public schools as needing $112 billion in repairs. According to the GAO about 14 million students attend schools in which water and fire damage, termite infestation, peeling lead-based paint, and unsanitary plumbing make attendance unsafe or even harmful.[5]

- A spokesperson for the Center for Defense Information (CDI) describes how money that could be used to address vital needs is squandered on wasteful military spending. The failure to eliminate thirteen unneeded weapons systems, CDI estimates, costs taxpayers $16 billion the first year and as much as $500 billion over the life of the systems.[6]

- Other witnesses describe hundreds of billions of dollars of tax money spent to bail out the architects of the Savings and Loan scandal, trillions of dollars in tax breaks to our richest citizens, and the tragic consequences of a market-dominated culture in which corporations spend nearly $125 billion each year on advertising[7] and in which programming and advertisements deliver messages of violence, sex, and empty promises of the good life.

Our children try to absorb the enormity of the testimony and the poverty of our excuses. Looking on from mean streets and malls they see the following:

- children faring better in most other industrial countries than in the U.S.;
- unneeded, costly weapons systems "defending" deteriorated schools and neighborhoods;
- bank bailouts and tax breaks for the rich alongside attacks against welfare recipients;
- welfare systems that fail to break cycles of poverty and dependency;
- market systems that generate poverty and inequality.

As our children name the emptiness in their souls that cannot be filled through misleading advertising and the seduction of TV programming, they cast aside the loud, persistent, and empty rhetoric of family values that dominates private and public discourse. Our children refuse to accept adult claims that we can't do better and that our society can't afford to break the cycles of poverty on which the well-being of families, neighborhoods, and society depend. The message they get from both parents and society is that children are expendable.

The verdict is in. On charges of personal parental irresponsibility and failed social policies, our children find us guilty on all counts. But as adults we are the real jurors. How will we decide? Guilty? Or not?

Chapter 4

Relative Privileges

In my day-to-day work as a physician, I get immensely discouraged, yet increasingly there seems to be no one readily available to blame. When I find myself angry at my patients, annoyed by their problems, irritated by some of the people I am to care for; when I find myself crossing the street or slipping out a side door to avoid them; when I find myself worn out at the end of even four hours of patient care, exhausted by the tragedy of these lives, I can no longer excuse myself by blaming them. If these are victims, oppressed people, those who have been "done to," on whom can I vent my frustration when their shortcomings enrage me? . . . Wherever I look I find fault — in my patients, in our institutions, in the wider society, in myself. Looking through the lens of "blame," however, is pointless. It allows little understanding and leaves no way out. To function as a physician among the poor of Washington's inner city, I have to view my responsibilities and those of my patients in a fuller perspective. And yet everything in our common circumstances works to obscure that view — to render the truth of my patients' lives invisible, not only to me, but often, I'm afraid, to themselves.

—Dr. David Hilfiker, *Not All of Us Are Saints*

It's possible that three more-or-less happy children, well cared for and loved, nurtured in good, stable homes, had a bad day, or a bad moment in a day. Therefore they saw a tricycle, took it, and trashed it. Call it a child equivalent of temporary insanity.

It's possible, but I doubt it. It's more likely that the kids who trashed Audrey's tricycle were angry. Their behavior was probably not a lapse in an otherwise normal socialization process in which children learn to deal appropriately with anger. These kids may have good reasons to be angry, and an anonymous tricycle may be a convenient target for the rage they feel toward both their parents and society.

Do you remember Shavon Dean and Robert Sandifer? Shavon was killed by the random bullet Robert fired into a crowd at the behest of his gang lords. She was fourteen. Three nights later Robert, an eleven-year-old African-American child who was four feet eight inches tall and nicknamed "Yummy" because he liked to eat cookies, was apparently executed by members of his own gang. According to a story in the *New York Times:*

> Neglected and abused by his family, bounced from group homes to squad cars and killed...by his own street gang, Robert was buried today, a symbol of the nation's most troubled children.... During most of his life, it seems, hardly anyone — except the same gang lords — paid him much attention.
>
> ...Before he was 3 years old, Robert, according to child welfare records, had been neglected and abused by his parents. He had belt marks and cigarette burns on his body. He was then raised by his grandmother. Last year, he was made a ward of the state because of neglect.[1]

When my daughter Naomi was twenty months old, "yummy" was one of her favorite words. The fact that "Yummy" is also the nickname of an eleven-year-old murderer and murder victim gets me thinking about relative privileges.

My wife and I chose to start a family somewhat late in life. Choice in such things, of course, isn't yet the norm. At present, for a variety of social, cultural, religious, political, and economic reasons, millions of parents, especially women, are denied access to family planning. The fact of choice, in family planning and other matters, is a privilege of the relatively powerful.

Even for those of us with choices, planning families is not as routine as we sometimes think. Just hours after telling family and friends the joyous news, "we're going to have a baby," our first pregnancy ended with a miscarriage. Our fourth was such a surprise that the sperm and egg earn our "miraculous culprits award" for overcoming overwhelming odds.

By the time our first child was born, most of our contemporary friends and family members had finished the early stages of parenting. They supplied us generously with numerous essential items, from cloth diapers to baby clothes, strollers, and tricycles. In this sense, hand-me-downs remind us of how rich we are even though we choose to limit our family income.

Our relative good fortune as a family is evidenced by many things beyond access to hand-me-downs. We live in a city where housing is, relatively speaking, affordable. Our family has adequate shelter, and all of us at the time of this writing are healthy. We have health insurance, paid for in roughly equal proportions from family income and my wife's employer. Our neighborhood, though far from free of violence and crime, is reasonably safe and well organized. My wife and I work in situations that offer flexibility. This, coupled with the fact that we have set our sights on a lifestyle that requires a modest income, enables each of us to work part-time, meet the material needs of our family, and share equitably in the myriad tasks of parenting.

Our work as parents is made easier because we have supportive family members living nearby and participate in a well-run cooperative day-care center a few blocks from our home. We also are part of a strong, neighborhood-based ecumenical faith community in which families help each other. What all this suggests is that our children, through a convoluted convergence of luck, inheritance, choice, and circumstance, have started out privileged. They have both parents involved intimately in their daily care and access to the material things and social services they need. Many parents and children aren't nearly so fortunate.

Around the corner from our house in South Minneapolis live a mother and five children. Each child apparently has a different father. The youngest, who is five, spends many of her days wandering between a few safe-houses and yards in the neighborhood. Her mother, who has many emotional problems and probably several addictions, is unable, unwilling, and seemingly uninterested in caring for her children. The Minneapolis office of child welfare services does nothing. A list of our family's benefits and advantages over this child, "Yummy," and other children facing similar problems is a long one. It includes adequate housing, health care and child care, flexible work, adequate resources, two parents active in the care of children, sympathetic extended family members, a "safe" neighborhood, and strong community support. It is an impressive list and, on the surface at least, appears to be a reasonable agenda to strive toward for many families.

As I look at the list, I feel good about the choices we make: to value time more than income or the things that money can buy, to co-parent, and to nurture our children in the context of community. These choices *are* good for our family. The list can obscure, however, the many ways in which our good fortune and choices are possible because of our privileges. They can also mask our vulnerabilities, the fact that a major illness, job loss, or other unexpected problem could precipitate a crisis. Perhaps most important, in spite of our good fortune, good choices, and all the benefits named above, as parents we feel inadequate some if not much of the time. Our children are often delightful. They can also be inconsiderate and self-centered in spite of our efforts. Parenting has its rewards, but it is also hard work with parental responsibilities claiming our time and attention twenty-four hours a day, seven days a week.

Our decision to co-parent is good for every member of our family. Our children benefit from time spent with both Mom and Dad, and as parents we benefit from time both with and away from our children. Co-parenting is helpful, but it doesn't automatically make us good parents. Nor does it provide us a blueprint of how to parent or to live in the context of growing insecurities about the future symbolized in global problems of hunger, poverty, crime, indebtedness, racism, and environmental decay. Like all parents we contend with a society that says in hundreds of ways that it doesn't value kids and that parents are responsible for children independent of broader social forces. One advantage of co-parenting is that we face these issues and problems together.

There are many reasons to be concerned about the well-being of children, including other people's children. One obvious concern is that neglected or abused children are often problem children who become troubled adults. A growing number of prison studies, for example, including those at the Minnesota State Prison and the Massachusetts Treatment Center for Sexually Dangerous Persons, show that 60 to 90 percent of all inmates, and nearly all of those on death row, were abused as children. The most conservative study by the National Institute of Justice estimates that 40 percent of all violent crimes are associated with offenders who were abused as children.[2]

We might also wish to elevate the needs of all children because today's kids are tomorrow's workers. Without adequate nurturing, training, or education, my social security is in danger. And yours. Today's kids will also have to help solve difficult problems, including those they inherit from us, from debt to depletion of the ozone. "The proposition is that poverty in childhood has such heavy long-term costs that money spent to prevent it would yield far better returns than extant welfare policies," writes Penelope Leach, and "that any extra costs incurred, over and above current budgets, would be more apparent than real, and that focusing on children would ultimately produce more caring and creative societies."[3] The fact is we all benefit from personal and social investments in children, and we all suffer the consequences when we fail to make them.

Our decision to devote significant time to our kids doesn't insulate our family from the consequences of other people's poor parenting practices or society's neglect, one other reason I want other kids to be nurtured and cared for adequately. As tempting as it may be, it is difficult if not impossible to separate our family from the broader problems of crime, violence, a destructive TV culture, peer pressures, advertising, and a myriad of other social problems common to a society marred by deepening social inequalities and family disruption. It's not unusual for me to have to "parent" other people's children in order for my own to feel safe enough to enjoy a family activity. This makes me resentful.

I was playing with my children at a park one day in a suburb near where their grandparents live. Boys and girls, including my own, were having fun. Parents were talking amiably as they watched or helped their children on the playground. The scene seemed as it should be until two boys, one in particular, kept playing out of control. He ran over children, my daughters included, and was oblivious to any concept of taking turns or respecting other children's needs or space. He was verbally abusive and obnoxious.

I made my way around the small park asking each of the parents if they were responsible for this child. They all said no but shared my concern about the boy's behavior. At that point the boy, who was about eight and spoke in almost unintelligible "sentences," began bragging about the knife he had in his pocket. "Me got knife. To cut you with," he said to another child.

With no parental figure monitoring his inappropriate behavior, I spoke to him. My words of caution had no impact. I intervened again, telling the boy that if his behavior continued I would impose what I deemed an appropriate consequence. Out of the parking lot there eventually emerged a bedraggled woman who looked to be in her late thirties or early forties who said she was the boy's grandmother.

As in the case of seeking an answer to Audrey's question about why someone would trash her tricycle, I found myself searching for reasons behind this boy's behavior, trying to imagine the life of this child. What was his home like? Were a mother and father in the picture? How poor was the family? What would this boy be like in the future?

I also thought again about how my children, who are privileged to have two caring parents in their lives and adequate economic resources, are nonetheless deeply affected by the consequences of other people's poor parenting and a society that seems not to value children. At whom or what should we be angry? At ourselves? Other parents? Society? And what should we be doing differently?

Dr. David Hilfiker, quoted at the beginning of this chapter, works as a physician with some of the poorest residents of Washington, D.C. He is not the only one who wrestles with the question of responsibility and blame. There seem to be so many appropriate targets for my feelings of frustration about dysfunctional children's lives that it often leaves me bewildered. What is clear is that the quality of my parenting is important to others beyond my immediate household, and other people's parenting will either add to or diminish my insecurity as a parent and my feelings of parental success and failure. The quality of parenting also impacts society, either positively or negatively, and is influenced positively or negatively by broader societal forces.

If my encounters with poor parenting happen often enough to make me resentful, they also trigger sympathy. Even with the many advantages we enjoy, sometimes we still feel overwhelmed and inadequate. We can only imagine the struggles of single parents, or of parents and children living in poverty or with serious illness or disabilities, or of families where both parents work full time.

If we stand on the threshold of insecurity in our stable household, where husband and wife communicate well, work part time, love each other, and share intimately in matters big and small, then what of households devastated by unemployment or low-paying jobs, abuse, the trauma of illness aggravated by no health insurance, or stresses of poverty, violence, divorce, drugs, or incest? Although our neighborhood has its share of crime and other problems, I wonder about meaner streets and recognize that parents for a variety of personal and social reasons can be easily overtaxed, desperate, lonely, angry, or out of control. All of this takes a brutal toll on children. And on society. Meeting the basic emotional and physical needs of any child and all children in these circumstances is a daunting task. A good-faith effort to do so will require significant changes in personal, family, and societal choices. We must go beyond assigning blame and allow the needs of children to guide us. Concern for children could unite us in a common effort to strengthen families and overcome poverty. Children's needs, in other words, could be a catalyst that helps us transform both parenting and politics.

Awareness of the relative privilege my family enjoys shaped my initial response to Audrey's "unanswerable" question. I told her that it was okay for her to feel angry or sad. I too felt sad because her tricycle was wrecked. I also said I felt sorry for the kids who wrecked it. I took her hand, looking directly into her tearful eyes. "Audrey," I said, "I don't know why those boys destroyed your tricycle. But anyone who does something like this must not feel very loved." Our conversation ended as we prayed for the children who had turned the most exciting tricycle ride of her life into a nightmare.

Chapter 5

Failing Children

Listening to many of the public conversations here in the U.S., you would think the secret to world peace, or at least the key to solving almost all of our internal problems, is family values (FVs). . . . Now keepers of patriarchy of all stripes have practically made it their mantra. They lament the loss of our FVs and cite it as cause for everything from teen sex and eroding educational standards to street crime, urban blight, and poverty. Lost family values, not militarism and the legacy of Cold War policies. Not racism and the capitalist reverence for market forces. Not more than a decade of Reagan and Bush. Not the plethora of guns and the steady diet of violence spooned up as entertainment. Not the male rage that makes so many homes unsafe. And most definitely not patriarchy.

— MARCIA ANN GILLESPIE, *Ms.* MAGAZINE EDITORIAL

In the United States the evidence that we are failing our children is overwhelming. Whether we look at child poverty, infant mortality, attempted suicide, violent crime, homelessness, high-school dropout rates, alcohol and drug abuse, and other adult violence against children, or any number of other factors, our nation's youth are faring poorly. The trends are bad and worsening.

As parents and as a society we fail our children and yet seem surprised when our children fail us. Consider the following:

- Homicide is the major cause of death among young African-American males.[1]

- More than 3.6 million high-school students are assaulted yearly, most of them by other adolescents.

41

- Ten times each day gun violence takes a child's life in the United States. More teenage youth die of gunshot wounds than all other causes of death combined.

- Violent crime among fifteen-year-old American males rose 264 percent over the past four years.

- Every nine minutes a child is arrested for a drug/alcohol offense.

- Every minute of every day an American teenager has a baby.

- The dropout rate from high school is approximately 25 percent.[2]

- According to the 1994 National Household Survey on Drug Abuse, nearly one of five teens reported being approached by someone selling drugs in the month before the survey.[3]

Our failures and those of our children are even more pronounced when we make international comparisons. Sylvia Ann Hewlett writes:

Children in America are at much greater risk than children elsewhere in the advanced industrial world. Compared with other rich countries, children in the United States are much more likely to die before their first birthday; to live in poverty; to be abandoned by their fathers; and to be killed before they reach the age of twenty-five. Although the United States ranks No. 2 worldwide in per capita income, this country does not even make it into the top ten on any significant indicator of child welfare.[4]

There is a volatile debate under way about why families in our society are in trouble and about the causes of the broader social crisis gripping the nation. In an effort to assess or deflect blame, divergent groups offer competing explanations. Differences in approach can be seen clearly through the following sound bites in a heated discussion.

During the presidential campaign of 1992, then Vice President Dan Quayle blamed declining family values and the breakdown of the family for the growing list of social problems plaguing the nation. In a speech delivered shortly after the verdict in the Rodney

King trial set off a wave of violent disturbances in Los Angeles, he chose TV character Murphy Brown as a symbol of what was wrong with America. "It doesn't help matters when prime-time TV has Murphy Brown," Quayle said, " — a character who supposedly epitomizes today's intelligent, highly paid, professional woman — mocking the importance of fathers by bearing a child alone and calling it just another lifestyle choice."

The targeting of Murphy Brown was in some ways brilliant. She was a white woman, but she indirectly or vicariously symbolized a "woman's equivalent" to Willie Horton, a black man who raped a white woman while on furlough from a Massachusetts prison and whom the Bush campaign turned into a racist symbol of the failure of liberalism during the 1988 election. Cast in the shadow and racist overtones of the Rodney King verdict and subsequent rebellion, the attack against Murphy Brown was intended, I believe, to raise the issue of irresponsible single motherhood without naming directly single black mothers, the real target of the attack. Focusing on a well-known TV character, a white one at that, avoided charges of racism and had the added advantage of challenging the values projected by television and movies.

The initial response to Quayle's criticism of Murphy Brown was largely negative. Many critics were outraged because the constituency Quayle represented blamed feminism for the dissolution of family structure and numerous other problems. In the view of his critics, Quayle's constituency had a "Father Knows Best" solution to the family crisis in which Mom stayed home and Dad brought home the bacon — and the wisdom — on which the family depended. An example of the perspective that fueled the ire of Quayle's critics is provided by an informational brochure from Focus on the Family, a national family advocacy organization associated with the religious right:

> While feminism and some psychological views may maintain that the sexes are identical except for a few physical differences, males and females are in fact different from one another in every cell of their bodies, because they have a different chromosomal pattern. Further, the biblical view maintains that

maleness and femaleness are not merely the result of social conditioning but express God-designed differences.... Attempts to obliterate or minimize the differences between the sexes can only be destructive to individuals, marital relationships and the family structure. Scripture maintains that the sexes are equal in value but different in nature. Consequently, the sexes have different roles within the family.... The husband is called to provide leadership and love, while the wife is called to follow the responsible leadership of the husband, nourishing and loving the family.[5]

Other progressive voices found Quayle an unlikely spokesperson on family values and the decline of the family because the social policies and economic priorities of the Reagan–Bush, Bush–Quayle years were particularly harsh on families (a point I will address in detail in later chapters, particularly chapter 12).

Lost in the initial defense of Murphy Brown and Murphy Brown's own eloquent statements on behalf of single or unmarried mothers is the fact that the life of this TV character is unusual, not typical of single mothers. Only one-tenth of 1 percent of unwed mothers have, like Murphy Brown, incomes greater than $50,000 a year. Most of them face enormous problems, especially financial ones: half of all single mothers now live below the poverty line.[6]

I believe Dan Quayle understood that Murphy Brown was atypical of single mothers. His focus on Murphy Brown not only provided a means to scrutinize Hollywood-inspired values, it was part of a strategy to attack all single mothers, especially, by implication, black ones. Births to unwed mothers, according to Quayle, and the resulting changes in family structure are destroying the country. Casting the explosive issue of dysfunctional families in this light, he hoped to put progressives, many of whom had been silent about the issue of family disruption and family values, on the defensive.

The initial, largely negative reaction to Quayle's comments about Murphy Brown seemed to indicate his failure. As an unpopular politician linked to a constituency that was anti-feminist and to so-cial policies that hurt families, he was easy to criticize. The debate shifted considerably, however, when some time later the moderate *Atlantic Monthly* graced its cover with the following lead-in to its major story:

DAN QUAYLE WAS RIGHT. After decades of public dispute about so-called family diversity, the evidence from social-science re-search is coming in. The dissolution of two-parent families, though it may benefit the adult involved, *is harmful to many children, and dramatically undermines our society.*[7]

The article, written by Barbara Dafoe Whitehead, describes how family disruption in the U.S. not only impacts individual fami-lies and children negatively; it is a central cause of many of our most pressing social problems, including poverty, crime, and declin-ing school performance. In the post–World War II generation, 80 percent of children grew up in a family with two biological par-ents married to each other, but by 1980 the figure was less than 50 percent. This decline in two-parent households is problematic, Whitehead says, because children in families disrupted by divorce and out-of-wedlock birth do worse than children in intact families.

Single motherhood is rarely economically viable, Whitehead says, and it often leads to debilitating dependency. Children of single-parent families are six times as likely to be poor and more likely to stay poor longer. Of the never-married mothers who receive welfare benefits, nearly 40 percent remain on welfare for ten years or more. The children of these women are more likely to repeat this pattern, resulting in a kind of "intergenerational poverty."

Children in disrupted families, according to Whitehead, are two to three times as likely to have emotional and behavior problems; they have a harder time achieving intimacy in relationships, forming stable marriages, and holding a steady job. They do more poorly in school, are less likely to be high achievers, and are more likely to be late or truant. Increases in teen suicide rates, juvenile crime, and poor school performance are each linked to changing family structure. So too is the incidence of childhood poverty that increased dramatically from 15 percent in 1970 to 20 percent in 1990.

Whitehead is also concerned with family disruption triggered by divorce. Hollywood, she says, affirms divorce and out-of-wedlock birth while presenting "the married two-parent family as a source of pathology."[8] In the real world, however, the fact that many divorced fathers are both emotionally and financially absent from their children's lives takes a devastating toll. Many children never recover from the trauma of divorce.

Whitehead notes that although changes in public policies (stricter enforcement of child support; expansion of the Earned Income Credit, a federal program that increases the real or non-taxable income of the working poor; changes in the welfare system; and promotion of better jobs in poor areas) can help our nation's children, it will be important to restigmatize divorce and out-of-wedlock birth if we are to alter behavior patterns that encourage disruption of families.

The importance of the debate, Whitehead implies, cannot be overstated:

> If we fail to come to terms with the relationship between family structure and declining child well-being, then it will be increasingly difficult to improve children's life prospects, *no matter how many new programs the federal government funds.* Nor will we be able to make progress in bettering school performance or reducing crime or improving the quality of the nation's future workforce — all domestic problems closely connected to family breakup. Worse, we may contribute to the problem by pursuing policies that actually increase family instability and breakup.[9]

I find much of Whitehead's perspective logical and compelling. Many years ago I was struggling within a bad marriage that after seven years ended in divorce. I was out of touch with many things, but somehow I understood that it was important for my wife and me not to have children. Some people counseled that having a child would bring us closer together, advice that, fortunately, we did not follow. I know through the experiences of close friends that divorce is often traumatic for both the children and the adults involved. Who can doubt that single parents living in poverty face staggering odds in providing for the emotional and material needs of their children, or that absent fathers create emotional holes in their children's lives, or that poor parenting, whether by choice or circumstance, has an impact that extends from child to child and family to family until negative social consequences are apparent as well?

The most important, controversial, and perhaps weakest elements in Whitehead's analysis are assertions that changes in family structure are the principal *cause* of social breakdown and poverty, not vice versa, and that solutions depend *primarily* on changes in personal behavior. For Whitehead the social, political, and economic environments in which families live become secondary and, sometimes it seems, relatively unimportant concerns. In her view, government social programs can and often do make problems worse.

Raising three daughters within a major urban center, I see many dysfunctional families who are incapable of nurturing their children and who contribute directly or indirectly to many social problems in my city, including crime and delinquency. I also see that economic decisions at local, state, national, and international levels and state and federal tax policies often push people into poverty and put enormous strain on families. Naming family breakdown as the principal causal factor in social distress obscures complicated relationships between families and society. It seems logical to me as a concerned parent *that the deep crises of family and society require changes in both personal behavior and social policies.*

The *Atlantic Monthly* article drew a harsh response from Judith Stacey. Writing in *The Nation*, Stacey criticized Whitehead's conclusions and the work of other "centrists" whom she saw as a dangerous group of "new family values crusaders."

> The centrists have it backward when they argue that the collapse of traditional family values is at the heart of our social decay. The losses in real earnings and in breadwinner jobs, the persistence of low-wage work for women and the corporate greed that has accompanied global economic restructuring have wreaked far more havoc on Ozzie and Harriet Land than have

the combined effects of feminism, sexual revolution, gay liberation, the counterculture, narcissism and every other value flip of the past half-century.[10]

Stacey noted that the "old-style family values warriors like Quayle, Pat Buchanan and Jerry Falwell are reactionary Republicans and fundamentalist Christians" who are "overtly antifeminist, antigay and, at least at the moment, on the defensive." However, they are being replaced by "the revisionist family values campaign" that is "explicitly centrist and coming on strong."[11]

By declaring the principal source of family disruption over the past three decades as cultural, Whitehead and other centrists, Stacey said, had "mounted a crusade to restore the privileged status of lifelong, heterosexual marriage." The centrists "claim that two married, biological parents is the passport to a child's welfare, and thereby to society's welfare.... They identify fatherless families as the root of everything — from poverty, violence, drug addiction, crime and declining standards in education and civility to teen pregnancy, sexually transmitted disease, narcissism and the Los Angeles uprising."[12]

According to Stacey a family's structure, whether a single-parent or two-parent household, is less important than the quality of its relationships. "Research indicates that high-conflict marriages are more harmful to children than low-conflict divorces," she writes. "The research scale tips toward those who stress the quality of family relationships over their form." She also notes, without acknowledging the relatively rare convergence of the conditions she names, that when "other parental resources — like income, education, self-esteem and a supportive social environment — are roughly similar, signs of two-parent privilege largely disappear."[13]

Stacey largely dismisses Whitehead's charge that choices made by parents in favor of personal fulfillment or career goals are often harmful to children. Whitehead's perspective, she argues, betrays a class bias that ignores "the family realities of working people — married or single, lesbian or straight, employed, laid off or retired.... Few can enjoy the luxury of a 'new familialism' that places children's needs above the demands of a job."[14]

Finally, Judith Stacey indicates that she shares many concerns with the centrists, although her solutions differ dramatically:

> We should also recognize that in most industrial societies teenage motherhood (married or not) often does not augur well for the offspring. Without rejecting the view that most teens now lack the maturity and resources to parent effectively, we might note that this is as true of those whom [sociologist] Charles Murray would shame and starve into shotgun marriages as of those whose dads lack shotguns.... The drive to restigmatize "illegitimacy" demands a renewed struggle to destigmatize abortion and make it accessible, along with contraception and sex education. It seems time to revive Margaret Sanger's slogan, "every child a wanted child." To show solidarity with single mothers, we need not deny that two responsible, loving parents generally *can* offer children more than one parent can. Of course, three or four might prove even better. Programs encouraging child-free adults to form supportive ties with children of overburdened parents (a category from which few parents are exempt) might give many kinds of families common cause.[15]

I find much to commend in the perspective of Stacey and the *Ms.* editorial cited at the beginning of the chapter. My household is part of a broader society. My parenting choices are framed by personal decisions made within the family. These decisions, however, are made within a broader social context that is influenced by economic policies and governmental priorities. Like Stacey I fear some of the anti-democratic impulses of the fundamentalist family-values crusaders, their bias against gay and lesbian people, their tendency to blame the poor for poverty, and their emphasis on personal accountability apart from wider social influences. There is little doubt, for example, that most family-values advocates divert attention from key economic and political policies that reward the privileged few at the expense of the majority of families. Family values and personal choices are nevertheless important. Citing family breakdown as the principal causal factor in social distress obscures complicated relationships between families and society. It is also true that naming dysfunctional social policies as the principal cause of family breakdown can serve to minimize the importance of personal responsibility and, whether intended or not, to deflect attention away from important issues concerning values.

Penelope Leach sorts out the various claims and offers resolution by stressing cumulative risk factors that influence child welfare:

> Different studies in various countries have shown...that children reared by lone parents are at a serious disadvantage; that they are not necessarily at any disadvantage; that they may have advantages over children brought up in two-parent households. The conclusion to be drawn is not necessarily that some or all of the research is flawed but that "it depends." And what the results of lone-parent rearing (or any other specific factor) depend on is *other* factors.
>
> It is the concept of cumulative risk factors in children's lives that makes research findings like these comprehensible. In post-industrial Western countries where family patterns are in flux and their reality is often at odds with the ideals of the society in which they are located, lone-parenting *is* a risk factor for children. But the magnitude of the risk depends on a wide range of family relationships and circumstances....Gradually we are learning to identify some of the risk factors that, piled one upon the other, make rotten results for children cumulatively more likely. The more we learn, the clearer it becomes that, in post-industrial societies at least, poverty is the biggest risk of all....In study after study, conducted in country after country, family poverty has been shown to be inexorably correlated with premature delivery; postnatal, infant and childhood mortality, malnutrition and ill-health; childhood neglect; educational failure; truancy; delinquency; school-age pregnancy and the birth of babies who are victims of premature delivery, post-natal, infant and childhood mortality, malnutrition and ill-health...and so on. Each of these is, in itself, a risk factor. Each can and does occur, singly or in combination, where families are in privileged socio-economic circumstances.

But poverty increases the statistical chances of those risk factors accumulating and the difficulty of dealing with any one of
them.[16]

It seems clear that any efforts to resolve the crisis of families
without addressing the issue of poverty are doomed to fail. At the
same time, those who minimize the importance of personal responsibility are likely leading us on pathways littered with obstacles to
the well-being of our children.

Chapter 6

Character Flaws

I know what the black man is, and I have no hesitation in declaring that he is incapable of the art of government, and that to entrust him with framing and working the laws for our islands is to condemn them to inevitable ruin.
—British Envoy Sir Spenser St. John, 1889

It's May 1994, a month after the election of Nelson Mandela as president of the Republic of South Africa. My home for the past several days has been a church retreat center in the black township of Soweto on the outskirts of Johannesburg. The compound is surrounded by a fence, and at night the main gate is locked. We have been warned not to venture out at night as the streets are not safe for blacks or whites after dark.

This morning's walk through an impoverished neighborhood with community leaders provides ample evidence that the changes sweeping through South Africa, although monumental, haven't yet begun to touch the poverty, poor housing, and joblessness that bind the majority of black South Africans like an unwelcome chain. Children, some naked, others barefoot and wearing little more than rags, go in and out of shacks to view the spectacle of visitors. Young men gather on street corners, restless and seemingly with nothing to do and no place to go. Older men and women sit on tree stumps surrounding old crates playing cards. The smiles of the children etch themselves in my memory.

Later that night I'm sitting in a small theater in downtown Johannesburg. Tonight's performance, *Josie Josie,* is a musical production about life in the "new South Africa" by a theater company with an all-black male cast. It depicts life in the black townships surrounding Johannesburg in a totally unflattering way, portraying daily realities of abusive, self-destructive behavior: drugs and alcohol, violence, the rip-off of vulnerable people, gambling, and crime.

Josie Josie, as I interpret it, offers a brutally self-critical look into the dysfunctional behavior of blacks who were the primary casualties of apartheid. It screams out with deafening clarity that although political apartheid is fallen, its legacy is alive and well, persistent and painful. The brutal consequences of apartheid are seared into the hearts, minds, and character of all South Africans, particularly black South Africans who were apartheid's principal victims.

The apartheid system (apartheid means separateness) utilized the labor of black workers to provide six million white South Africans with one of the world's highest standards of living while impoverishing most of the thirty-seven million blacks whom it confined to homelands or segregated in townships. In addition to race-specific economic development and impoverishment, the geography of apartheid insulated whites from visual images of their own brutality. In many cases whites did not see the human faces of poverty, inequality, and injustice that the apartheid system fostered.

Blacks could live and work only in areas designated by whites. Political power was confined to whites; blacks could not vote. The state police and military had a near monopoly on the instruments of violence, which they used frequently to maintain order in a system that in all its forms of structural violence gave rise to social turmoil. The system collapsed finally due to persistent black resistance, international sanctions, and the weight of its own contradictions.

On this particular night, *Josie Josie,* challenging in its own right, is of keen interest to me because I'm sitting next to two white South Africans. My brief exchange with them before the play begins provides ample evidence that they were not involved in the anti-apartheid movement. I marvel that they are here and cast glances occasionally in their direction as they watch many of their worst fears about the "new South Africa" acted out before them.

We talk further during intermission and after the production. They tell me that many whites resisted the formation of one-person-one-vote democracy because they believed the inevitable aftermath of any black-led government would be a bloodbath against whites. (I wonder if they have projected the values and behavior of previous white governments onto blacks. I also sense that at an unconscious level they are aware that the injustices of the apartheid system would make such a bloodbath a lamentable but understandable act of revenge. On the other hand, the violent and dysfunctional behavior of blacks depicted by blacks in *Josie Josie* lends legitimacy to their fears.)

My white South African theater companions tell me that they, unlike many whites, support the recent changes. They may not embrace Nelson Mandela, but they accept him as president, a prospect that not long before would have been unthinkable. "It was," they say, "unrealistic for things to continue on as before." They also are encouraged because the economy remains firmly rooted in the hands of whites, and many of their privileges are still intact. Even whites far more skeptical, they tell me, have been pleasantly surprised that the transition from apartheid to a black-led government has gone smoothly. "It's a miracle," one of them says.

This is perhaps the tenth time in as many days that people I've met, black and white, have used the word "miracle" while describing recent events. The anxiety white South Africans feel toward the future is still apparent in the faces of these theater companions as clearly as the shadows cast by a harvest moon on a cloudless night. Respect for Mandela is reluctant but real. Yet for these whites to embrace a "new South Africa," all blacks would need to be like Mandela, not like the blacks in *Josie Josie*.

Mandela is, of course, exceptional. Imprisoned for more than twenty years, cut off from his people, yet persistent, faithful, determined, gracious, competent, and forgiving. The "miraculous" transition is so much tied to Mandela's integrity that it is hard to envision a new South Africa without him.

But for my white theater companions Mandela is not only exceptional; he is the exception. Most disturbing, they see no connection between the dysfunctional behavior of blacks described in *Josie Josie* and the apartheid system. The play is for them not a play at all. The men on stage are not actors portraying the marred character of apartheid's victims. They are a representative group of blacks revealing the innate character of all black South Africans: drug and alcohol abuse, violence, prostitution, and crime are racially defined, the twisted consequence of genetic inferiority.

Josie Josie triggers a sense of doom in my theater companions. The immediacy of fear blinds them to their own wounds and to distortions in their own character resulting from apartheid. They identify race with dysfunctional behavior and downplay the reality of the white brutality that was the predominant feature of the apartheid order.

As we're leaving the theater, one of the South Africans speaks to me as an unhappy slaveholder expecting sympathy based on our common racial superiority: "I think your blacks are much more civilized than ours."

Two nights after seeing *Josie Josie*, I have a conversation with black women in Soweto. The township is famous for student-led uprisings against apartheid, depicted in the movie *Seraphina*. It is late, dark, and dangerous for these women who have come to meet with us at a local church. For several hours women whose faces are engraved with dignity and pain tell stories. Apartheid destroyed their lives and their families, and its terrible legacy continues to stalk them daily in the unwelcome shadows of dangerous streets and through crime, rape, unemployment, restless youth, and fear.

Apartheid, which separated blacks from whites, also separated blacks from one another: husbands from wives, women from men, mothers and fathers from their children. Women and children were often legally and, if necessary, forcibly restricted to homelands, areas in South Africa comprising about 13 percent of the country's land but home to nearly 87 percent of its people. Men went to work in the gold and diamond mines or in factories. Following work opportunities, many were confined to single-sex hostels, hell-holes of despair and violence. Movement within the country was regulated strictly.

The mothers with whom I am speaking were given passes to travel to Johannesburg to work during the day but had to return to Soweto to sleep. One of the most bitter fruits of apartheid is that the care they provided to the families for whom they worked was at the expense of their own children. One mother describes rising early each morning in order to travel to Johannesburg where she cares for a white family's children and household. She returns late at night to Soweto where her own children are attended by the street. "It's sad," she says. "We have lost our young people. They blame us because apartheid lasted so long. Young people no longer see us as other people's mothers. We are the targets of their hatred."

These women, their experiences, and their fears bring me back to *Josie Josie*, both to the power and to the inadequacy of the play. It describes the "new South Africa" through the lens of problems rooted in the apartheid system. So far, so good. But it is performed by an all-male cast. No women appear in the play, and the only "women" characters appear in a brief scene in which men dress up as prostitutes in order to deceive and rob foreigners.

On the positive side, an all-male cast, whether by design or not, draws attention to the troublesome and often violent behavior of men. Yet the depiction of "life in the new South Africa" without reference to women and children projects a powerful message of the "invisibility" of these groups.

Men in and outside South Africa, including those within institutions of a dominant society and those within marginalized communities, understand and exercise power in ways that are often destructive not only to themselves but to women and children. Not surprisingly, the all-male cast performing *Josie Josie*, although showing the problematic behavior of black men, ignores the fact that women and children are directly and indirectly victimized by the violent and socially destructive behavior of men. The obvious and yet often ignored relationship between men and violence is never named specifically.

As I listen to these women of Soweto, I am struck by how the "worst fears" of the white South Africans with whom I watched *Josie Josie* are daily realities for these women. There is a difference in perspective, however, and it is striking.

The white South Africans blame the victims, ascribe deviant behavior to race, and blind themselves conveniently to the consequences of apartheid and their role in it. The women of Soweto live with the consequences of apartheid, including crime and violence; they understand the dysfunctional behavior of many young people, particularly young men, in the context of apartheid; they lament the destruction of their own families, which they felt powerless to arrest; and they express both love and sadness, hope and dismay when they describe the young men who terrorize them, young men who are victims of apartheid, who must be given opportunities in the "new South Africa," but must be held accountable, too.

So many times as I walk the streets of my own city or reflect on my experiences in South Africa or Central America, I find myself looking at life through the eyes of children. Tonight as I speak with women of Soweto the weight of being a parent overcomes me. Within the context of apartheid, men and women put food on the table by sacrificing their children and in many cases without fully confronting the unjust apartheid order. Their children hated them for it. These women were not only victims of apartheid; they have become easy targets for the violence of other victims: the disgruntled youth who have lived without hope for so long.

Children in our society, too, are both victims and perpetrators of violence. Our children can rightfully find us guilty on many personal and social counts, but increasingly they are guilty, too. What's more, these women in Soweto remind me that parents concerned about injustice and their children's immediate needs walk a fine line between social responsibility and family neglect.

I have worked against hunger, poverty, and militarism all my adult life. These concerns predated the birth of my children and live on in the present and into the future. Ironically, the immediate needs of parenting make it more difficult for me to do this work while at the same time the love I feel for my children provides added motivation for doing so.

An additional insight hounds me throughout my stay in South Africa, preventing me from judging my white theater companions too harshly: the hideous consequences of apartheid in South Africa are paralleled in my own society. South Africa is a mirror in which I see my city and country, the global economy, the choices of my parents, my father, a smashed tricycle, family values, debates about welfare reform, and myself in new and disturbing ways.

Chapter 7

The Axman

===

If a man happens to be 36 years old, as I happen to be, and some great truth stands before the door of his life, some great opportunity to stand up for that which is right and that which is just, and he refuses to stand up because he wants to live a little longer and he is afraid his home will get bombed, or he is afraid he will get shot . . . he may go on and live until he is 80, and the cessation of breath in his life is merely the belated announcement of an earlier death of the spirit.

—Martin Luther King Jr.

I remember my grandfather describing an acquaintance in his small town as "a pretty good guy — for a Catholic." There were no Jews or blacks in the Swedish Lutheran enclave of Center City, Minnesota, and so Catholics were the objects of prejudice.

I grew up in two suburbs outside Minneapolis. Through grade three I lived in Brooklyn Park, a blue-collar, working-class neighborhood. Apart from missing my father, who worked long hours as a printer, and the time a neighbor tried to make me eat a bug, my memories of these years are positive. There were lots of kids, families, and fun. As kids we lived outside on bicycles, at the local park playing baseball, or shooting baskets in our driveway even in the dead of winter. Our family houses and lots were small, but our homes were revolving doors in which neighborhood children were always welcome. No one had fences, nearly everything was shared, and picnics and pot-lucks were common.

I was in the fourth grade when my family moved to Coon Rapids, a "nicer" suburb. The lot was beautiful, the house larger and new, but almost everything that had made Brooklyn Park a neighborhood, including close friends, shared meals, common struggles, and open doors, was absent in this isolated development.

Race may have been a dynamic in my neighborhood of Brooklyn Park, but I have no such memories. Within the homogeneous environment of Coon Rapids, prejudice and race also seemed like nonissues. Almost. When I was a sophomore in high school I was a starting guard on our basketball team. One night we were playing against a local school with an African-American player, a rarity in our suburban conference. Unknown to me, my teammates, and the crowd in attendance, our center hurled quiet racial slurs at this player throughout the game. His capacity to endure the constant barrage of insults was finally exceeded, and a shoving match ensued between the two players. This was perhaps my first experience that justice isn't color-blind. The African-American player was assessed a technical foul and, if I remember correctly, ejected from the game.

In another case a disk jockey on a Twin Cities radio station referred frequently to my home town of Coon Rapids as "Nigger Falls." The label was both disgusting and ironic, as there were no blacks in my community. There was sufficient protest to get the radio station to pressure him to stop. His racial slurs, however, did inspire a brief discussion in the city council about changing the name of our fair city.

For council members, the derogatory label "Nigger Falls" was symbolic of a broader image problem that was impeding their efforts to attract business and wealthy whites. "Coon Rapids" wasn't a sophisticated enough name for a ring suburb of Minneapolis. I realize in retrospect that in all likelihood they found "Nigger Falls" objectionable not so much because of its racist overtones but because it gave the false impression that blacks lived in Coon Rapids.

The council suggested "Flower City" as an alternative, but the name change faltered. Some of us joked that the mighty Coon Rapids Cardinals football team, which finished the season in my junior year with an impressive zero wins and eight losses, almost became the formidable Flower City Orchids. Adding to the absurdity, there were very few flowers within the city limits. What our city did have was an overabundance of thorny "stickers" that thrived in the mixture of sand and clay. The-ever present "stickers" account for my preference even today for wearing shoes instead of going barefoot, even in mid-summer.

If race was an issue that seemed unimportant where I lived, then it is also true that racism was not something I associated with or discussed with my family, including my father. When I was growing up, I loved sports, and I remember my father as a great athlete. On his fortieth birthday he challenged his children (four sons) to a running race and beat each of us handily. He flirted with professional boxing and was cut by the St. Louis Cardinals only on the final day of spring training.

As I remember the legend, he was let go after striking out most of the starting lineup in his final spring game. They didn't tell him that his fastball lacked velocity or that his curve didn't dive sharply but that he was too small and his arm wouldn't stand up to a full season. I thought of my father in 1978 when I lived in New York City. That was the year a small Yankee pitcher by the name of Ron Guidry won twenty-five games and lost only three. For my father, World War II ended any possibility of a made-for-TV ending.

When I was twelve my dad showed me, after much pleading on my part, how to throw a curve ball. My first attempt broke so sharply, and unexpectedly, that my father stuck out his throwing hand in an effort to catch it, breaking his thumb in the process. Even though I was underage I pitched twenty-seven consecutive scoreless innings in a summer baseball league because almost no one had seen, let alone could hit, a curve ball.

My father cared deeply about his children. Recurring problems with the presses at work, however, left him with little time or energy to spend with us, except for occasional weekends and a two-week vacation that our family spent together at the cabin he and my grandfather had built. I missed my father growing up, and the quality time we had together at the cabin compensated only partially for his absence in my life much of the rest of the time.

❖

The overriding goal of my parents was to provide a good life for each of their children, including opportunities for a college education. I respect and appreciate these goals, but even they are not as unqualified an object of praise as one might think. During the years of my childhood and youth, "the good life" for my family was defined too readily in material terms. The money for a cabin, for a new house in a "nicer suburb," and even money that helped with college was earned at the expense of relational time with each of my parents. Although I could not have articulated it to them then, I realize now that I loved my parents more than the things they wanted to give me or the things I felt I needed.

My mother went to work as an insurance underwriter when I started kindergarten. Ours was a traditional household. After becoming a full-time worker, she remained the person most responsible for cleaning, laundry, and cooking. Working mothers average three hours of home-maintenance work a day compared to twelve minutes for working fathers, statistics that were borne out in my childhood home.[1] My mother accepted these traditional roles but was overwhelmed by the amount of work that went with them.

That made the family cabin a mixed blessing. It was the place I spent good time with my father, but it added to the stress of our family and detracted from my relationship with my mother. Not only did a cabin necessitate my parents working more to increase family income; it added considerably to my mother's work load while "on vacation"; she was now responsible for two homes.

My mother is one of those people who likes things very orderly, clean, and neat. Now there were two sources feeding and frustrating that compulsion: four rather typical sons sometimes helping but more often undermining her efforts, and an overworked husband, stretched physically and emotionally. My mother, exhausted by it all, had high blood pressure and suffered a heart attack before she was forty. Consequently my mother, who is one of the kindest, gentlest, and most loving people on earth, was in my childhood often irritable and unpleasant to be around.

Mother wanted desperately to have a daughter for reasons that went well beyond a desire to have someone with whom to share the work. Had she had the daughter of her dreams, however, I have no doubt strict roles for boys and girls would have been reinforced. I was the fourth and, as it turned out, final child, as my mother's last pregnancy terminated with a miscarriage. The fact that I was a boy was something of a disappointment. She loved me dearly and still does, but she called me Jackie until I was five. One of my earlier memories is of the time when she bought me a new pair of red girl's shoes. I put my foot down instead of into the new shoes. "My name is Jack," I told her. "I'm a boy."

One interesting development in our male-dominant household that later had a significant impact on my approach to parenting is that as boys we did help with cooking and cleaning and other tasks assigned traditionally to girls. These patterns might have been truncated if my mother had been blessed with the daughter she longed for.

My father was tired and withdrawn and sometimes irritable out of sheer exhaustion, but I remember him as kind, gentle, and compassionate. He died of cancer at the age of fifty-nine, his lungs unable to withstand his many years of smoking and the lethal chemicals he inhaled at his unventilated workplace. Several people at his funeral told me he "was the finest human being" they'd ever known. I never heard my mother or father utter a derogatory joke, use racist language, or categorize or overtly stereotype any group of people. It was only recently that I began thinking about my father's prejudices. Because he was a very decent human being, it's hard to think about him and racism at the same time. As I watch *Josie Josie* and listen to my white South African theater companions, however, my father joins me as an unexpected guest:

"Dad?"

"Yes, son."

"Do you remember when I was about six or seven? You were having trouble with a new press at work. I hardly saw you. You didn't even sleep."

"I remember," my father says. "We were in Brooklyn Park then. Those were difficult days at work."

"But you never complained," I say.

"I was too tired to complain," he says with a smile.

I loved my father's smile. He smiled most when he was fishing — that is, if my brothers and I kept our lines out of the motor and our hooks out of his skin. "Do you remember a job offer in Milwaukee?" I ask.

My father grimaces along with my other theater companions as another fight ensues on stage. Black taxi drivers are settling a dispute over proper routes and fares. "I remember," he says, unable to pull his eyes from the actors. "It was a good job."

"When you and Mom talked, I thought it sounded great. You said the pay was good, the job less stressful, and the work-week shorter."

"You have a good memory," he says. "Do you see that?" he adds. "The guy's got a knife as big as a machete."

"What I don't understand," I say to him, "is why you didn't take it. It was a better job. You would have earned enough money, worked fewer hours, and spent more time with me, with our family."

I feel my pulse rising and tears forming in my eyes. "Maybe if you had taken that job," I continue, "then you wouldn't have worked yourself into a heart attack that forced you away from the printing presses and into that room without ventilation where you breathed too many chemicals. Maybe at the new job you wouldn't have breathed all those chemicals. Maybe if you hadn't been so stressed out at work you could have quit smoking earlier. Maybe you'd still be alive and I could call you for advice, we could go fishing, and my kids would have another grandfather. I miss you, Dad."

I'm not sure my father can hear me above the brawl on stage. Finally, he looks deep into my tearful eyes and then away. He knows the question that is coming. "Why didn't you take the job?" I ask.

My father won't or can't answer, and so I answer for him.

"I remember why you turned it down. You said 'Milwaukee is too close to the problems of Chicago.' That's what you said. I'm not sure I knew what that meant. Until now."

I glance at the stage and then back again, but my father is gone. All that remains are creeping memories. Not long after refusing a job in Milwaukee my mother and father uprooted our family from our neighborhood in Brooklyn Park. Against the wishes of the children, we moved about fifteen miles to the almost exclusively white suburb of Coon Rapids. My parents, working hard already to make ends meet and to pay for a cabin, were forced by mortgage payments on a new house to work even harder. They were therefore even less available to us. Our family changed houses and neighborhoods. My father kept the job that killed him.

My father died at home, the beneficiary of a hospice program that enabled us to care for him during his final weeks of life. We set up a bed in the dining room, where he could look out the sliding glass doors onto the backyard. Although my father hated the hospital, it was a difficult decision to leave. As long as he was at the hospital, there was a part of him that clung to an irrational hope of being cured. Coming home marked a turning point in my father's dying process. It meant full acceptance of the fact that he was going to die. Soon.

From the moment of his arrival it was clear that home was a better place to die. My father seemed remarkably free. Our house was built on a flat area at the top of a hill. Behind the house the lawn sloped downward gradually for fifty feet or so and then cascaded abruptly, leading to a small creek. From his bed he could enjoy the sight of green grass, oak trees, birds, and squirrels.

I sat with my father for many hours during his final days. Sometimes we would talk lucidly about his life, our life together, our love, his feelings about dying, and his ongoing hope for each of us. Other times I would quietly play my dulcimer, an instrument he loved, which seemed to soothe him. More often than not, especially toward the end, we sat in silence as my mother, one of my brothers, or I held his hand. Touch was important for us in those final days, as important as it is for parents and a newborn baby. It was as if by holding hands we kept each other in the same world for a few more precious moments.

There were several times during my father's final days that relative peace gave way quickly to panic. He sat up, looked intently out the back with fear across his face.

"Do you see him?" he asked with terror.

"See who?" My confusion was the other side of his own.

"Him," he said pointing.

"I don't see anyone, Dad. There's no one there."

"Yes, there is," he countered urgently. "He's coming for me."

"Who? Whom do you see?"

My father pointed again in the direction of the oak tree at the edge of the backyard. "Don't you see him, that big black man carrying the ax? He's coming over the hill to get me."

My father eventually calmed down, either convinced by our assurances or entering gradually a more lucid space. The scene repeated itself several times before he died. My father saw the angel of death coming for him, a black man carrying an ax.

Prejudice is common to most if not all peoples and cultures. It crosses religious, racial, economic, and national divides. However troublesome and widespread prejudice is, it becomes far more damaging when unequal power relationships allow one group to act out its prejudices at the expense of others considered less worthy. For this reason racism is often understood as prejudice plus power.

In South Africa, whites were able to institutionalize their prejudices against blacks because whites controlled sufficient economic, political, and military power to impose unjust systems on those they defined as inferior. The same can be said of slavery and Jim Crow laws in the United States. In both countries, therefore, it is necessary to speak not only of prejudice but of white racism.

Most of us are familiar with and disgusted by the Holocaust, where prejudice, reinforced by genetic theories of superiority and demonic power, resulted in the murder of millions of Jews and numerous homosexuals and Gypsies. Some may not know that Hitler, who published *Mein Kampf* in 1924, was so impressed with the U.S. Immigration Restriction Act, which prohibited people with hereditary illnesses and entire ethnic groups from immigrating to the United States, that he used it as a model for his program of racial purification.

In our turbulent world, deadly prejudice need not be based on race. Yugoslavia disintegrated in the context of bitter rivalries, prejudices, and hatreds among Serbs, Croats, and Muslims, who are racially indistinguishable. Prejudice and racism, whether subtle or blatant, personal or institutional, always have negative consequences. In times of economic crisis and dislocation, in fearful times, problems of prejudice and racism become still more entrenched, pervasive, and dangerous.

There is something deeply troubling to me about my father seeing death coming for him in the vision of a black man carrying an ax. It tells me that racism is a seed-bed in our subconscious on which others can sow seeds of hatred and fear quite purposefully. When the Bush presidential campaign wanted a symbol to illustrate that Michael Dukakis and the Democrats were "soft" on crime and criminals, they chose Willie Horton. Perhaps less conscious, but equally troubling, was Robert Kaplan's choice of black Africa as emblematic of the coming global chaos.

My father's death taught me many things. It showed me first of all that there is no hope without honesty. He had started coughing up blood a year before he died. The doctor's faulty diagnosis, "chronic bronchitis, not cancer," led us all to breathe a deep sigh of relief. We had heard what we wanted to hear. When the bronchitis didn't improve, he was finally and belatedly diagnosed and died a month or so later. This need for honest assessment, including the fact that hearing what we don't want to hear may be essential to life and healing, has social significance as well. As I have argued throughout this book there is no hope of solving the crisis of children and families in our society unless we are willing to take an honest and uncomfortable look at our personal and social priorities.

Ironically, my father's racist image of death's henchman made me think of the powerful words of Martin Luther King quoted at the beginning of this chapter. King, who was killed because he challenged both the economic and social aspects of racism, understood the horror of dying in the midst of life. I had been "dying" in a bad marriage for seven years, and my father's death helped me come to terms with that painful fact. His death taught me how precious life is. It should not be wasted or lived dishonestly. Each of us must awaken from our slumber, take risks at home and in the workplace, and place our lives clearly on the side of hope and healing — within our families, our communities, and the society that binds us together. Or tears us apart.

Chapter 8

Poverty-fed Prejudices

How does it feel to be a problem?... A sense of being a problem people rather than people with problems; of having one's humanity problematized rather than having the problems facing one highlighted; dealing every day with the subtle and sometimes not too subtle white supremacist's assaults on black beauty... attacks on black intelligence, guilt before proven innocent, or if you meet the standards, exceptional negro, different than the rest....Attacks on black moral character. Metaphors like welfare queen, a symbol of laziness and ripping off the nation state and one looks at the history of black women in this country, 60 percent in 1900 working in white households raising white children as well as working in their own households raising their own kids and they become the symbol of laziness, and idleness. How absurd. The sense of being cast as part of an undifferentiated blob, a monolithic and homogenous conglomerate. That's what it is to be cast as a problem people.
— Cornel West

Dion* is an African-American child who attends kindergarten with my daughter Hannah at a public school in Minneapolis. Dion's name comes up during my after-school conversations with Hannah. Her references to Dion are infrequent but negative. There is nothing harsh in her comments, just a general sense that she doesn't have much to do with Dion and several other children of color in her classroom.

Hannah is the youngest child in her kindergarten class of 1992–93, and she is extremely shy. We are pleased that she loves both her

---

*This and some of the other names of actual persons mentioned in this book have been changed.

teacher and school. She seems to thrive in her new environment, embracing new opportunities for learning and improving her social skills. My concern is that Hannah's only negative comments about school have to do with Dion. I wonder why she doesn't seem to care for him. I receive an answer when I work as "parent helper" in her classroom.

I arrive at Hannah's class about an hour into her school day, excited to see her in a new environment. Most of the children are busy at various tasks. Hannah is playing a matching game with another child. Others are painting, drawing pictures, or working on a project that has something to do with their teeth and whatever experience they may have had at the dentist. Her teacher asks me to work with Dion one on one with what seems to be a simple task of putting items in sequence. Red peg, blue peg, red peg, blue peg, red peg, blue peg.

As Dion sits across from me I introduce myself and try to engage him in conversation. I'm a recovering introvert and understand that having a stranger assigned to work with him might be awkward for him. Dion, however, is almost totally withdrawn and barely notices my presence. He yawns every few seconds, and lengthy blank stares are interrupted occasionally by darting glances as his attention seems to shift suddenly from random space to the immediacy of a particular object. Within minutes of "interacting" with Dion, I find myself wondering about his life. What gets in the way of his needed sleep? What is his home like? His diet? His family? His neighborhood?

Hannah and Dion attend a public Montessori school — a magnet rather than a neighborhood school, which means their parents choose to send them there. The sequential task that Dion is being asked to master is an essential stepping stone to other learning within the Montessori system. Many other students — black, white, red, and brown — successfully complete this task. Dion's difficulties, in other words, should not be dismissed as consequences of cultural bias in the curriculum.

A few minutes with Dion also help me understand where Hannah is coming from. My initial fear was that her lack of interaction with Dion, her vague expressions of discomfort, were signs of early prejudice. I am relieved to see Hannah interacting meaningfully with other children, including other African-American children.

Hannah's discomfort is not based on skin color but on the fact that she has almost nothing in common with Dion. Dion and several other children of color in her classroom are lethargic; Hannah and the others animated. Dion is tired; the others energetic. Dion is withdrawn; the others engaged. Dion is uninterested in school; the others engrossed, eager to learn, excited by the various projects and tasks with which they are involved. His elbow on the table, his head resting precariously on his hand, I try to get Dion focused on the task before us.

"Look at the pegs," I say. "Do you see the pattern?"

No response.

"Red, blue, red, blue," I add, putting more pegs into the board in sequence. "Red. What color peg should come next?" I ask.

Another yawn. Dion's eyes dart away and then return. "I want to go home," he says.

"School is over in another hour," I respond. "Red, blue, red, blue, red. What color comes next?"

Finally, Dion seems to track my words. He looks at the pattern before him and picks up a peg. "Green?" he asks, putting a green peg next to the red.

I repeat this exercise with another student with the same result. She too is an African-American child. Although less withdrawn than Dion, she is unable to complete the simple task and seems equally uninterested in being at school. She and Dion are already far behind Hannah and the other students in the class. It is a tragedy for their lives and for our society that they have started out behind and are unlikely to ever catch up.

The last day of school I get partial answers to my questions about Dion's situation. I sit next to his mother at a class picnic, and she tells me that the family is living in a shelter for homeless persons. Their apartment has been condemned because of dangerous levels of lead. One of her children is in the hospital with acute symptoms of lead poisoning. She looks at Dion and says: "I'm afraid it has affected him, too."

❖

One of my hopes for my children is that they learn to respect diversity. I want them to have friendships that cross racial, cultural, gender, and religious lines. I long for them to experience the rich diversity of cultures and to learn appropriate ways of dealing with problems, differences, and conflicts. These may be illusive dreams in a city and society segregated along class and racial lines and in which antagonism toward homosexuality is growing.

Our children and family benefit from our involvement in an ecumenical Christian faith-based community that, although mostly white, is diverse in other ways. We are Catholics and Lutherans, Mennonites and Quakers, Methodists and Presbyterians, young and old, single and married, married with and without children, worshiping and acting together. Perhaps our closest friends and neighbors are a lesbian couple, Julie and Linda, and their two children, John and Lucy. Our friendship, our proximity, our involvement in the same faith community, and the fact that Hannah and their daughter are best friends mean that our lives are woven together with threads of love, mutual help, and appreciation.

Divorce is often hard on children. Tension between former spouses doesn't end when divorce papers are signed. Conflicts over values, approaches to discipline and caring, issues of time and money linger on. Children of divorced parents face relational challenges that are enormously complex even under the best of circumstances. John and Lucy spend one night a week and every other weekend with their father, who recently remarried. The children must deal with their mother and father, now living separate lives except for their common bond to the children. They must also relate to the new life partners each has chosen.

John and Lucy's situation is more complicated because their mother is a lesbian in a society uncomfortable with sexuality and particularly troubled by homosexuality. They are fortunate to have the benefit of a supportive community in which John and Lucy are not singled out for ridicule or hate-inspired language because they have "two moms." They also are blessed because they have a loving mother who is an excellent parent, and their step-mom is sensitive, committed, and caring. Julie and Linda know the importance of male role models, particularly for John, and so he and I get together regularly, something each of us looks forward to. Julie teaches Hannah piano. Our families share meals and child care frequently.

Julie and Linda have claimed the right to commit themselves to each other for life in a public marriage ceremony, which our community embraced and celebrated. The closeness of our families means my children have two positive role models for parenting, one in which their own parents are a committed, married heterosexual couple and the other a committed, married lesbian couple. To my children, Julie and Linda are not sexual misfits. Homosexuals are not fags, queers, or dykes. Hannah has said on more than one occasion that when she gets older she may marry Lucy or Matthew.

Matthew is a young boy with whom Hannah shared child care two days a week for more than five years. They were five years old at the time they had the following "argument." "No, they can't," Matthew says emphatically. "Yes, they can," Hannah counters. "No, they can't," he repeats. "Yes, they can," she says once again. Finally, I ask what the heated discussion is about. "Matthew says women can't marry women and that men can't marry men, but I say they can." Hannah seems exasperated by Matthew's inability to comprehend what for her is obvious. "I told him about Julie and Linda's wedding and that Lucy is my best friend but he still doesn't believe me."

Hannah is learning about gay and lesbian people, not as abstractions but through the lives of real people, through relationships, mutual friends, and daily living. Can anyone seriously doubt that these are far better teachers than the bigotry and closed-mindedness evidenced by so many parents whose legitimate concerns for children get drowned in a sea of their own prejudices?

I wish I could tell similar stories about my children's interaction with black children and other children of color, helping to nullify or derail prejudices. But Hannah's experiences with children of color in her classroom, although not uniform, regrettably tend to reinforce prejudices.

When I speak in various places around the country and tell people I'm from Minneapolis, they often respond that "Minneapolis is such a wonderful city." Well, yes and no. Minneapolis has good parks, lakes within the city limits, bike paths, and a relatively good public school system. Others cite a history of progressive government, a civic-minded corporate culture, good cultural events, and professional sports teams as further evidence of an attractive city.

There is, however, another side to my city and state. Minneapolis is one of the most segregated cities in the country. People of color are more likely to live in poverty here than in any other major city in the United States.[1] In Minnesota, 54.2 percent of black children ages five and under live in poverty, a rate five times higher than that of white children. The overall poverty rate for blacks in the state is 37 percent, nearly four times the rate of whites. For Native Americans the rate is 43.7 percent; for Hispanics, 25.6 percent; and for Asians, 31.7 percent.[2] People of color in Minnesota are both poor and imprisoned in numbers disproportionate to their total number in the population, compared to whites. In fact, Minnesota's arrest and incarceration numbers are the nation's highest in racial disproportion. Black Minnesotans ten and older had a one-in-three chance of being arrested last year; for whites, it was one in twenty-two. Black adults are 27.7 times more likely to be locked up in state prisons than white adults, more than three times the black-to-white arrest ratio.[3]

With people of color disproportionately poor and concentrated in the Twin Cities, and with many affluent whites moving to the suburbs, more than one of two children in Minneapolis public schools are from families living on incomes below the poverty line. Hannah's kindergarten class is a microcosm of our broader society and world in which it is easy to confuse issues of poverty with those of race. Hannah did not dislike Dion because he was black. She was cool toward him because of the problems he brought with him to the classroom that resulted in his being lethargic, exhausted, and unable to focus on learning.

We would do well to recognize, however, that in a society in which people of color are disproportionately poor, Hannah's experience with problematic behavior rooted in poverty can easily become a foundation for racism. It may not take long before Dion's behavioral problems are linked to his race. If that happens then Dion, a child with many problems, will be seen as a problem child who is part of a problem people.

Chapter 9

Poor Perceptions

Prevalent among many who choose this work is the myth that the poor are to be our teachers. Perhaps it originated in the Gospel's Beatitudes, perhaps it derives in part from Liberation Theology, but according to the myth the poor are the simple ones, the salt of the earth. Their poverty has taught them humility; their suffering has given them wisdom. We who come to "help" should learn from their elemental values, from their long-suffering in the face of intolerable odds. For the political radical or community organizer, the myth differs somewhat: "The poor" are for them the authentic source of resistance to the dominant order, the source of revolution.

These are attractive fantasies. Sometimes I find myself propagating elements of them, too. But Deloris Taylor [a difficult patient] seems far from being the "salt of the earth," and all she teaches me is how difficult caring for the poor can be, how angry I am at having to deal with her damaged self. Those who have suffered the emotional and physical deprivation of the ghettos are not automatically "beautiful souls." It is still a shock to discover that I cannot handle the powerlessness and not even faintly edifying helplessness of the people I have come to serve. Coming face-to-face with unpleasant, ungrateful, and manipulative poor people is a misery all its own; and when I find that I cannot love my patients, or even serve them without resentment, I invariably wonder what's wrong with me.

—DR. DAVID HILFIKER, *Not All of Us Are Saints*

Several years ago I spoke with Jon Sobrino, a Jesuit priest and liberation theologian who teaches at the Catholic university in San Salvador. Sobrino has spent much of his life defending the interests

74

of poor people in a society marred by greed, violence, and brutality spearheaded by the rich and their backers in the military. He and his colleagues teach at the university, but they also work directly with people in poor communities. In many ways, they both encourage and echo voices of the poor.

Proponents of liberation theology say that poverty and injustice are signs of human sin rather than God's will and that people and communities of faith have a responsibility to work for greater justice. Sobrino, like the theology he espouses, is profoundly hopeful. Inspiring hope in others, however, particularly the poor, is dangerous. In the 1980s wealthy Salvadorans claimed that liberation theology was a deceptive cover for Marxism. U.S. foreign policy planners agreed. Together they targeted liberation theology as an enemy. The tragic consequences became clear to me during the years I lived in Central America. They are illustrated in the following story told to me by a Salvadoran *campesino,* or landless peasant, whose son was brutally tortured and killed:

> By a miracle I am able to tell you the story of my grand crime for which they threatened me with death. They took my son who was 18 years old, shot him ... and hung him from a cross in a tree.... They did this to warn me because I was a celebrator of the word of God. That was my crime.... We had to leave because they persecuted the whole land.
>
> Our crime is to be poor and ask for bread. Here the laws only favor the rich. However, the great majority of people are poor. Those who have jobs are exploited daily in the factories and on the farms. Without land we cannot plant. There is no work. This brings more hunger, more misery. We are without clothes, schools or jobs. And so we demonstrate. But to speak of justice is to be called a communist, to ask for bread is subversive. It is a war of extermination.... It is a crime to be a Christian and to demand justice."[1]

In November 1989 U.S.-trained elite soldiers entered the Catholic university and brutally murdered six Jesuit priests and two women workers. Sobrino avoided their fate because he was outside the country. The "crime" of his massacred friends is the same as other murdered religious workers in El Salvador, including Archbishop Oscar Romero, four U.S. church women — Maura Clarke, Jean Donovan, Ita Ford, and Dorothy Kazel — and hundreds of lay religious leaders who suffered fates similar to that of the *campesino* just quoted: they awakened hope in the poor and defended their interests.

Father Sobrino told a group I was traveling with in El Salvador that "anyone who idealizes the poor or poverty hasn't spent time with either. Poverty is ugly," he said, "and it does ugly things to people and to the communities where they live. Poverty means death." Given his history of work with the poor, his articulation of a theology in which justice is a central attribute of God, given the deaths of his friends and the risks he takes, I believe Jon Sobrino's words about poverty should be taken seriously.

Sobrino has received many North American visitors. He understands our capacity to take a powerful theology and idealize it, thus diminishing it. And he along with Dr. Hilfiker quoted at the beginning of this chapter must know that while some people vilify the poor, others mythologize them. When I hear Sobrino's cautionary words and listen to those of a committed D.C. doctor, I gain important insights into myself and the poor. I realize that many people, myself included, have been inspired through encounters with poor people in Central America but often feel overwhelmed and discouraged by poverty closer to home. If I am honest, I admit that I am thoroughly uninspired by many poor people I see in my own city, including the homeless man often seated next to me at the library who carries on a conversation with himself about the devil and Liberace. This contrast between my experience of poor people near and far reminds me that those who give me inspiration in Central America are the *organized* poor.

Poverty, as Father Sobrino, Dr. Hilfiker, the poor themselves, and most of the rest of us know, is ugly. The struggle to survive can be a desperate one. Brokenness at some point does away with all niceties. Poor people often behave in ways that are destructive to themselves and others. Situations of poverty are often marked by crime, murder, drugs, prostitution, violence, malnutrition, infant mortality, broken families, and abuse. The *organized* poor, whether in the

United States or Central America, inspired by a new understanding of themselves and in some cases of God, are not transformed into saints. But many do regain a sense of dignity, purpose, and possibility. The poverty they fight against is still ugly, but there is power in their personal transformation and the social movements they are struggling to build at a grass-roots level. I think, for example, of the Christian communities in Central America who find courage in cooperative Bible study and action, or of homeless people in Minneapolis who work with the Alliance of the Streets on housing and other issues. The organized poor are unfortunately a distinct minority who somehow have managed to at least partially transcend enormous personal and social obstacles standing in the way of hope itself.

The life situation of Hannah's classmate Dion amplifies the concerns of a Salvadoran priest and a D.C. doctor. Together they remind me that poverty is destructive and unpleasant. Poverty takes a brutal toll on its victims. This does not mean that wealth is beautiful or that wealthy people are incapable of behaviors destructive to themselves and others. The wealthy people in El Salvador directly or indirectly gave the orders to murder priests and fashioned an ideology that found it acceptable to torture *campesinos*. Money has a profound impact on U.S. politics, and it is wealthy people and their political allies at home and abroad who shape economic policies that fill their coffers while emptying the plates of the poor. And it is the economically powerful who bring us our news, focus attention on street crime rather than corporate crime, provide us images of the "good life," and widen divisions among the economically insecure in ways that consciously or unconsciously divert attention from their own role in destructive public policies.

The "ugly things" relatively rich people do are in some cases less visible but not necessarily less problematic. A battered suburban wife and her violent husband are more hidden than a poor woman and her attacker on the sidewalk. An emotionally neglected child of Nintendo is less apparent than a homeless child begging on a street corner. The businessmen chugging mixed drinks on early-morning flights or in airport lounges are both less noticeable and more acceptable to us than a drunk swaggering down Broadway carrying a bottle inside a paper bag. Corporate crimes, like the Savings and Loan or insider trading scandals, get less media attention and capture fewer of our fears than the gruesome murders on the nightly news, and yet they may be more costly and far-reaching in their negative impact on society.

A focus on the relationship between race and poverty is important because it reveals something about the nature of our society: Blacks and other people of color are disproportionately poor. However, such a focus may divert attention from the main power brokers in our unequal system, thus obscuring more than illuminating the causes of our interrelated crises of family and society.

Hannah's "prejudice" against Dion may best be understood as a reasonable prejudice against poverty or against problem behaviors linked to Dion's tragic economic circumstance, and not his race. Because poverty correlates closely with street crime, delinquency, and poor academic performance, however, and because people of color in our society are disproportionately poor, then over time it may be difficult for Hannah, and ourselves, to distinguish between problems rooted in poverty and those rooted in race. When we focus on race rather than poverty, we lose track of vital issues.

William Julius Wilson, an African-American sociologist, argues that although racism is important in explaining poverty in America, the key variable in understanding segregation, poverty, and crime is jobs. Segregation, he says, is now linked to concentrated poverty because of joblessness. In the Brownsville area of Chicago, for example, Wilson notes that in 1950 nearly 70 percent of men age fourteen and over were employed, whereas in 1990 only 37 percent of those sixteen and over had jobs. Both the number and the quality of jobs have declined.[2]

People concerned about violent crime and the problems of unwed teenage mothers, Wilson says, must look at the issues of jobs, unemployment, and low salaries. Black and white youth who are eleven years of age, Wilson points out, are equally likely to commit violent crimes, but by their late twenties blacks are four times more likely to be offenders. However, blacks and whites who are employed differ little in violent behavior.[3] Wilson also sees a direct link between joblessness and births to unwed mothers as the number of employed men able to meet family responsibilities has diminished.[4] He is not alone. "Until we invest heavily in our inner cities," Sylvia Ann Hewlett writes, "until disadvantaged youths are given the...opportunity to join the mainstream of society, out-of-wedlock births to teen girls will continue to spiral out of control."[5]

If we see the links between dysfunctional behavior and economic deprivation, then our search for solutions for children with problems in a troubled society will force us to look at the causes of economic inequality, including racism. If on the other hand we focus attention on problem peoples and lose sight of the ugliness of poverty and its causes, then we are increasingly likely to become a racist people and culture prone to scapegoating and to the mean politics it fosters.

Charles Murray, embraced by many family-values crusaders because of his praise of two-parent families and his position advocating an end to welfare, argues that blacks are poor because they are genetically inferior.[6] He along with Richard Herrnstein co-authored *The Bell Curve*, a book with a simple, flawed, and seductive message: that low IQ *causes* people to be poor rather than poverty causing low IQs. If poverty can be blamed on the deficient IQ of the poor, then we need not pay much attention to the social roots of poverty. Whites who are convinced that poverty is rooted in the inherent deficiency of the impoverished need not feel guilty or examine racism. In the present political climate, old arguments about racial inferiority are being rekindled in pursuit of objectives such as punitive welfare reform and the crackdown on Latino and black immigrants who, according to Murray and Herrnstein, are "putting some downward pressure on the distribution of intelligence."[7]

In *Amazing Grace*, a book in which Jonathan Kozol shares conversations with many poor people, mostly living in the South Bronx, the bitter irony of genetic-based research into low IQs is laid bare:

In the light of all these socially created injuries to intellect, most of which could be corrected by a fair-minded society, it may seem surprising that scarce research funds should be diverted to investigations of "genetic links" between the IQ deficits of certain children and their racial origins. There is something wrong with a society where money is available to do this kind of research but not to remove lead poison from the homes and schools of children."[8]

Jim Naureckas, writing in *Extra*, a publication of Fairness and Accuracy in Reporting, speculates as to why a book with many fundamental flaws could receive so much attention:

Why is *The Bell Curve* suddenly an "important book" that needs to have cover stories, news broadcasts, even whole magazines devoted to it? In large part, because the book is well-timed to take advantage of a resurgence of racism in U.S. media and society — a racism that does not want to face up to its own identity.[9]

As time goes on and economic divisions between the races widen, as highly visible criminal and other dysfunctional behaviors associated with poverty manifest themselves throughout society but with disproportionate frequency within communities of color, our racial stereotypes are likely to harden. Jonathan Kozol writes:

The statement... heard so often now as to assume the character of incantation, that embattled neighborhoods like the South Bronx have undergone a "breakdown of the family," upsets many women that I know, not because they think it is not true, but because those who repeat this phrase, often in an unkind and censorious way, do so with no reference to the absolute collapse of almost every other form of life-affirming institution in the same communities.... Perhaps this is one reason why so much of the debate about the "breakdown of the family" has a note of the unreal or incomplete. "Of course the family structure breaks down in a place like the South Bronx!" says a white minister who works in one of New York City's poorest neighborhoods. "Everything breaks down in a place like this.

The pipes break down. The phone breaks down. The electricity and heat break down. The spirit breaks down. The body breaks down.... Why wouldn't the family break down also?"[10]

Whether we are talking about the "breakdown of the family" or crime, addressing "ugly behavior" will require a willingness to examine the underlying issues of poverty and social inequality. Our track record of doing so is not encouraging. In South Africa my theater companions refused to see a relationship between the problematic behavior of blacks depicted in *Josie Josie* and the apartheid system. In El Salvador the United States and its allies among Salvador's business and military elite waged a repressive war against the organized poor, including progressive religious workers. A similar phenomenon is at play within the United States, where public policies that aggravate and even cause poverty go largely unscrutinized while the destructive behavior they help to foster is widely condemned and attributed to matters of race and personal character flaws. Completing the circle, the dysfunctional behavior of the poor then becomes the explanation for poverty and other social ills. Instead of putting on trial the economic system and public policies that generate so much poverty, we judge the poor harshly. Instead of using the inadequacy of present welfare programs as a lens to focus attention on alternatives capable of breaking the cycles of poverty, we challenge and undermine the assumption that government has a responsibility for the well-being of its citizens.

When they assess the reasons why families are in crisis, both conservatives and progressives generally fail children. People on the right tend to blame the poor and big government while minimizing the negative consequences and false promises of the marketplace. People on the left often avoid issues of personal responsibility and fail to advocate a different role for government or meaningful alternatives to present economic priorities and systems. Neither approach is capable of renewing communities and offering authentic hope to children.

Reverend Gregory J. Boyle, director of Jobs for a Future and Homeboy Bakery, has buried forty young people from his Los Angeles community. He writes:

The violence that has us in its grip has always indicated larger problems: poverty, unemployment, racism, the great disparity between the haves and have-nots, dysfunctional families and, above all, despair. This week, I must bury a homeboy who, unable to find his way clear to imagine a future, put a gun to his temple and ended his life. This desperate act... sidestepped the inner city's more acceptable mode of suicide — the irrational battlefield of a gang war. He chose instead to make explicit the wish for death long implicit among our youth. Within the first 100 days of the 104th Congress, House Speaker Newt Gingrich with his GOP Contract with America hopes to revisit the crime issue... [with] the "Taking Back Our Streets Act." ... They will eliminate $5 billion in crime prevention.... For those of us who live and work among the urban poor, the urgency is not to "take back our streets." What the crime and violence among our youth signals is something more urgent than the reclaiming of our streets. We need, rather, to infuse them with hope.... Poor, unemployed youth are hard-pressed to conjure up images of themselves as productive and purposeful adults. The 15-year-old girl, bounding ecstatically into my office with news of her pregnancy, explains, "I just want to have a kid before I die." She says this not because she's been diagnosed as having a terminal illness, but because she lives in my community — a place of early death and where the young lack the imagination to see something better.[11]

When we look at Dion, we have many choices about what to see. It is both difficult and imperative that we see beyond the classroom where an uninterested child sits, lethargic and indifferent, unable to put a colored peg in its proper sequence. To understand Dion we need to understand his individual situation and family, but we need to do more. We must enter the shelter and visit the hospital where his brother lies ill with lead poisoning. We need to examine his neighborhood and find the landlord in order to ask some hard questions. We need to examine why so many people lack safe, affordable housing and to look at corporate decisions that drive wages down and eliminate jobs. Finally, we need to probe the nature of a society that allows a spiral of devastation and neglect to continue until a child like Dion loses his childhood, his hope, and his interest in life and learning.

Chapter 10

Conflicting Perspectives

A civil war of values is raging across North America. And in its wake lie thousands of crumbling households.

—FOCUS ON THE FAMILY BROCHURE

Conflicting perspectives on family crisis and social breakdown resemble the classic chicken-or-egg argument. Which came first, the breakdown of the family or social decay? Are the erosion of family values and the breakdown of the family responsible for deepening societal problems such as violence, crime, and poverty, as suggested by Dan Quayle, much of the religious right, and the so-called centrists represented by Barbara Dafoe Whitehead in the *Atlantic Monthly* article? Or are deepening societal problems rooted in poverty and inequality responsible for the breakdown of the family, as Judith Stacey and the *Ms.* magazine editorial argue?

Looking at the issues in this either/or way may not always be helpful, but so much of the debate is framed precisely in this manner that I would like to highlight key features in each approach as well as the weaknesses and strengths they harbor. At the heart of the debate are differing views on the interplay between social causes and individual responsibility and action. For the sake of simplicity and clarity I refer to the perspective of Quayle, the religious right, and the centrists as a *personalist* approach. At odds with the personalist view is the perspective of Judith Stacey, *Ms.* magazine, and other similar voices, which I call a *social* approach. Both personalists and advocates of a social approach address issues of personal responsibility, and both groups are concerned with societal forces. They differ profoundly, however, both in the relative *weight* they assign to social forces when examining dysfunctional individual behaviors and over *which social forces are of primary concern* when assessing the crisis of children and society.

In chapters that follow I look at both approaches and within the framework of a simple question: what would we do differently, as parents and as a society, if we cared about the unmet needs of children? Although they share a common concern over the plight of children, advocates of these competing perspectives answer this question in radically different ways.

Chapters 10–12 examine both the personalist and social perspectives with an emphasis on limitations in the personalist perspective. The present chapter looks at broad characteristics and how points of apparent convergence on negative media influence end up looking different through personalist and social lenses. Chapter 11 ("Men and Violence") explores differences in perspective over another apparent common concern, that of violence; and chapter 12 ("Public Policy") highlights differences regarding the role of government.

Proponents of the personalist approach place blame for the dismal plight of children, families, and society primarily *on parents themselves.* Other contributing factors they cite are government policies that encourage parents to make decisions that are harmful to children and society and negative cultural factors such as media violence. In a simplified form, the personalists argue that many parents, particularly single mothers and divorced adults with children, are unable or unwilling to parent responsibly and therefore put children at risk and society in peril.

Personalists claim that erosion of family values has led to changing family structures that are harmful to both kids and society. They are concerned about the large increase in the number of children raised by unwed mothers or divorced parents and about efforts to "redefine the family" to include same-sex partners. Focus on the Family, an organization with a $100 million annual budget and two-million-member mailing list, says in one brochure: "The fabric of society itself and the foundations of our culture are built upon the family, and tampering with its legal definition must necessarily tear that fabric and undermine those foundations."[1]

The personalist road is often littered with rhetoric about traditional family values. It puts "us" (good parents, good values) against "them" (bad parents, bad values), married against unmarried, two-parent against single-parent households, straight against gay, and, directly or indirectly, whites against blacks and other people of color.

The personalist approach has several strengths. Foremost among them is that it takes values, children, the family, and parental responsibility seriously. Personalists also aren't afraid to acknowledge that the behavior of the poor is sometimes problematic. When I hear advocates of this perspective make sweeping generalizations about "welfare cheats," "lazy" AFDC recipients, and "irresponsible unwed mothers," usually with racial undertones lurking crudely beneath the surface, I get angry. They are turning people with problems into problem peoples, and doing so is a large step in the dangerous direction of scapegoating.

However, if I'm honest and if I put fears of being labeled a racist aside, then I can acknowledge that personalists tell part of a story that is validated by my own experience. The three crack houses opened and eventually shut down in my neighborhood during the past year were operated by poor blacks. Students having or causing trouble in my daughter's school are often poor children, disproportionately children of color. Friends in the medical field, who like Dr. Hilfiker are sensitive, caring people, are troubled by many of the poor, young, and predominantly African-American patients they see: a fifteen-year-old girl sucking her thumb during prenatal visits; women with minor ailments arriving in taxi cabs at the emergency room for treatment; a twelve-year-old girl showing off her Norplant (implanted birth control patch) while her peers ask whether it is best to have the patch installed before or after they begin menstruation; young girls asking for workups because they have been trying for several years to get pregnant but unlike most of their friends haven't succeeded; a pregnant woman on crack who plans to have four more children to make up for four others who have become wards of the state.

These are not isolated stories, and the behaviors they depict trigger concerns within diverse communities throughout our society: inner city and suburban, rich and poor, black and white. They are examples of a real and deepening crisis of young women *and* men in our society that cuts across racial and economic lines but that disproportionately affects people living in poverty. Within the African-American community, two-thirds of births are to unwed mothers. My medical friends, it is true, tell me stories about teenage mothers pulling their lives together and finding hope, intimacy, respect, and direction for their lives in the context of caring for a child. These stories are, however, the exceptional ones.

However flawed their proposed solutions might be, personalists at least talk about these issues and define them as problematic. It is important, for reasons I will discuss in chapters 15–16, for more progressive voices to deal with these issues honestly and forthrightly. Personalists also share common ground, at least nominally, with more progressive or radical critics of family disruption about the impact of divorce on children and the destructive influence of films, music, and television on children's lives and on the broader society.

Regrettably, these commendable features in the personalist approach flounder in a sea of biases. At the extreme, personalists seem to say that the main causes of poverty, besides the poor personal values displayed by the poor themselves, are anti-poverty programs. Most family and societal problems, they affirm, can be solved by:

- ridding our country of homosexuals;

- banning abortions;

- getting tough on crime (imposing mandatory sentences and the death penalty for numerous crimes, putting more police on the streets, and building more prisons);

- fighting off gun-control efforts and allowing citizens to carry concealed weapons (so good people can be armed);

- teaching creationism and allowing prayer in public schools;

- reestablishing Mom's place in the home within the framework of a two-parent household in which women follow the leadership of their husbands;

- restigmatizing divorce;

- teaching abstinence;

- adding a balanced-budget amendment to the U.S. Constitution; and

- ending welfare and other government programs in order to instill in former recipients values of work and discipline and to tackle the budget deficit.

The personalists are harshly critical of television, films, music, and other forms of popular culture. Once again, this concern is justifiably widespread: black or white, rich or poor, urban or suburban, single or married, almost any parent who pays attention to what passes as entertainment in our culture, from Saturday-morning cartoons to video games and slasher films, would be hard pressed to disagree with the assessment that the values being conveyed are generally in conflict with the health and well-being of children and society. The problem is only compounded by the fact that many parents don't or can't find time to "pay attention to what passes as entertainment."

I require students in several college classes that I teach to spend several hours watching Saturday-morning cartoons. Initially some are reluctant to do so because they don't see a relationship between this assignment and the topic of the course, which is U.S. foreign policy. With very few exceptions, however, these students, who may or may not have children, are shocked by what they see. In cartoon after cartoon, one incident of violence is followed by another. Saturday-morning cartoons, according to my students, often depict more than twenty acts of violence in an hour. The message conveyed is that superior force allows good to triumph over evil. This is an early part of our children's socialization in redemptive violence, where violence is presented as acceptable, normal, and expedient. Toy commercials are equally troubling as dozens of advertisements encourage boys to purchase toys that encourage violent play while socializing girls in the art of makeup and glamour.

The violence in many video games exceeds that of cartoons. Reading descriptions from the rating system for video games from the Recreational Software Advisory Council (RSAC) provides a picture of the problem. RSAC has established three ratings for computer-game software:

- Benign Immobilization "refers to an act that stops or restrains the actions of a sentient being (any being or object depicted as feeling, thinking or self-aware) in a way that does not demonstrate any death, discomfort, harm or pain."

- Gratuitous Violence "refers to depictions of continuous aggressive violence that causes harm or death to a sentient being once that being has been rendered helpless. It may include physical torture and continued attacks on or damage to corpses."

- Blood and Gore depicts "a great quantity of a sentient being's blood . . . or depiction of innards, organs, and or dismembered body parts. The depiction of blood or vital body fluids must be shown as flowing, spurting, flying or collecting in large amounts or in pools. To be classified as Blood and Gore, there must be more than just simple dismemberment; the dismemberment must be accompanied by tendons, veins, bones, muscles, etc."[2]

Barbara Dafoe Whitehead's article in the *Atlantic Monthly*, in a section on "The View from Hollywood," reflects a deep anxiety felt by many of us concerning the harmful influence of the media. Particularly troubling to Whitehead, is the media portrayal of the family itself in which divorce and unwed motherhood are defended and the married two-parent family is depicted "as a source of pathology."[3]

I find most television programming and advertising offensive, whether or not they are specifically targeted to children. Sex, violence, and unlimited consumption as the key to happiness are the dominant images. I don't want my daughters to think casual sex is fine, that affairs are acceptable or normal, that relationships involve little commitment, that use of drugs and excessive drinking are socially acceptable, that the "good life" is centered on having more and more things, that if something is pleasurable it is automatically acceptable or that violence is an appropriate means of resolving conflicts. Yet this is what they are being taught through popular music, television, videos, and movies. The TV is rarely on in our household, and our children's viewing is limited almost exclusively to public television. But this is only a partial solution to a far-reaching problem.

Values communicated to children through TV, movies, music, and videos are an area of common concern between advocates of the personalist and social approaches to family and social crisis. Profound differences separate them, however, differences that in my view illuminate many of the pitfalls in the personalist approach.

In *Selling Out America's Children*, Dr. David Walsh, an advocate of the social approach, highlights one point of similarity with the personalists when he notes that during formative years the average child receives forty-five thousand messages from television about sex.[4] He cites a *TV Guide* survey showing that 94 percent of the sexual encounters portrayed on daytime TV soap operas are between people not married to each other. "The implied message," Walsh says, "is that sexual relations outside the context of marriage are the norm." This, he notes, "implies a standard of behavior" and "is a very subtle yet powerful value message about sexual behavior."[5] Crime, particularly violent crime, and TV violence are other worries shared by both groups. Walsh says that as a society we encourage the use of violence for entertainment despite an undeniable correlation between violent entertainment and violent behavior. Targeting violent entertainment at children promotes the violent behavior we fear. Walsh notes that by age eighteen the average child sees two hundred thousand acts of violence on television. They also receive messages about sex and wealth, including rewards without work, and are flooded with largely attractive images of drugs, alcohol, selfishness, and disrespectful behavior.[6]

Walsh is not the only progressive voice who shares this concern with the personalists. Dr. Myriam Miedzian in her excellent book *Boys Will Be Boys* notes that boys who on average watch about twenty-eight hours of television each week will by age eighteen see about twenty-six thousand TV murders, a vast majority of them committed by men.[7] According to Miedzian, we have allowed our children "to be raised on tens of thousands of TV murders, detailed depictions of sadistic mutilations on the screen, and song lyrics that advocate rape."[8] *Citizen*, a publication of Focus on the Family, a voice of many personalists, agrees. It condemns "gangsta rap's field of screams," in language similar to that of Miedzian.[9]

Another progressive voice, that of Sylvia Ann Hewlett, echoes their anxiety. In *When the Bough Breaks*, Hewlett notes that international surveys measuring educational achievement show American kids are at or near the bottom. At the same time, the U.S. ranks number one in the percentage of thirteen-year-olds who watch five or more hours of TV every day, with a typical eighth-grader spending four times as many hours watching TV per week as on homework.[10] Time spent in front of a television or video screen is the single biggest chunk of time in the waking life of an average American child.[11] By age eighteen our children have watched fifteen hundred hours of commercials, witnessed two hundred thousand acts of violence on television, and seen forty-five thousand messages about sex.[12]

The convergence of interest between personalists and advocates of a social approach is both real and limited when it comes to assessing the implications of the media in shaping children's values. Each group sees a series of common problems, but the personalists seem unwilling to broach related issues. Their hope of limiting the damage caused by the media is precluded by the limits of their social lens. Two examples can illustrate this point.

First, the political and economic agenda of many personalists was reflected in their support for many of the reforms carried out in the 1980s under Presidents Ronald Reagan and George Bush. One such reform was deregulation, which had a profound impact on TV programming. Sylvia Ann Hewlett writes:

> By 1974 each broadcaster was required to make a "meaningful effort" to provide special programs for preschool and school-age children in the late afternoon hours. In addition, restrictions were placed on the amount of advertising allowed during

children's programs, and host selling (using program characters to promote products) was prohibited.... Ronald Reagan
was elected president and a new administration came to power
that was committed to deregulation and a greater reliance
on free enterprise.... By 1984 the FCC [Federal Communications Commission] had removed virtually all guidelines on
general program content and had abolished the limits on advertising in programs targeted at young people. As a result
of these decisions, children's programming has become much
more commercialized. The networks now air entire programs
whose sole purpose is to market commodities.... Educators call
these shows program-length commercials.[13]

Hewlett notes that in most other countries late-afternoon hours
are given over to programs that are tailored to the needs of children and that if the United States wants to "catch up to the rest of
the civilized world" our government needs to devote more money to
children's programming and impose "reasonable controls over what
children are able to watch."[14] Instead of protecting our children
from potentially harmful shows and advertising and instead of expanding publicly financed alternative programming, recent decisions
in Washington have targeted public television for cuts while under-
funding public schools. This has resulted in restricted programming
options in the home and has placed many school districts in a position of welcoming commercial messages into classrooms in exchange
for free television sets and programming.

This illustrates how the commitment of personalists to broad
deregulatory policies, which are central features in a business and
government strategy to redistribute wealth upward within our society, led to deregulation of television with disastrous consequences
for children. Concern for children, in other words, was and is being
sacrificed in favor of broader economic objectives, a pattern that is
accelerating within the present political and economic climate.

The personalist view is further undermined by social blinders in
the way its proponents allow and even approve the commercializa-
tion of our children. Stated crassly, it is profitable to sell violence,
sex, and other elements in the "civil war of values" and to use

violence and sex to stimulate sales. Instead "of treating our children as our most precious national resource," Myriam Miedzian writes, "we have allowed them to be treated as a commercial market. A major part of their enculturation is now in the hands of people whose primary interest is in profit-making rather than in the well-being of children."[15]

The truth about children and economics is that children are valued in our society as consumers. That helps explain why we abandon them to market forces. The commodification of our children explains both their neglect and exploitation. During their early years children aren't valued in a market society because they don't produce anything. On the other hand, the market does value the dollars that children spend and likewise values their influence on the spending patterns of their parents. The "worthlessness" of children may explain why family values often do not translate into personal and social policies that result in valued families. The consumerist value assigned to children by the commercial sector helps explain why we don't protect them from the horrible consequences of a largely unregulated marketplace.

The concerns that personalists profess for children are undermined by a deep commitment to broad market forces that victimize children. They are disturbed by the sexual values communicated by TV but are unwilling to confront the fact that sexual images are used to sell things beyond movies or programs about sex. They are troubled by violent TV images, and they are upset that music lyrics and films that glamorize violence garner huge profits. Yet they seem unprepared to wrestle with the fact that violent programming is of central importance to the market economy. Violence, like alluring sexual images, attracts both audiences and advertising dollars. Violence, therefore, is used to promote the consumption of cars, beer, food, and nearly every advertised product in America.

The goal of profits through selling is not only at the heart of the TV and broader media industry but is central to the values of the U.S. economy as a whole. David Walsh reminds us that violence, sex, images of wealth, rewards without work, appealing portrayals of drugs and alcohol, selfishness, and disrespect are the values communicated through television. Many of these values and their TV portrayals are not chosen arbitrarily. They are used by the architects of our TV fare, including corporate sponsors, because they elicit consumer desires. He writes:

> For the most part, TV sticks to the themes that sell [especially violence, sex, and humor], because selling things is what television is all about.... The goal ... is to sell things. Therefore, values that are good for children are not the guiding principles for TV. The marketplace provides TV's guiding principles. Our society has developed an extremely powerful teacher, but the teacher has only the values of the marketplace driving it. *And the value messages of the marketplace are increasingly at odds with those values which are important for healthy children and a healthy society.*[16]

It is a sobering reflection of these marketplace values that the United States is the leading exporter of violent weapons used in conflicts throughout the world as well as the leading exporter of violent toys and violent programs aimed at children. Violent programming is a problem in itself because it legitimizes and encourages violent behavior. It is also problematic because our reluctance to curb violent programming is due to the fact that violent shows attract audiences and therefore major advertising budgets, which trigger broad-based consumption. Exporting violent programming is also easy and profitable because violence is becoming a universal language that cuts across other linguistic barriers.

"What would we do differently, as parents and as a society, if we cared about the unmet needs of children?" The personalists' answer would likely include the following:

As parents we would stay married for the sake of the children, even if the marriage is riddled with conflict. Mom would stay at home. Dad would exercise leadership in the family while working to support it. We would monitor closely our children's TV viewing and other media images they receive. We would teach our children abstinence.

Our parental concerns would also push us into the political arena with an ambitious agenda. We would condemn homosexuality and fight efforts to "redefine the family"; we would seek control of local school boards in order to teach abstinence and creationism, block sex education, and allow prayer in public schools. Our broader political agenda would include banning abortions, getting tough on crime, and blocking gun control so that parents can defend themselves and their children against criminals. Based on our belief that social programs aimed at helping the poor are in fact a principal cause of poverty and a major factor in promoting the problematic behavior of the poor — including especially the escalating number of pregnancies among single young women — our political agenda would include ending welfare or enacting punitive welfare reform. Values, however, would remain subservient to the market.

Chapter 11

Men and Violence

*[Many] of the values of the masculine mystique, such as tough-
ness, dominance, repression of empathy, extreme competitiveness,
play a major role in criminal and domestic violence and underlie
the thinking and policy decisions of our political leaders. The masculine mystique manifests itself differently in different environments
but the end result is the same. For a poor ghetto youth, proving
that he is a man might involve a willingness to rob, assault, or
kill someone. (Homicide is the major cause of death among young
African-American males.) For a group of middle- or upper-class
boys, it might mean participating in a gang rape, or going on a
hundred-mile-an-hour joy ride. (Automobile accidents are the major cause of death among young white males.) For the men in our
National Security Council, proving manhood might mean showing
how tough they are by going along with a military intervention
that is not really necessary for our national security. (In the case of
Vietnam this led to the death of at least fifty-eight thousand Americans and well over one million Vietnamese.) For the men in our
nuclear think tanks, it might mean making sure we have at least as
many nuclear warheads as "they" do, regardless of whether we need
them or not.... Our nation can no longer relate to foreign powers
the way boys related to each other in the school yard.*

— MYRIAM MIEDZIAN, *Boys Will Be Boys*

Families Valued begins with a simple story about several boys stealing
my three-year-old's tricycle and taking turns smashing it to pieces.
I named the gender of the perpetrators because I think it is important that we address issues related to boys, men, and violence.

96

The unfortunate and generally unspoken truth is that violence is overwhelmingly a male problem. Violence would be of concern to me regardless of the gender of my children, but the fact that I have three daughters prompts a greater sense of urgency. If as my daughters grow up they become involved in heterosexual relationships, then I want those relationships to be healthy, respectful, and free of violence. If they are homosexuals and choose life partners of the same sex, then I would like them to be able to live out their commitments without triggering the irrational fear and hatred of others. Present patterns of male socialization, including behaviors already common among young boys whose lives intersect with my children, frighten me. Audrey's tricycle was trashed by boys. Hannah has returned more than once from school upset because a boy punched her during class, and violent behavior by boys on school buses has become a serious problem throughout my city.

In *Boys Will Be Boys* Myriam Miedzian argues convincingly that our distorted understanding of masculinity is a major value problem at the root of our family and societal crises. Her concern is illuminated in the subtitle of her book, *Breaking the Link between Masculinity and Violence.* Miedzian points out that most acts of violence, including 89 percent of violent crime and most child abuse, are perpetrated by men. Approximately 1.8 million women each year, she says, are physically assaulted by their husbands or boyfriends, and "wars have always been, and continue to be, initiated and fought almost exclusively by men."[1]

The problem of male socialization and male violence in our culture is a value issue that is never addressed under the otherwise broad umbrella of "family values." Its absence, in my view, is a gaping hole that needs to be filled. Despite ample evidence that violence is a men's problem, personalists and many others ignore the link between men and violence because *both violence and male behavior* are considered normative. Twenty scientists from around the world were so alarmed by the widespread assumption that violence and war were inevitable for human beings that they wrote a statement for the United Nations to refute the logic of such claims. *The Seville Statement on Violence: Preparing the Ground for the Construction of Peace,* was disseminated by decision of the General

Conference of UNESCO (United Nations Educational, Scientific, and Cultural Organization) at its twenty-fifth session in November 1989. It has been endorsed by many organizations of scientists around the world, including anthropologists, ethologists, physiologists, political scientists, psychiatrists, psychologists, and sociologists. It says in part:

- IT IS SCIENTIFICALLY INCORRECT to say that we have inherited a tendency to make war from our animal ancestors.

- IT IS SCIENTIFICALLY INCORRECT to say that war or any other violent behavior is genetically programmed into our human nature. While genes are involved at all levels of nervous system function, they provide a developmental potential that can be actualized only in conjunction with the ecological and social environment.

- IT IS SCIENTIFICALLY INCORRECT to say that in the course of human evolution there has been a selection for aggressive behavior more than for other kinds of behavior.[2]

Refuting claims that violence is inevitable inspires hope, as the writers of the *Seville Statement* make clear:

This Statement is a message of hope. It says that peace is possible and that wars can be ended. It says that the suffering of war can be ended, the suffering of people who are injured and die, and the suffering of children who are left without home or family. It says that instead of preparing for war, we can use the money for things like teachers, books, and schools, and for doctors, medicines, and hospitals.[3]

If violence is not inevitable among human beings but is instead conditioned by ecological and social environments, then we must look at the social causes of violence and more specifically to the social roots of male violence. The acceptance of violence as inevitable and male violence as normative impedes efforts to deal with problems ranging from domestic abuse and street crime to war. To recognize violence as a male problem would lead us to look not only at the factors that encourage men to be violent, but also at the behavior of women. According to Miedzian, delegitimizing male violence and elevating patterns of women's behavior could change our entire perspective. Despite the obvious link between men and violent crimes, and despite the fact that nations led by men engage endlessly in armed conflict, there is little awareness that we face a men's problem, rooted not in genetic inevitability but in male socialization.

According to Miedzian, boys are not destined to be violent, but they are biologically more predisposed to violence than are girls. This predisposition to violence must be taken seriously by both parents and society because it will be encouraged or discouraged, depending on how boys are socialized.

> Violence is best understood as developing out of an interaction between a biological potential and certain kinds of environments. In comparing males and females...it is the *combination* of evidence from such diverse and independent sources — studies in the United States, cross-cultural studies, hormonal and animal studies — which leads me to conclude that the potential for violence appears greater in males.[4]

Regrettably, parents and society both tend to reinforce the male predisposition to violence at every turn. Violent behavior in boys is encouraged through violent play and sports; through social conditioning that romanticizes war; through violence on TV, in films, and in popular music; and by bolstering the masculine mystique of toughness, dominance, repression of empathy, and extreme competitiveness. In a graphic example of inappropriate socialization, Miedzian notes how in "slasher films as in the endlessly violent 'adventure films'...it is young boys in particular who are being reinforced to commit acts of rape, murder, and sadism."[5]

Boys are also socialized to be warriors:

> The prevailing feeling is that going to war is exciting, patriotic, and proof of courage and manhood. Boys are raised to be soldiers. They are prepared from the youngest age to view war as a thrilling adventure. Their play with war toys is great fun without pain. The books they read (and today the TV shows and films they see) focus on exciting violence. In schools all

over the world, little boys learn that their country is the greatest in the world, and the highest honor that could befall them would be to defend it heroically someday. The fact that empathy has traditionally been conditioned out of boys facilitates their obedience to leaders who order them to kill strangers.[6]

Women have a profoundly important role to play in breaking the cycles of violence, because throughout history they have been predominantly nonviolent. Therefore, Miedzian says, it makes sense to look to women to play a larger role in the political arena and to provide men with different role models.[7]

Identifying violence as a predominantly male problem points to another troubling inconsistency or blind spot in the personalists' perspective about the media and values discussed in the previous chapter. Male violence is simply not a topic for discussion within the "family values" debate. And for at least the segment of the personalist camp identified with the religious right, gender-role differences are God-given. "Maleness and femaleness are not merely the result of social conditioning but express God-designed differences," Focus on the Family argues. The husband is called to "provide leadership" and the wife "to follow the responsible leadership of the husband." If "the wife launches off in defiant independence from her husband and belittles his masculinity, this transforms the marriage into a chaotic insurrection."[8] Although personalists seem genuinely concerned about violence and other values portrayed in the media, they are committed to defending the traditional masculine role of husbands within the traditional family.

The concerns expressed by many personalists about children, family, violence, crime, and other social problems are largely undermined by patriarchy and by solutions that reinforce strict gender roles. Obviously, neither the religious right nor other proponents of a personalist approach to family and social problems advocate domestic abuse. Focus on the Family describes "mutual sacrificial love" between marriage partners as a key to family well-being.[9] However, their failure to probe the relationship between violence and contemporary understandings of masculinity in my view hurts both children and society. I also believe that the predisposition to seeing a women's role in the family as God-given makes it difficult if not impossible for such personalists to understand the plight of working women and the relationship between economic and family stress.

The emphasis of the religious right on strict gender roles within the family spills over into society and reinforces the tragic consequences of the masculine mystique. The results are far-reaching. The same groups who fear violence and crime in our neighborhoods actively block gun-control efforts while supporting aggressive foreign policies and military adventurism. The Christian right by way of example mobilized support for the apartheid government in South Africa and on behalf of the Nicaraguan contras despite ample evidence of horrendous abuses in both countries. Women who bring compassionate values to the political arena are dismissed or vilified. Men who need role models that build on empathy and on the traditional nonviolent behavior patterns of women remain entrenched in their worlds of hierarchical men's power. Children, particularly boys, who need empathetic male role models struggle without them because their fathers are physically absent, violent, or emotionally distant. Even the important issue of teenage pregnancy is distorted by a focus on mothers and a corresponding lack of recognition of the problematic behavior of fathers. According to U.S. Public Health Service reports, 71 percent of all teenage parents have adult partners over age twenty. Men over age twenty cause five times more births among junior-high–age girls and 2.5 times more births among high-school girls than high-school boys do.[10]

The reluctance to address issues of men and violence may be linked to the religious right's image of God. The Bible, as theologians have demonstrated convincingly, was written in a context of patriarchy, so that what passes as "God's word" is sometimes a man's word. Although it is beyond the scope of this book to seek answers to the following questions, I think it is important to raise them. Why is it that many of the values of the masculine mystique that are pervasive in our homes and in our society mirror distorted images of God? Are problems of abusive power and male violence encouraged by belief in a God whose "maleness" is authoritarian, patriarchal, jealous, and vengeful? Would violence toward women be as prevalent if these images of God were challenged? Is pervasive violence in our society linked to the fact that many of us who call ourselves Christian ignore the nonviolent coming of God in the person of Jesus in favor of a God who is both powerful and patriarchal? Dorothee Soelle writes:

> As a woman I have to ask why it is that human beings honor a God whose most important attribute is power, whose prime need is to subjugate, whose greatest fear is equality....Why should we honor and love a being that does not transcend but only reaffirms the moral level of our male-dominated culture? Why should we honor and love this being, and what moral right do we have to do so if this being is in fact no more than an outsized man whose main ideal is to be independent and to have power?[11]

The unwillingness to deal with the implications of male violence may or may not be rooted in images of God, but unfortunately it runs deep within our society. When President Bush ordered the U.S. invasion of Panama in December 1989, R. W. Apple, Jr., writing in the *New York Times* called it "Bush's Presidential Rite of Passage." "For better of for worse, most American leaders since World War II have felt a need to demonstrate their willingness to shed blood to protect or advance what they construe as the national interest," Apple wrote. For President Bush, "a man widely criticized as recently as a month ago for his purported timidity," shedding blood and thereby "showing his steel had a particular significance," Apple said. It "has shown him as a man capable of bold action."[12] "The Panama invasion," a senior Pentagon official said after the invasion, "was a test of manhood and all G.I.s...passed the exam with flying colors."[13]

Years after the Panama invasion, on the day the 104th Congress met for the first time and Newt Gingrich was sworn in as Speaker of the House, the children of members of Congress were entertained by the "Mighty Morphin Power Rangers," particularly violent TV characters. Gingrich, who had rallied the Republican faithful around the theme of "family values," shook hands with the Power Rangers and hailed the characters as "multiethnic role models."[14] Equally ironic, and toward the other end of the political spectrum, I find it troubling that many proponents of women's rights who are legitimately concerned about domestic abuse advocate full participation of women in the military. Military organizations perhaps more than any other are bastions of the masculine mystique of toughness, dominance, repression of empathy, and extreme competitiveness. They are paradigms in which male violence is not only considered normative but is praised and rewarded. Tragically, yet not surprisingly, women in the military are more likely than their civilian counterparts to be raped or to experience sexual harassment. It is symptomatic of a deep crisis in this country that during the time frame encapsulating the Vietnam War, a war in which more than fifty thousand young American men died fighting a senseless war, a similar number of American women died as a result of domestic violence.

Breaking the cycle of violence depends on modeling alternative behaviors through empathetic socialization. Miedzian describes various programs in which schoolchildren from kindergarten through high school have regular contact with children and parents in the classroom. These programs reinforce empathy, particularly in boys, reduce violence, enhance conflict-resolution skills, and prevent teenage pregnancies as young people learn the joys and difficulties of caring for infants and children.[15] Each summer my ecumenical faith community organizes a "peace village" for children in the neighborhood where conflict-resolution skills are taught. These types of programs need to be expanded dramatically.

The centrists associated with the personalist approach reveal a less blatant disdain for feminism than does the religious right, but they tend to place disproportionate blame for family and, in their view, societal breakdown on women. Their perspective conflicts sharply with that of Miedzian, who argues forcefully that breaking cycles of violence will require validating the experiences of women, not obscuring and thereby reinforcing notions of masculinity that distort the behaviors of men in personal, political, military, and economic arenas where they exercise power.

Placing disproportionate blame on women for the failure of children is convenient in a society dominated by men. As fathers we need to play important financial and emotional roles in the lives of our children. We need to parent, not abandon or baby-sit, and we need to learn and model behaviors that reinforce alternatives to violence.

Two controversial movements are emerging in the United States that are attempting to elevate the roles and responsibilities of men that offer both promise and pitfalls. The Nation of Islam, in which there has traditionally been a strong emphasis on male leadership and responsibility, played a dominant role in organizing a black men's march on Washington in the fall of 1995 that focused attention on the plight, importance, and power of black men. Significantly, a central theme of the march was a confessional stance whereby black men asked for forgiveness concerning their abandonment of women and children and their failure to assume meaningful roles in the much-needed renewal of their communities. It is regrettable that within the Nation of Islam women are clearly assigned subordinate positions.

The same weakness may limit the effectiveness of the second movement as well. Promise Keepers has grown dramatically since its modest beginning in 1990. An organization of Evangelical men, Promise Keepers is the brainchild of Bill McCartney, head football coach at the University of Colorado and outspoken critic of legal rights for gay and lesbian people. The premise of Promise Keepers is that each participant must follow certain worthwhile promises, including pledges to honor Jesus, nurture family and marriage, build relationships with other men, and be active in community affairs. Promise Keepers has thus far attracted an overwhelmingly white constituency but is committed in principle to racial reconciliation. Although Promise Keepers' commitment to help men "take back the family" may play a positive role in helping men share meaningfully in family and community life, it is unlikely to do so in ways that challenge racial and gender stereotypes and the masculine mystique. There are disturbing signs that Promise Keepers may fall prey to anti-gay, anti-feminist biases and become another outlet for white male frustration.

One other promising movement is the Families Against Violence Advocacy Network. Expressing horror at "the prevalence of violence in our culture," and acknowledging that "increasingly violence touches every community and practically every family," the Network is committed to "eliminating violence, one family at a time." Coordinated by the Parenting for Peace and Justice Organization, the Network hopes to have one million families sign a "Family Pledge of Nonviolence" by the year 2000. Although the Network's manifesto and Family Pledge of Nonviolence do not specifically address the relationship between men and violence, they do address the multiple sources of violence that are tearing families and communities apart. The Family Pledge of Nonviolence calls for family members to commit themselves to respect self and others; share feelings honestly; look for safe ways to express anger; work to solve problems peacefully; listen carefully to others; forgive others and keep from holding grudges; treat the environment and all living things with respect; select entertainment and toys that support one's family's values and avoid entertainment that makes violence look exciting, funny, or acceptable; and to be courageous, that is, to be willing "to challenge violence in all its forms whenever I encounter it, whether at home, at school, at work, or in the community, and to stand with others who are treated unfairly."[16]

My daughters benefit from the role models of women who touch their lives: loving grandmothers and aunts; a judge, a pastor, doctors and nurses, social-change advocates and volunteers known as neighbors, family, and friends; leaders in our ecumenical faith community; teachers and softball coaches; their mother, who blends part-time work, volunteerism, and their personal care; and many others who take time from busy lives to give personal attention to children who aren't their own. They also benefit from seeing men integrally involved in the care of children: full-time, stay-at-home dads; mentors; Sunday-school teachers and day-care providers; and the example of their own father.

Each year as part of a ritual within our community I recommit myself to nonviolence, including a pledge to work continually "to create just relationships in our world, our community, and our personal lives...by refusing to participate in acts of violence or to retaliate in the face of provocation, and by seeking creative responses to conflict." As a father of three daughters and as someone who knows that violence lurks within me despite my best intentions and public commitments, I find Miedzian's book on the relationship between masculinity and violence disturbing and challenging. Her critical insights bring to light the limitations of the approach of the personalists, whose concern about unhealthy media influence is undermined by deeper contradictions.

How would we change our behavior as parents and as a society if we took the problem of violence seriously? In the view of the personalists, we would presumably have less domestic violence if husbands and wives embraced their "God-given" roles within the family. Less TV viewing might also discourage personal violence. Moving to the suburbs could help reduce the threat of societal violence. So might owning a gun. Beyond these solutions, one senses that the social vision of how to reduce crime and violence is punitive: we need more police, more prisons, longer sentences, and the death penalty.

Chapter 12

Public Policy

Judging by the headlines that have been leading the news for the last several years, public debate in the United States at the end of the twentieth century has become a war of words among the disaffected minorities that so often appear on the never-ending talk show[s]. . . . Conservatives at war with liberals; Christian fundamentalists at odds with liberal Jews; blacks at war with whites; whites at war with Hispanic immigrants; men at war with women; heterosexuals at war with homosexuals; and the young at war with the old. . . .

The noise is deceptive. Off-camera, beyond the blazing lights, past the ropy tangle of black cords and down the hall, in the corner offices (on Capitol Hill as well as at General Electric, The Walt Disney Company, and CBS News), people in expensive suits quietly continue to go about the work of shifting the center of gravity of wealth and power in the United States from the discounted many to the privileged few. While public attention has been diverted to controversies as inflammatory as they are trivial — Should the Constitution be amended to ban flag-burning? Should dirty pictures be allowed on the Internet? — the American elites that subsidize and staff both the Republican and Democratic parties have steadfastly waged a generation-long class war against the middle and working classes.

— MICHAEL LIND, *Harper's Magazine*

Personalists earn their name because they see irresponsible *personal behavior* and values as the principal cause of family stress and social breakdown and because they promote *changes in personal behavior*

107

as the key to rescuing families and society. This does not mean personalists are unconcerned with government. Many personalists view government initiatives aimed at helping the poor as key causes of poverty and significant contributors to the problematic behavior of the poor. The personalists' selective disdain for government implies support for public policies that reward personal initiative and rejection of those that do not. That, at least, is the theory.

My categorization of this perspective as personalist is, in fact, misleading. The personalist approach is highly politicized. Included among the personalists are the well-financed grass-roots lobbies of the religious right. Personalists have a lengthy political and legislative agenda that includes ending or "reforming" welfare, banning abortions, establishing creationism and prayer in public schools, denying equal rights to homosexuals, building prisons, passing a balanced-budget amendment, and maintaining a "strong defense." Many of these political actions, they say, reflect family values and are motivated by concerns for the family.

In its centrist variation, personalists see family breakdown as the principal *cause* of social decay. Government programs, no matter how many or how well funded, are of limited value, according to this view, without prior, dramatic changes in parental behavior. Increasingly, however, personalists, including centrists, entertain extreme positions such as those of conservative sociologist Charles Murray, who advocates an immediate end to welfare, food stamps, and other social programs.[1] Murray sees the low intelligence of the poor, black and white, as a reason to abandon remedial efforts to improve their skills because "for many people, there is nothing they can learn that will repay the cost of teaching."[2]

Implicit in the personalist approach are the ugly specters of racism and homophobia. If blacks are disproportionately impoverished, on welfare, and filling our prisons, if two-thirds of black babies are born to unwed mothers, and if the causes of poverty and crime are overwhelmingly personal, then blacks or, more generally, people of color have certain personal, cultural, and even genetic characteristics that lead to social deviancy. This perspective is not unlike that of the white South African theater companions who see *Josie Josie* as descriptive of the innate character of blacks, a convergence in views that isn't surprising, given the religious right's long history of support for the apartheid system in South Africa.

Personalists do a disservice to families, not only because the solutions they propose are punitive and therefore likely to hurt children, but because the adults who advocate them pass on prejudices. Many white personalists betray a deep intolerance for the diversity that is essential to a democratic society. Radical intolerance is apparent, not only in their racist treatment of blacks and immigrants, but also in vicious attacks against gay and lesbian people.

David Boaz, executive vice president of the conservative Cato Institute, wrote recently that the "right ought to focus on families and not on gay rights." He noted that "self-styled 'profamily' groups" correctly state "that America faces some real social problems, and that many can be attributed to the deterioration of families." However, according to Boaz, many legitimate issues are overlooked by conservatives "because they are too busy attacking gay men and lesbians."[3]

Boaz looked at articles in the leading conservative journals and concluded:

> *The American Spectator* has run 10 articles on homosexuality in the past three years, compared with two on parenthood, one on teenage pregnancy and none on divorce. *National Review* has printed 32 articles on homosexuality, five on fatherhood and parenting, three on teenage pregnancy and just one on divorce. The Family Research Council, the leading "family values" group, is similarly obsessed. In the most recent index of its publications the two categories with the most listings are "Homosexual" and "Homosexuals in the Military" — a total of 34 items (plus four on AIDS)....
>
> As for the Christian Coalition... its current *Religious Rights Watch* newsletter contains six items, three of them on gay issues. The July issue of the American Family Association's newsletter... contains nine articles, five of them on homosexuality.[4]

The religious right's attacks against gay and lesbian people are motivated by money as well as conviction. Floundering efforts to ban abortions, which coincided with the end of the Cold War, generated a crisis of identity — and of cash. Anti-communism and patriotism that defined America as God's chosen nation were foundational for the key organizers of the religious right's family values coalitions. Mel White — who served as a ghost writer for Jerry Falwell, Pat Robertson, Oliver North, and many other leaders of the Christian right, and who acknowledged recently and publicly that he is gay — describes how the end of the Cold War and a diminished communist threat led to a financial crisis. "With all the celebrating, no one even dreamed that the end of communism would mean the beginning of a whole new era in the history of gay bashing by the religious right," White writes. "Their television and radio ministries had been financed in large part by using the communist threat to raise funds and recruit volunteers. Without communism,..." he continues, they "had only two issues hot enough to mobilize their forces: abortion and homosexuality." According to White:

> During the 1990s, when the religious right shifted the focus of their fund-raising appeals from the "evil communist empire," I began collecting samples of their terrible lies against us. One of my early hate-mail "treasures" was an emergency Jerry Falwell fund-raiser sent in an oversize envelope...with a bold red banner across its face stating simply: "Declaration of War....Official Notice." Jerry Falwell was officially declaring war against gay and lesbian people. Why? Because, according to Jerry, homosexuals "have a god-less, humanistic scheme for our nation — a plan which will destroy America's traditional moral values." He went on to claim that our "goal" as gays and lesbians was the "complete elimination of God and Christianity from American society...."
>
> It was the same tired old lie that Adolf Hitler and Heinrich Himmler had used in 1936 when they created a Reich Central Office for the Combatting of Homosexuality and Abortion. The Nazis, like the religious right, stirred up that ancient pool of misinformation and hatred against homosexuals to recruit new volunteers and mobilize their troops....

Without knowing it, Jerry was using a page right out of Hitler's book to take advantage of people's fear and confusion about homosexuality to raise funds and recruit volunteer "soldiers" for his cause. In that fund-raising letter to an estimated 5 million people...there was a "Declaration of War" form asking Christian Americans to sign up in Jerry's battle against gay and lesbian Americans. Those who donated $35 or more to "keep the Old Time Gospel Hour on the air" would get an antigay videotape as well.[5]

In fairness, homophobia, an irrational hatred of gay and lesbian people, is pervasive in our society. It crosses race, gender, social class, and denominational boundaries with discouraging ease. Homosexuals are too often treated as second-class citizens, despite growing evidence that sexual orientation is genetically determined. My own denomination, the Evangelical Lutheran Church in America, says that "human sexuality is a gift from God" and then limits enjoyment of this gift to heterosexuals. My point in stressing the anti-gay hysteria of the religious right is simply to show how some groups who say they are committed to family values spend much of their time, energy, and political capital in the despicable and profitable enterprise of attacking gay and lesbian people, many of whom have children and all of whom are connected to families. This bias, as we shall see in this and chapters that follow, obscures the role of destructive public policies and corporate decisions that undermine the well-being of families. It also diverts attention from important family issues and does enormous harm to children struggling with issues of sexuality, to families with gay or lesbian children, and to children with gay or lesbian parents. "Most of us gay and lesbian people," Mel White writes, "are just normal folk who try our best to live respectable, productive lives in spite of the hatred and the condemnation heaped upon us."[6]

I see attacks against homosexuals through the lens of our family's relationship with Julie, Linda, John, and Lucy, the lesbian couple and their children who are our neighbors and friends. This wonderful, loving family would benefit dramatically if child-support payments came on time and if Julie and Linda received the same tax benefits as heterosexual couples. And they like most families would benefit if present public policies and corporate practices that block initiatives for universal health coverage, adequate day care, progressive tax policies, good schools, and an economy capable of generating decent-paying jobs were changed. Unfortunately, destructive corporate practices and public policies rarely come to light in the heat of the inflammatory and diversionary controversies described by Michael Lind in his essay in *Harper's Magazine*.

Personalists take a dim view of efforts to provide gay and lesbian people with legally protected rights. They also attack welfare and other government programs that they say encourage irresponsible behavior, social breakdown, and moral decay. These attacks against government are both selective and counterproductive. They obscure the many ways in which corporate and government policies in the 1980s rewarded certain sectors of U.S. society while penalizing others, including families and most particularly middle-income earners and the poor. Many personalists were so preoccupied with issues like homosexuality and so focused on the problematic behavior of the poor that they failed to notice what rich individuals and corporations and their political allies were doing. The key support some personalists offered to former Presidents Reagan and Bush translated into policies that resulted in unimaginable rewards for the richest of our citizens, vulnerability for those in the middle, and untold misery for those at the bottom. "The United States of the 1980s," writes Republican strategist Kevin Phillips in *The Politics of Rich and Poor*, meant "new wealth in profusion for the bright, the bold, the educated and the politically favored; economic carnage among the less fortunate."[7] According to businessman Paul Hawken:

> Even though the GNP of the United States grew considerably during the 1980s, three-fourths of the gain in pretax income went to the richest one percent. The majority of Americans had less money and lower incomes than they did when the decade began. Primarily, what growth in the 1980s produced was higher levels of apprehension, violence, dislocation, and environmental degradation.[8]

The failure to come to terms with how their preferred public policies in the 1980s favored a powerful but narrow segment of U.S. society while proving disastrous for the majority of families may constitute the biggest blinder in the personalist position. According to the Congressional Budget Office the gap between the after-tax incomes of the richest and poorest fifth of the U.S. working population increased from a ratio of 8 to 1 in 1980 to 20 to 1 in 1989.[9] The Census Bureau reports that the national share of income held by the top 1 percent of U.S. households now equals that of the bottom 40 percent.[10]

The contrast between professed concern for children and public policies that undermine their well-being is as stark as if I were to tell my children I love them, send them off to their classroom, and then dismantle the public walkway they use to cross the freeway on their way to school. The 1980s were like that for children and families, and the carnage continues today. During the 1980s, corporate-led government policies resulted in the largest internal transfer of wealth in the history of the United States, from poor and working-class citizens to the upper 1 to 5 percent of the population. According to Kevin Phillips, who as a Republican strategist was concerned that Republican candidates would be hammered in upcoming elections if the electorate learned the truth about what happened in the 1980s, the top personal tax-bracket rate dropped from 70 percent to 28 percent over seven years, the rate of federal tax receipts from corporate income tax earnings continued to plummet, and the burden of taxes shifted further onto low- to middle-income households through a variety of means, including hikes in regressive Social Security taxes.[11] I described the results in *Brave New World Order:*

> In the first five years following the passage of the 1981 Economic Recovery Tax Act, the superrich "shared a half-trillion-dollar victory." These tax changes translated into deepening disparities between the incomes of the rich and poor. Between 1977 and 1988, according to the Congressional Budget Office

report, the incomes of the wealthiest fifth of U.S. households increased 34 percent, the incomes of the middle fifth grew 4 percent and the incomes of the poorest fifth dropped by 10 percent. The top 1 percent benefitted most. Their incomes rose by 122 percent.... According to the 1991 *Green Book* from the House Ways and Means Committee, *the after-tax income of the richest 1 percent of all U.S. citizens in 1988 was as great as the combined after-tax income of the bottom 40 percent.* By way of contrast, the after-tax income of the bottom 40 percent in 1977 was more than double the total after-tax income of the richest 1 percent.[12]

Personalists dislike welfare, food stamps, and other government programs that they say discourage recipients of such aid from working. They seem unconcerned, however, that policies that contribute to the massive upward redistribution of wealth are at the expense of jobs, wages, benefits, and other needs of common working people and have a particularly devastating impact on children.

I discussed earlier how deregulation hurt children because it resulted in market approaches to TV programming and advertising. This aspect of deregulation is upsetting to personalists because of the media's admittedly harmful role in the "civil war of values." The deleterious impact of deregulation on children and families, however, goes much deeper.

Deregulation fuels a kind of "casino capitalism," an economic environment in which money isn't invested in new production but chases after money through raids on pension funds, hostile takeovers, junk bonds, and mergers. Between 1981 and 1990 more than 11.7 million workers lost their jobs. One-third of them remained unemployed or left the workforce. Of those who found jobs, about half took part-time positions or cuts in pay.[13] As a result of declining wages and benefits, the number of *working adults living in poverty* rose by a third between 1978 and 1989. Not surprisingly, as the number of working adults living in poverty increased significantly, so too did the number of children living in poverty. From 1979 to 1989 the incidence of childhood poverty increased from 16 to 20 percent, with 2.25 million more children living in poverty than in 1980, a total of 13 million.[14] The working poor not only suffer the burden of low wages; they also are often without benefits, including health insurance. The number of uninsured Americans grows by about 1.2 million a year and stands currently at about 43.4 million.[15] More than two of every three poor workers have no employer-based or union-subsidized health insurance.[16]

In October 1994 I spoke to representatives of food-delivery and service providers whose agencies respond to issues of hunger and homelessness in Montana. A theme that emerged repeatedly throughout the conference is that mothers using AFDC (Aid to Families with Dependent Children) prefer jobs over welfare. They want to work. Regrettably, there are few jobs available, and what jobs exist pay minimum wages and offer few if any benefits.

One provider talked about being discouraged following the defeat of health-care reform. Most of the women she works with prefer work to welfare, but taking a minimum-wage job, if available, means losing health-care benefits and putting their children at risk. Without health-care reform, this provider said, she couldn't in good conscience make a case for why these women should work. Exemplary of deep contradictions between rhetoric and policy, many personalists, including those among the religious right, lobbied successfully to block health-care reform while at the same time they condemned those welfare recipients who didn't work (because working would have meant a loss of health benefits for their children).

The hostility to health-care reform was rooted in part in distorted fears of big government that precluded meaningful discussion of a "single payer" health care system similar to that which functions effectively in Canada. Big government can be a problem, but there are occasions when big government may be justified. General condemnations are counterproductive. Both the General Accounting Office (GAO) and Congressional Budget Office report that a single payer system would save enough in administrative costs to immediately offset the cost of universal coverage for the then estimated 37 million Americans who were uninsured. The *New England Journal of Medicine* reports that private U.S. insurers spend 13 percent of every dollar for overhead, while Medicare and Medicaid combined average 3.5 percent overhead. Canada's single-payer system has overhead of less than 1 percent.[17]

Children pay the price when personalists cast a blind eye to the public policies and economic forces that put severe strains on families. In 1981, the beginning of the "Reagan revolution," thirty soup kitchens and food pantries in New York City served meals, mostly to single men with substance-abuse or mental problems. By 1992, according to Bread for the World (a faith-based citizen lobby organization concerned with hunger), 750 emergency food providers in New York served an estimated 2.5 to 3 million meals a month.[18] Did millions of New Yorkers suddenly get lazy or experience family breakdown, as the analysis of personalists implies? I doubt it. Bread for the World offers an alternative view. "Extensive coverage of hunger within the United States [in the 1960s] . . . helped mobilize the public to make substantial gains in addressing domestic hunger," the organization writes in its publication *Hunger 1994: Transforming the Politics of Hunger.* "Twenty years later, many of those gains had been reversed. Anti-hunger organizations proved to be no match for the budget cuts of the Reagan administration."[19]

In all eighty-seven counties in my state of Minnesota, according to a study by Congregations Concerned for Children and Children's Defense Fund of Minnesota, the well-being of children declined in the 1980s. The report measured eleven indicators of child welfare on a county by county basis, including poverty rates, risks at birth, and levels of violence and neglect. "Except for one indicator, violent deaths among children," the report says, "the trends for Minnesota's children are moving in the wrong direction."[20] Bread for the World says that part of the reason for dramatic increases in hunger is our distorted perception of the problem. "Structural obstacles are frequently ignored," it says, especially by journalists who "personalize poverty and hunger" and ignore real causes that should be named.[21]

The importance of the nurturance of children points to yet another instance of how personalists ignore the relationship between family stress, public policies, and economic forces. Personalists are right when they say children in our society need better care and that meeting their emotional needs involves a major commitment of time from parents. I also agree, as do Judith Stacey and other advocates of a social approach, that in many cases two-parent families offer advantages over single-parent households in meeting the needs of children.

Some personalists prefer Mom to stay at home; others acknowledge important roles for fathers both in and outside the home. My own experience is that children and parents do well when both Mom and Dad share intimately and equitably in providing care. For the purpose of this discussion, however, let's assume that under "the right circumstances" nurturing children is possible through any of these configurations.

But what are the right circumstances? Personalists would likely stress the need for significant parental involvement and adequate time for nurturing. Although right so far as it goes, this response ignores important connections between adequate material resources, time, and nurturing. All families must somehow garner sufficient goods to provide for their children. If they do not, then the well-being of families, children, and society are put in peril. Personalists downplay obvious connections between economic health and nurturing, between adequate wages and time available for meeting the emotional needs of children. The cumulative impact of economic and social policies in the 1980s was to make life difficult for many families. Generally speaking, more and more parents are spending longer hours at work and less time with children, while in many cases earning fewer dollars.

There is a deep and troubling incongruity in the position of personalists who ignore how the political and economic changes they support contribute to the deterioration of families and society. They ignore any connection between dramatic increases in homelessness and severe federal spending cuts for low-income housing (from $32.2 billion in 1978 to $9.8 billion in 1988). They condemn unwed mothers yet supported during the Reagan years a 50 percent cut in federal funds for programs to prevent teen pregnancies. They express disdain for the dysfunctional behavior of the poor but seem blind to the ways that cuts in AFDC, food stamps, Head Start, education, child nutrition, and health programs throughout the 1980s harmed children and families and contributed to a social environment conducive to crime and violence.[22] And they decry "wasteful" government expenditures and failed government programs while supporting massive military spending increases, including a 38 percent rise from 1982 to 1986.[23] Personalists express concern about children but seem unconcerned when federal spending on the elderly rose 52 percent between 1978 and 1987 while that for children declined 4 percent, contributing to poverty rates that are now six times higher for children than for older Americans.[24]

Perhaps even more troubling, personalists who advocate family values, point fingers at "lazy welfare moms," and deplore feminists who enter the workforce at the expense of children are blind to the economic forces that push people into poverty, into low-wage jobs, into situations in which material survival is often at the expense of the emotional health of children. "It is extremely important to stress that *growing economic pressure on families with children* — particularly young families and single parents — is at the heart of the parental time famine," Sylvia Ann Hewlett, writes. According to Hewlett since 1973 male wages have fallen 19 percent, and the workweek increased from 41 to 47 hours. Decreased earning power translates into longer working hours, more financial stress, and the loss of a significant block of time, which is no longer available to spend with children. Low wages for women compound the problem. Hewlett says that full-time women workers average only 71 percent of declining male wages. Even more desperate are mothers with dependent children who earn, on average, 46 percent of the male wage. The number of women holding two or more jobs quintupled between 1970 and 1989.[25]

"Lazy welfare moms" constitute a common image of America's poor. A more accurate image may be that of heroic mothers, not unlike the women of Soweto, who sacrifice their children in order to feed them. Sociologist Christopher Jencks from Northwestern University estimated that the average single working mother in 1995 needed $1,500 a month to get by without government assistance.

If subsidized child care and national health insurance were available, then this figure could be reduced substantially but would still involve the need for wages significantly higher than minimum or near-minimum-wage jobs currently available.[26]

After a decade of "casino capitalism," U.S. corporations were deeply in debt and concerned about their "competitive position" within the international economy. One pillar in their strategy to improve "competitiveness" is massive layoffs. A Chicago-based employment consulting firm reported that major corporations announced 108,000 layoffs in January 1994 — the highest monthly figure since it began tracking layoffs in 1989.[27] Between 1991 and 1994 just five companies — IBM, AT&T, GM, Sears, and GTE — announced layoffs of 324,650 employees.[28] Downsizing remains a fundamental strategy for U.S. corporations. As a result, worker insecurity increases along with stock prices on Wall Street.

Another pillar is to further reduce wages. Through initiatives such as the North American Free Trade Agreement (NAFTA) and the General Agreement on Tariffs and Trade (GATT), corporations are becoming more "competitive" by taking advantage of low-wage labor in Mexico, in China, and throughout the Third World. The availability of "cheap labor" abroad facilitates a ratcheting down of wages at home as a significant segment of U.S. workers are forced to compete with lowest-common-denominator wages determined within the context of a global marketplace. "As globalization progressed and more corporations fled to the Third World through the 1980s, into the 1990s," Charles Derber writes, "the American poor lost their usefulness as a reserve labor force, becoming permanently expendable."[29] Many are left with no possibility of worthwhile employment and few options beyond service-sector jobs at McDonald's or Wal-Mart. Between 1989 and 1994, 80 percent of American men and 70 percent of women experienced declining or stagnant wages.[30] Nearly all income growth is flowing to the wealthiest 5 percent of the U.S. population.[31]

The Center on Budget and Policy Priorities estimates that 4.2 million hourly workers in 1993 earned the minimum wage or less. According to center estimates, 70 percent of minimum-wage workers are white and 62 percent are women.[32] As the rich feasted on tax breaks in the 1980s, the purchasing power of minimum-wage workers declined significantly. The value of the 1994 minimum wage of $4.25 an hour was at its second lowest point, in real terms, since 1955, 26 percent below its average in the 1970s and 35 percent below its peak value in 1968.[33] Jodeen Wink, a single parent, notes the catch-22 many single mothers face:

> Too many of us are caught between the rock and the hard place: Stay home and be impoverished or work and be impoverished. Neither is good for children. Welfare reform is easy. If we expect people to get off welfare, they must find jobs that pay the same amounts earned by people who don't need welfare. If there aren't enough of those jobs to go around, we need to admit it instead of degrading the dignity of our citizenry *ad nauseam*. . . . Let's accept the fact that people will work if it betters them and they won't if it makes their situation worse, especially if they have to be responsible for children. It's common sense.[34]

Speaking at the Montana conference I mentioned earlier, sociologist Paul Miller noted that over the past several years Montana has had the highest growth in per capita income of any state in the country *and* the second highest increase in child poverty. The reason for this paradox, he says, is that in Montana and much of the country there exists a two-tier economy. There are a sizable number of good jobs at the top, a substantial number of minimum-wage, no-benefit jobs at the bottom, and a rapidly shrinking number of jobs in the middle. This, he says, does not bode well for families, particularly at a time when government resources for the poor are diminishing or are drying up. Welfare reform in such a context will be punitive, he warns, because the problem of poverty is principally a problem of the working poor.[35] A *Star Tribune* editorial advocating a boost in the minimum wage notes that by 1992 "more than 14 percent of adult workers earned wages below 75 percent of the federal poverty line, triple the 1979 percentage.[36] Today, nearly one in five *full-time* U.S. workers earn poverty-level wages! According to a 1994 Commerce Department study, the number of people working for poverty wages has increased 50 percent since 1979.[37]

The Minnesota Jobs Now Coalition estimates that in 1995 the number of Minnesotans seeking "livable-wage jobs" outnumbered job openings six to one. Fewer than half the state's jobs pay the necessary wage needed by a family to cover basic necessities such as health care, housing, and food for a family of three.[38] A "livable-wage job" is defined as $20,000 per year for a family of three. According to the Coalition, 53 percent of jobs created in Minnesota between 1990 and 1993 were in the low-paying service sector with a median wage of $12,800 per year.[39]

Cornel West described the paradox of prosperity for some and economic insecurity for others in a speech in Minneapolis in October 1994:

When I look at America 1994, it strikes me as quite sad, frightening, terrifying...[I see] relative economic decline, undeniable cultural decay and political lethargy all conspiring together to make it difficult for...the democratic tradition...to stay alive. The relative economic decline, the slow motion silent depression in our urban centers, the levels of unemployment and underemployment. The part-time job with hardly any benefits and no pension...[is] more and more paradigmatic as a permanent job with decent living wages gets more and more difficult to procure.

The redistribution of wealth upward and the redistribution of the tax burden downward. The vast gap and disparity between the well to do and the vast majority of Americans. The top twenty percent doing fairly well, professional managers, the top one percent doing very, very, very well. Forty-two percent experiencing wage deflation.... [And what of] the working poor.... Twenty percent of all Americans in the labor force work more than forty hours a week [and] do not receive one penny from the federal government but still live in poverty. The working poor, if they do not embody the Protestant ethic who does? Deferred gratification, thrifty, frugal, work hard, still living in poverty. And of course, twenty percent of our children live in poverty, across race and forty-two percent of our young brown brothers and sisters under ten live in poverty and fifty-one percent of young black brothers and sisters under ten live in poverty. What sense of future can they have?[40]

What would we do differently, as parents and as a society, if we cared about the unmet needs of children? The personalist response to the social dimensions of this question are clear: talk incessantly about family values while cutting federal spending of every major program designed to help children; condemn the values of the poor while elevating market values to the status of gods; punish the working poor and create economic insecurity while offering those who are fearful about the future cultural explanations for the plight of the poor that feed hatred of blacks, women, and homosexuals; treat people with problems as problem peoples; redistribute wealth upward, shift the tax burden downward, and let the market decide who will feast and who will die.

The personalists' concerns about dysfunctional families, single mothers, crime, and violence are legitimate, but their social agenda causes and compounds these and other problems. Sylvia Ann Hewlett names part of the contradiction:

> During the 1980s child poverty became entrenched in the United States on a scale unprecedented in the postwar period and unmatched in the advanced world. Close to 13 million children are currently growing up in families that live below the poverty line, and this exacts a huge price whether measured in moral or economic terms. Family poverty is relentlessly correlated with high rates of infant mortality, child neglect, school failure, teenage childbearing, and violent crime.
>
> Despite the severity of these problems, they share one hopeful characteristic. They can all be ameliorated by an infusion of funds.... There are ways to halt that "fateful march from unmet needs to joblessness and crime."
>
> ...It's just that we have chosen not to allocate significant resources to these problems. Quite the reverse — as children's problems have mounted, we have cut deeply into the social supports that underpin families with children.[41]

An "infusion of funds," if properly used, will be a key component in helping our children. But the problems we face and the solutions called for require more than money, more than better government programs. They challenge every aspect of our lives.

Chapter 13

Buckle Up, Bake Bread

═══════════════════════════════════════

The parental time deficit has so far been discussed as a decline in the amount of time parents spend with their children. But the parent-child relationship depends on qualitative as well as quantitative factors, and... [today] severe time constraints are compounded by mounting job-related stress. In contemporary society a majority of children not only have two parents who work; they have mothers as well as fathers who routinely work fifty-five-hour weeks, who come home preoccupied and stressed out, unable to give much of anything to their children.

—Sylvia Ann Hewlett, *When The Bough Breaks*

I would have trouble isolating a single event among so many to choose from, but my wife, Sara, to this day can recall her worst experience as a parent as vividly as if it happened yesterday instead of many years ago. Hannah, then two years old, and Sara boarded a plane in Seattle when our usually pleasant daughter decided to throw the tantrum of all tantrums. Hannah bit, clawed, screamed, wrestled, and flailed for about thirty minutes in this closely confined space. Sara somehow kept her composure, something I may not have done, as anguished passengers looked on thinking no doubt that only an incompetent mother and an abused child could be involved in such an episode. I can only guess what they must have assumed about the father. To add to Sara's embarrassment, her boss was on the same flight.

It is through experiences such as these that parents learn to be tolerant of other parents and children and hope for understanding from others. Parenting is humbling and sometimes even humiliating. Therefore it is with a bit of trepidation that I approach this chapter, which looks at several symbols of good and poor parenting, including assumptions about the role of men in children's lives and issues of seatbelts, supermarkets, and bread. Each of these symbolic issues illustrates the importance of time. Children need our time — routine, qualitative time. Lots of it. When parents are pressed for time, unfortunately, children are too often the losers.

My first concern is the widespread belief that men shouldn't be expected to spend much time with children. Sara and I make choices about work and money that allow each of us to share meaningfully in all the tasks of parenting. We are a team. Sara does a bit more than her fair share of cleaning and laundry. I do most of the cooking and nearly all of the shopping. As a father who tries to participate fully in the raising of my daughters, it bothers me when I'm with my kids at the supermarket or park and someone approaches me and says, "Baby-sitting, huh?" Having someone smile and say "Baby-sitting, huh?" is not like being cursed, and there is no offense intended. Yet I hear it often, and what bothers me is the underlying assumption: women parent; men "baby-sit." My response to "Baby-sitting, huh?" is usually simple and polite: "No," I say with a smile, "I'm parenting."

This response may seem trivial or arrogant, but important issues are at stake. As we saw in previous chapters there are profound differences of opinion as to why families and children are in trouble and concerning the relationship between troubled families and the broader social crisis in the United States. According to one school of thought, the breakdown of families and of society is caused by women or, more specifically, feminists.

Casting blame on women obscures or minimizes the degree to which men should be accountable to children: men who sire babies but don't raise children; men who after a divorce abandon their kids, financially and emotionally; men who occasionally "baby-sit" but rarely parent; men who model violence in the home, on the streets, and in the foreign policy citadels of the nation; men who control disproportionately the levers of political and economic power and whose decisions often put women and children and, ultimately, all of us at risk. When someone assumes I am baby-sitting rather than parenting, they reveal a widely accepted bias that runs deep within our society about the limited role of men in children's lives.

I am also concerned about seatbelts or, more accurately, that so many children and adults in cars speeding down our roadways don't wear them. As in the previous example, there is more to my frustration than immediately meets the eye. Not wearing seatbelts not only puts our children's health at risk; it is for me a mark of poor parenting that is rooted once again in the illusion that it is possible to parent well without devoting sufficient time to the numerous tasks that good parenting requires.

Using seatbelts is essential for safety, and in my state it is also the law. Look around, however, and you will see an appalling number of cars, perhaps a majority of those with children, in which seatbelts are not being used. Recently my wife and I shook our heads as a van loaded with children pulled away from a supermarket parking lot with none of the passengers wearing seatbelts. That night the local news reported a traffic accident with three fatalities. None of the dead, including a child, was wearing a seatbelt at the time of the accident.

I can understand from my own experience how this happens. There were times our family got into the car and one or more of our children announced that they were not going to buckle up. "It hurts." "It's too tight." "I hate seatbelts." These and other complaints were coupled with whines, threats, tears, and screams. But we established a rule from the very beginning that in our car each person must wear a seatbelt. Now wearing seatbelts is something each member of our family does without thinking, fussing, or fighting.

To understand how wearing seatbelts became natural rather than a source of conflict, it may be helpful to look at five different parental approaches to the problem of kids not wanting to wear seatbelts. Each approach, or definition of the problem, leads to a logical solution, and each solution has consequences — some predictable, some not.

Problem Definition 1: I want to get somewhere, and my kids won't put their seatbelts on.

Solution 1: Give in and get on with the trip.

Problem Definition 2: My kids don't want to wear seatbelts, and their whining, fussing, and screaming are driving me crazy.

Solution 2: Give in and they will stop whining.

Problem Definition 3: I need to get somewhere, the kids won't buckle up, and their whining is driving me crazy.

Solution 3: Bribe them. If they buckle up and stop whining, they get ice cream or candy as compensation.

Problem Definition 4: I need to get somewhere, the kids are whining, and I want them to wear seatbelts.

Solution 4: Use intimidation or violence. Slap them around until they buckle up.

Problem Definition 5: My children are whining, aren't wearing seatbelts, and must do so. I want them to understand the importance of seatbelts, to buckle up, and to stop whining. I want them to do all these things without me resorting to physical coercion.

Solution 5: I tell my children the following:

> You must wear your seatbelts because I love you and I want you to be safe. Not wearing your seatbelts is also against the law, but this is not nearly as important as the fact that it is my responsibility as a parent to keep you safe. I would feel terrible if you were hurt or killed in a car accident because I was a careless parent who gave in to your whining. When you're older you can choose for yourselves whether or not you and your children wear seatbelts. For all of these reasons, the car won't move until we're all buckled in.

The advantage of the first three solutions is that the immediate crisis is solved easily and quickly and without lingering negative feelings on the part of the children. But each one becomes a long-term nightmare for parents because it leads to similar behavior again and again. The fourth solution, using force, offers parents a quick fix and shares the advantage of number 3 in that the kids end up wearing seatbelts. But it also encourages abusive parental behavior and creates fearful, intimidated children.

Giving in to inappropriate behavior, whether through acquiescence or bribes, or using violence that can undermine a child's self-esteem are temptations that all parents, including this one, face. It will likely lead, however, to a cycle of frustration. In the first two cases and possibly the fourth, kids eventually will not wear seatbelts. They are unsafe in the car, are breaking the law, and have learned that whining pays. They may no longer need to whine about seatbelts, but anything else becomes fair game.

In order to resolve an immediate crisis quickly, it is easy for parents to make an unacceptable behavior acceptable (not wearing seatbelts, whining, bribes). In the fourth instance, an unacceptable behavior, violent coercion, is used to achieve a desired outcome. As frustrated parents looking for an easy way out, we deny our children a valuable lesson in the importance of boundaries, demonstrate the utility of violence, and in the first three cases set in motion patterns of negative behavior that our children learn from experience will be rewarded. It's also likely that solutions to our seatbelt dilemma that leave children unprotected also mean they are freer to bother each other, thus leaving open the possibility for other conflicts that are likely to be "resolved" in similarly inappropriate ways.

The advantages of the fifth approach are obvious. On the down side, explaining the importance of seatbelts to children and refusing to start the car until all are wearing them has undoubtedly made a frustrated parent late on more than one occasion. Yet children and parents have both learned valuable lessons. Parents are reminded that good parenting takes time and that children have the right to know why we ask them to do certain things. Children learn that parents respect them enough to talk through an issue even if it means being late. They also learn why it's important to wear seatbelts (safety, the law, parental responsibility), and that parents require them to do so because they love them and want them to be safe.

One benefit of resolving the crisis through explanation and demonstration rather than by giving in or through force is that the debate over seatbelts becomes for the most part a nonissue. It is expected and accepted that one buckles up when traveling in a car.

Not everyone has a car, so let me offer a similar example from the supermarket. I do most of the grocery shopping for our family. I often take one or more of our children with me when I shop. This means frequent visits to local supermarkets, places marked by a genuine absence of gentleness between parents and children. It is not unusual for me to see children screamed at or hit at the super-market.

I can offer no scientific reason why supermarkets are generally unfriendly to children in the extreme. I do offer the following observations, however, the threads of which are not unrelated to the previous discussion of seatbelts.

First, parents are often in a hurry when we shop. If we are in a hurry ourselves and surrounded by others in a similar state, then it adds to the overall anxiety of shopping. Children are affected by our moods, particularly our anxieties.

Second, children at the supermarket are surrounded, bombarded visually, and I would say overwhelmed by thousands of tantalizing, colorfully packaged cereals, snack foods, and other goodies on store shelves. Hundreds of tempting items like candy bars, gum, and other sweets are positioned intentionally near the check-out counter. This adds to their anxiety and can easily trigger stress between parents and children.

Third, when a child whines and fusses, whether because she doesn't want to wear seatbelts or because he wants the candy bar staring him in the face, the easiest way out is to give in. But the quick way out becomes a curse. This helps explain the inordinate number of temper tantrums thrown at supermarkets.

Fourth, anyone wanting a preliminary look into the power of advertising to distort children's lives can find a good deal of supporting data in supermarkets. In addition to problems of product recognition ("I want X"), there is the more general message of advertisers that we are incomplete without their product, miserable and worthless until our happiness is restored through consumption.

I would venture that there is a high correlation between temper tantrums and other child-parent conflicts in supermarkets and the number of hours that children spend watching TV, and thus the number of commercials they are exposed to. One consequence of parenting without devoting time to our children is that television serves too often as a surrogate parent. As a result the average preschooler watches four hours of TV per day, and by age eighteen our kids have been exposed to fifteen hundred hours of commercials.[1] It is fair to say that media influence is significant, and one of the places it rears its ugly head is the supermarket.

I am not the world's best parent. I lose my patience and my focus more often than I care to admit. Yet in all my years of grocery shopping, often accompanied by one, two, or three children, our experiences together have been remarkably pleasant. I think the reasons for this include the following:

First, when our children ask for this or that at the store, we generally say *no* and explain why: "We try not to buy things we don't need." "Too much junk food is bad for us." "We have 'special treats' at home." These "treats" would be shared after eating a "good supper." It's not that we never buy something special, or sweet, or spontaneously. But it is not an expectation that we do so. The one exception to this rule is that after shopping at the food co-op, filling our jars with rice, beans, lentils, oats, flour, and other items, we reward ourselves with chocolate balls at the total cost of about 20 cents for the entire family.

Second, we try not to reward whining, whether in the supermarket, in the car, at home, or anywhere else. On a number of occasions I remember telling my children, whose complaints were cascading into whining, that yelling, screaming, moaning, groaning, whimpering, griping, and wailing were all preferable to whining. When I said this I was sometimes calm, sometimes exasperated, and sometimes close to whining myself.

Third, our children are more interested in books and creative play than in television. They have seen very few commercials, and we have taught them that commercials rarely tell us much that is either truthful or helpful. Thus when they go to the supermarket, our children are not programmed to want advertised items.

Finally, food is important to our family for a variety of reasons that go beyond our basic nutritional needs. Sara and I *and the children* bake most of our own bread, make most meals from scratch, can tomatoes and applesauce, freeze Minnesota vegetables, donate food for the hungry, and belong to a community-supported farm in which we get seasonal produce in exchange for our paid membership. We have a small urban vegetable garden in our backyard, where the children have a section of their own.

Baking bread, gardening, canning, and cooking with our children take time that many parents don't have. For us, however, it is time well spent. This is particularly true when we view these endeavors as family activities that end up with a product rather than focusing on the product itself. Baking bread with Naomi, who covers herself and the floor with flour and who eats much of the dough before the bread enters the oven, is fun if I'm in a state of mind that is focused on spending quality time with her. The delicious bread is a wonderful side benefit of our time together.

Where we shop is also important. Buying from locally owned businesses is better for the local economy, because money spent is recirculated in the community rather than siphoned off to corporate headquarters. I confess that I still purchase cereal and cheese at chain stores because the price difference is so great. We usually buy most other items at the farmers' market, neighborhood food co-op, or local, smaller supermarket, even if the costs are somewhat higher.

Shopping at local outlets is not only best for the local economy; it is better for family dynamics. In each of these stores the incidence of family conflict, so common to larger chains, is greatly diminished. There may be a variety of reasons for this. Many shoppers in local stores, although not wealthy, carry fewer anxieties with them to the market than some shoppers at the big chains, who, in Minneapolis at least, are more likely to be poor. In my unscientific view the temper tantrums and other conflicts between kids and parents at the larger markets are common among all races and social classes. This suggests that other dynamics are at play. I suspect one reason for fewer squabbles between parents and children at local markets has to do with the fact that purchasing food in these settings involves a relationship with a farmer or grocer or at least with people whose faces and names are familiar.

Conflicts over seatbelts and in grocery stores are reflections of problems in parenting. Taking time to make bread or can tomatoes with our children may seem insignificant, but it has profound implications for both children and society. Homemade bread with carefully mixed ingredients, kneaded with sticky hands, rising with yeast and laughter, filling our houses with sensuous aromas, is a powerful symbol of parenting. It contrasts sharply with the competing symbol of commercial white bread. White bread, like so much of our culture, offers appearance without substance. It is like Styrofoam puffed up with air.

To raise healthy children requires time, care, and the proper ingredients of love, nurture, and discipline. Our lack of time to explain things to our children, our desire for instant foods and quick solutions, our failure to set and respect limits, our propensity to provide our children with candy rather than caring — all have profound consequences, most of them negative. These consequences flow not simply from the parental choices we make but from the broader society of which we are a part. Parenting is difficult under the best of circumstances; good parenting is a monumental undertaking. Penelope Leach writes:

> Everything parents can do is clearly not enough. Whatever the real scale and scope of horrors perpetrated on or by children, there are not hundreds, or thousands, but millions more who are being failed by Western society, and are failing it. We leave parents the responsibility for children's well-being and happiness, but do we also empower them to ensure it? . . . Our society is inimical to children and has therefore devalued parents to such an extent that individual good parenting is not only exceedingly difficult but, ultimately, insufficient.[2]

Part II

Chapter 14

Where Personal and Social Responsibility Meet

[Dan Quayle has] an insight but the ideology is wrong.... His insight is the family is in trouble. He's right. But even when the family was stronger and the nuclear family was in place it always took more than two to raise children. You needed aunts and uncles, and grandmothers and grandfathers, and rabbis and ministers and deacons and ... teachers and still a little luck and grace. You needed a thick web of social relationships for the nurturing and the caring.... What we are seeing is the systemic erosion, the family is but one site, one institution within that network. It is being emptied out and hollowed out by ... a market culture buying and selling, promoting and advertising.

—CORNEL WEST

I could explain Audrey's trashed tricycle by referring to the perpetrators of the act as "unloved children" or "victims of poverty." One answer would please personalists. The other answer would be received well by advocates of a social approach. Both answers may be correct, but each, if isolated from the dynamics that lie behind the explanation of the other, is flawed.

The social approach traces problems of children and families to society's doorstep. Disturbed kids and troubled families, this argument says, are a predictable product of a society marred by massive inequalities, racial divisions, market-defined morality, and economic dislocation. One strength of the social perspective is that it underscores how societal choices, including economic priorities, tax

135

policies, wages, and social spending impact all parents and children. If parents have the responsibility to teach their children to swim, this perspective argues, then society has a responsibility to make sure the lake in which they learn to swim is not polluted.

Cornel West, pointing out the major flaw in the personalist perspective and the relative strength of the social approach, says:

> Dan Quayle is right in stating that families are in crisis. But he is wrong when he fails to see at the heart of the crisis a breakdown of familial and social networks and forces that in combination undermine efforts to nurture our children. The breakdown is systemic with family disruption a symbol of a deeper crisis in which market morality and a market culture distort our values, our economy and our very definitions of life's meaning.[1]

Personalists wear social blinders. But how about those, including myself, who are more comfortable with the social approach? Do we wear personal blinders? Social ones? What are our strengths and weaknesses? These questions, which help frame a discussion of the strengths and weaknesses of the social approach, are the subject of chapters 14–17 and 20–21. The present chapter demonstrates the importance of holding personal and social concerns in balance when assessing family and societal responsibility for meeting children's needs. Chapters 15 ("Race, Poverty, and Politics") and 16 ("The Politics of Poverty") make a case for why it is important to look at issues of race and poverty head on; they examine the forces that are fueling, and alternatives needed to avoid, a mean politics. Chapter 17 ("Market and Nonmarket Values") describes the distorted values dominating present American life, the importance of refusing to cede the values debate to the religious right, and the imperative of assessing personal values while extending the values discussion into the arena of the market economy. In chapters 18 ("Luxury Hotel") and 19 ("Interests") I weave together personal stories from my travel journals with analysis that sets the stage for further discussion of the strengths and weaknesses of the social approach to understanding the twin crises of family and society. Chapters 20 ("Values, Debt, and the Environment") and 21 ("Values, Prisons, and Poverty") look at the tragic legacy that present personal and social priorities offer our children and the need for alternative vision and action. Chapter 22 probes the question "Are You a Good Parent?" "Toward a Better World for Children" and "Community" offer practical avenues for action, followed by the Epilogue.

There is much to commend in the social perspective. The best of this perspective, as Cornel West articulates above, sees the family in the context of a broader network of relationships and institutions that are in crisis while taking personal responsibility seriously. Healthy families depend on healthy communities, and healthy communities depend on wise personal choices and public policies.

David Walsh looks at the personal and social causes of violence in ways that correlate well with the reasons our children are failing. He says there "is no single explanation for the level of violence infecting every corner of our country. The causes," he writes, "are complex and numerous."

> Family factors, like the absence of fathers, poverty, and racism, all contribute to fostering the culture of violence. But there is no doubt that the reinforcement that violent behavior receives from our larger culture exacerbates it and increases the risk factor for everyone.[2]

Walsh says it is possible to assess the risk factors for violence by examining three concentric circles surrounding the child, including a family circle, a neighborhood circle, and a circle representing the larger society.[3] These are not separate categories but overlapping circles in which factors in each influence and are influenced by the other.

> Risk factors have a compounding and cumulative effect. In other words, a child who comes from a very healthy family and who lives in a community where violence is not condoned has less risk for violent behavior than one who comes from an abusive family and who lives in a crime-ridden neighborhood. The more risk factors, the greater the likelihood of violent behavior. Nevertheless, even the child who is raised in the healthiest

of families and neighborhoods is increasingly at risk because of the powerful influence of the larger society which . . . condones and even encourages violent behavior.[4]

Many parents seek refuge from violence and crime as my mother and father did: by moving to the suburbs. Walsh counters the prevalent notion that violence or other destructive behavior is confined to the poor or can be avoided through flight:

> Parents who think they can keep their children safe by moving away from "rough neighborhoods" are quickly discovering that violence is growing everywhere. In fact, the tendency to flee for safety is not only futile, it exacerbates the problem. When we flee rather than deal with the problem, there are fewer people left behind who are willing to confront the issues and work toward solutions. (Also, the sense of community is lost, and there is less value placed on preserving it.) The strategy of retreating and building walls is not working, because the decay is coming from within. The influence of a culture selling violence is flooding families and neighborhoods across the socioeconomic spectrum.[5]

Walsh's conception of interactive concentric circles is a helpful way of identifying common ground between the personalists and those who stress social factors. The notion of interactive circles is particularly helpful if we expand his category of "larger society" in ways that address both cultural influences and economic priorities that are shaped increasingly by a global marketplace.

There is in our society, according to Cornel West, an "undeniable cultural decay and that decay is inseparable from but not identical with the economic decline." The decline of every civilization including our own, he says, has to do with "the relative erosion of the systems for nurturing and caring especially for children. It is systemic. It is not just a family affair."[6]

The social approach offers many correctives to the positions of personalists, but it is not without dangers. The emphasis on social dynamics can consciously or unconsciously invite us to down-play or ignore individual choices. Judith Stacey is so infuriated by the social blinders of the personalists that she seems to ig-nore almost completely the personal dimensions of the family crisis.

To their credit, many advocates of a social perspective, including Sylvia Ann Hewlett, Myriam Miedzian, and David Walsh, place a strong emphasis on responsible parenting and the importance of val-ues and the choices we make. Each stresses the profound impact of a father's absence on children's lives and underscores how children among all races and social classes are in trouble, suffering physical or emotional neglect or both. David Walsh reflects the concerns of many advocates of both the personalist and social approaches when he notes factors that correlate positively with children doing well in life: parental involvement in school, consistent discipline, parents spending substantial amounts of time at home with kids, and pa-rental monitoring of behavior.[7] Myriam Miedzian also shows how a nurturing father is one key to mitigating potential violence in boys.[8] The personal dimensions of their analysis balance and strengthen their discussions of social causes.

Jesse Jackson, searching for a proper balance between personal and social responsibility when assessing family issues, says it is important to "look in the mirror at ourselves" and "out the window" at society:

> Often these discussions go in two directions. One is...some serious introspective looking in the mirror. And some in look-ing in the mirror go to the very nth degree in that direction and never get back to standing up to look out the window pane. [In these two directions]...are both the very subjective innermost dimensions of our being in this discussion about the family, and the roles that men must play, as well as the objec-tive world, with the conditions under which we live outside the window.[9]

Although poverty makes parenting more difficult, Jackson re-minds us that it doesn't absolve parents of responsibility for raising children. Nor are problem children confined to the ghetto. Speaking on the role of men in children's lives he says:

Manhood is a natural gift...but it is a taught art. Nature qualifies us to be a man effortlessly, but the moral and ethical and social attributes must be taught, and practiced and learned.... Fundamentally this issue is more about ethics than ethnicity, and whether black or white, suburban or inner city, very wealthy or very poor, there are some common-ground dimensions....

For men must be taught in their formative years that... raising the babies you make...[is] a reasonable expectation. Dogs raise their puppies, cats their kittens, cows their calves, eagles stir the eaglets in the nest until they can fly. It is a natural and reasonable expectation.[10]

Some advocates of the social perspective allow a strength in their analysis to become a weakness. While it is abundantly clear that poverty correlates closely with problem behavior for many kids, young people are in trouble in *all* communities and among *all* social classes. David Walsh earlier warned of the futility of trying to flee to the suburbs to avoid violence. Sylvia Ann Hewlett offers another caution, this time to upwardly mobile parents:

Over the long haul you cannot claw your way up the corporate ladder, work sixty hours a week, *and* be a good parent, spouse, and citizen. And you clearly cannot dump spouse and kids and move on to greener pastures without risking the coherence and viability of the children you leave behind. Self-absorption is bad news for families and, in the long run, is even destructive to individuals because it can leave personal relationships in shambles and the community at war with itself.[11]

In the circle of my life, which frames my concern about children and families, I see frequent examples where parents who love their children deeply have little time to spend with them. In some cases both Mom and Dad work full time, not out of necessity but because their careers are fulfilling and consuming. Among the seductive promises of our culture is the illusion that gifted, well-intentioned, highly motivated people can "have it all," implying that difficult choices can be circumvented by our stubborn will, determination, and unusual gifts. The truth is that there are only so many quality hours in a day and that the needs of children must be considered a priority.

There seems to be a rough parallel between the crisis of poor youth and their affluent counterparts. It is captured in a statement from progressive grass-roots Christians, *On the Way: From Kairos to Jubilee:*

> Our shopping-mall culture keeps consumers busy in an age of hitherto unknown materialism whose signs are emptiness, loneliness, anxiety, and a fundamental loss of meaning. A most revealing sign of the times is the blank, sad, or angry look in the eyes of the young who congregate both on the wasting corners of our urban mean streets or in the wasteful corridors of our suburban shopping centers.[12]

When Judith Stacey dismisses criticism of parental lifestyle choices as a misplaced concern rooted in a lack of appreciation of class privilege, it is symptomatic of a deeper problem in some leftist analysis. The fact that troubled kids often come out of privileged settings is a clear sign that individual choice and action, including choices made by relatively affluent or at least financially secure parents, profoundly impact children.

Parental choices matter to all children. The fact that some parents have sufficient resources to make more choices than others should be acknowledged openly, and we should work to more equitably distribute those resources. Acknowledgment of privileges should be used, however, not to judge those lacking similar resources and choices but to subject the choices available to us to close scrutiny based on the needs of children. If we care about troubled children, it is clear that we need to take a critical look both "in the mirror" at ourselves and "out the window" at society. Parental choices matter. So too does the systemic erosion of institutions and social networks that undermines community and diminishes our capacity to nurture children.

Family stress, neighborhood decline, and broader circles encompassing cultural violence and economic disparity compromise the well-being of our nation's children. Saving our children will require us to make significant changes within each of these overlapping spheres of influence.

Chapter 15

Race, Poverty, and Politics

===

*It has been among the white working and lower middle classes
that many of the social changes stemming from introduction of
new rights — civil rights for minorities, reproductive and workplace rights for women, constitutional protections for the criminally
accused, immigration opportunities for those from developing countries, free-speech rights to pornographers, and the surfacing of highly
visible homosexual communities — have been most deeply resisted.*
—THOMAS AND MARY EDSALL, *Chain Reaction*

Whenever I allude to issues of race in this book, in this and other
chapters, I am forced to ponder my own racism. I am the product
of a white suburb and a segregated city, of grandparents who found
it difficult to accept Catholics and of a father who refused a job in
Milwaukee because he wanted his children to be safe from blacks
and crime, and whose image of death was a black man with an ax.
It is not my intent to vilify my family, the many fine people I knew
growing up, or the communities where I have lived. My point is to
remind us that our nation, and each person within it, has a history
out of which racial prejudices are born and nurtured.

I know also that I enjoy many privileges: I've never been discriminated against when applying for a job or a loan; my neighborhood
hasn't been red-lined by banks; I haven't been pulled over and ques-
tioned by police nor have my children been taunted because of our
skin color; and the dominant society from which I receive my entitlement doesn't define me as part of a problem people. I receive
many other benefits from a white-dominated society, and the fact

that I am hard pressed to name many of them is undoubtedly part of the problem.

I also harbor many racist ideas. It's easy for me to see that children like Dion in my daughter's kindergarten class have problems, but it's also easy for me to slip into a mind-set that sees him as part of a problem people. The same is true when my black neighbors turn out to be drug dealers or when the kids who walk through my alley, who I hope are out for a stroll, end up stealing cars. When the evening news flashes through the upcoming stories, including the latest murder, I sometimes assume it is another incident of black-on-black violence. Often I am wrong, but adding to my confusion is the fact that too many times I am right. This reflects media bias as well as my own, but it also shows with some accuracy that the problem of black-on-black violence is real. Black males age fourteen to twenty-four make up 1.2 percent of our nation's population but they commit 30 percent of the homicides and are victims of 18 percent of those homicides.[1]

The difficulty of talking about race, poverty, and politics is clear. The importance of doing so is equally apparent, and yet many people avoid the topic like the plague. I am often among them. There are many factors that contribute to my silence. Part of me is afraid of being wrongly accused of racism or of having my actual racism challenged by others. I also have a sense that as a white man it is important for me to listen to the voices of African-Americans as they describe our society and the problems black people and others face within it. Listening is important if those of us who are white want to speak with integrity. This is one reason I lift up the voices of William Julius Wilson, Jesse Jackson, Cornel West, and Jacqueline Jones (in the following chapter) as they speak directly or indirectly about the crisis of families in our society.

When talking about race and poverty we must strive to keep a focus on the problems people face and guard against the impulse of labeling others as problem peoples. We must also be willing to look at social and political systems and how they influence the behaviors of individuals. In a society in which racism is never far from the surface of politics, whites often find it convenient to feed white fears and scapegoat blacks and other people of color. Obvious examples include President Bush's use of Willie Horton, a South Carolina woman killing her two young children and then telling police and much of the nation that they'd been abducted by a black man, a Boston husband shooting his pregnant wife and then claiming a black man had shot her in their car, or California voters blaming the state's economic crisis on immigrants.

Racism is unfortunately a "quick sell" to many whites. White supporters of a punitive social agenda, including many personalists, are on the political ascendancy. Born-again Christians, who dominate much of the family values debate, helped Republicans take control of the U.S. House and Senate in the mid-term elections of 1994. Buoyed by the influence of the Christian right, the new Republican-led Congress is pursuing economic and social policies that will likely lead to more crime, despair, inequality, violence, poverty, and hopelessness — the very things that fuel white fears, feed racism, and give rise to mean politics in the first place.

As I raise questions about what we would do differently as parents and as a society if we cared about children, I have come to see another potential pitfall in the social approach: *a failure to address issues of race and poverty head on.* By treating this as terrain walked on only by "racists," advocates of a social perspective contribute to the anger and alienation of fearful whites who now make up a key element in a political coalition whose policies are disastrous for families and the nation (chapter 12). White born-again Christians, who made up 22 percent of the voters in the 1994 election (up from 12 percent in 1988), offered critical support for the Contract with America. Seventy-eight percent of them voted Republican.[2]

In *Chain Reaction,* Thomas and Mary Edsall describe the important role working-class whites played in the elevation of Republicans to the presidency in 1980. Many white voters, historically tied to the Democratic Party, formed a coalition with Republicans, according to the Edsalls, because of matters of race. Working-class, moderate-income whites, their argument goes, were working hard but falling behind and feeling insecure. They looked around and saw blacks disproportionately committing crimes, living in poverty, receiving welfare and food stamps. These whites resented both the nonworking poor and the interventionist federal government, which in their view used the court system and their tax dollars to provide benefits to people they saw as increasingly unworthy. In the language Cornel West used earlier, the poor who had perhaps once been perceived as people with problems were now defined by many whites, particularly white men, as problem peoples.

Many of these working-class whites, according to the Edsalls, supported civil rights in the abstract — that is, so long as civil rights meant equal access rather than redress of historical wrongs. Whites who saw "their jobs" going to blacks because of affirmative action or whose children were being bused away from neighborhood schools, however, grew resentful of the whole "rights revolution."

The Edsalls describe alienated white voters, disturbed by the Democratic Party's connection to civil rights and its sponsorship of programs that benefitted blacks, eagerly embracing a Republican coalition that promised to favor taxpayers rather than recipients, the private sector over an intrusive federal bureaucracy, workers over the jobless, victims of crime over criminals, and advocates of a "meritocracy" over against proponents of entitlement. Reagan's victory was sealed by fear that the election of a Democratic president would mean raising "taxes from the largely white lower-middle and middle classes in order to direct benefits toward the disproportionately black and Hispanic poor — benefits often seen as wastefully spent."[3] In the 1980s, fearful whites with a conservative social agenda joined forces with the big-business and wealthy elites who have historically dominated the Republican Party. The Edsalls, confirming the analysis I presented in chapter 12, note that the Republican presidents elected by this coalition carried out policies that resulted in "what may well have been the most accelerated upward redistribution of income in the nation's history — a redistribution fed by the tax, spending, and regulatory policies of the Reagan and Bush administrations."[4]

Issues of race and poverty fuel tensions between poor or middle-class whites and poor blacks. According to Cornel West:

[When democratic societies unravel] ... it has much to do with increasing poverty that produces escalating levels of despair and increasing paranoia that produces increasing levels of distrust. And to talk about race in America, to talk about the legacy of white supremacy in America, is to talk about poverty and paranoia. Too many black poor people. Too many poor people in general.[5]

Our sense of common destiny is eroded by white fear, which is fed by economic insecurity.

Relative economic decline generates fears.... [Fears] of downward mobility, or experiences of downward mobility,... always bring out the worst in each and every one of us [and] lead us to scapegoating, lead us to look for conspiratorial theories to account for why things are out of control and we see it proliferating around the country.... Brother Rush Limbaugh speaks of something very real, the pain and the grief and the fear of so many white working-class and lower-middle-class brothers... as they feel as if they are becoming invisible with the women and the browns and blacks and yellows and reds taking over....

...Their pain is real and one needs to speak to it but it ought not to take the form of scapegoating. "Oh, if all the women had stayed in the kitchen the culture would be intact, if we were in control of black folk we'd actually have jobs." Do you think so? How many black folk own production units in your part of the country? "Oh, if the gay brothers and the lesbian sisters had just stayed in the closet the morality would be intact." Oh really? They're that powerful that when they stepped out, things collapsed. Really?[6]

It is important to talk about race and poverty. Because under the cover of such tensions, Republican administrations in the 1980s fleeced much of the electorate, doing immeasurable damage to families, neighborhoods, and our economic future in the process. Social programs were cut, the value of the minimum wage eroded, taxes were shifted onto poor and working-class people, the national debt skyrocketed along with military spending and tax breaks for the wealthy, casino capitalism drained pensions and tore communities apart, gaps between the rich and poor widened, and the middle class was squeezed. From 1971 to 1991 the combined Social Security and income-tax bills of median-income families grew by 329 percent while the combined tax bills of individuals and families with incomes of more than $1 million a year fell 34 percent.[7] The resulting resentment and insecurity fed fears and prejudices that triggered and trigger a political backlash.

Michael Lind, who traces the roots of economic insecurity felt by many Americans to the doorsteps of "America's oligarchy" or "overclass," describes how in the trenches of daily life affirmative action generates tensions among whites, people of color and women of all races. According to Lind, a black 1989 high school graduate in California with the minimum high school grade-point average had a 70 percent chance of being accepted to Berkeley, while a white student with the same score had only a 9 percent chance of admission. Not surprisingly, for many whites affected by such numbers, the consequence of such affirmative action is resentment. This resentment, Lind implies, is understandable, but it masks more unpleasant realities. First, it diverts attention from the "overclass," where real economic and political power is exercised by white men.

> Anybody choosing to see the oligarchy in its native habitat need do nothing else but walk down the street of any big city to an office tower housing a major bank, a corporate headquarters or law firm, or a national television station. Enter the building and the multicultural diversity of the street vanishes.... Step off the elevator at the top of the tower and apart from the clerical and maintenance staff, hardly anybody is nonwhite.... No matter what your starting point, the closer you come to the centers of American politics and society, the more everyone begins to look the same ... Almost exclusively white, disproportionately mainline Protestant or Jewish, most of the members of the American elites went to one of a dozen Ivy League colleges or top state universities.[8]

Lind also points out how the children of the overclass often get into elite schools through "legacy preference" and not on their own merit.

What he doesn't add is that the elite are almost exclusively male. Although women make up nearly half of the U.S. labor force, it is men who hold 95 percent of senior management positions in business,[9] a fact lost on the many white men who all too frequently displace fears rooted in economic insecurity onto women and people of color.

A second problem with resentment over affirmative action is that it diverts attention from issues such as corporate downsizing and other strategies pursued by the overclass that cause job losses and put downward pressure on wages. "As the number of black and Hispanic students at selective universities and partners in prestigious law firms is artificially maintained," Lind notes, "the average wages of black and Hispanic workers, along with those of white workers, continue to stagnate or decline. The tokenism embodied in racial preference and multiculturalism is thus about as threatening to the American elite as an avant-garde sculpture in the lobby of a bank."[10]

In recent years, as economic insecurity has become more pronounced, political power has shifted increasingly to more affluent, white suburban voters and to other fearful whites who seek to isolate themselves both geographically and fiscally from blacks in the inner city. A profile of voters from the November 1994 elections suggests that many white voters bring their fears and economic interests with them into the voting booth at the same time that many people of color are alienated from the political process itself. Less than 40 percent of eligible voters cast ballots. African-Americans, who make up 11.8 percent of the population, cast 9 percent of the votes while Hispanics, who are 9.6 percent of the population, cast only 3 percent of votes. The profile of income paints an even starker picture of why the Republican Contract with America, with its punitive policies toward the poor, was popular among many of those who voted. Although only 4.6 percent of the U.S. population have incomes of more than $75,000, they cast 16 percent of the votes. Only 12.8 percent of Americans make more than $50,000 a year; however, they accounted for 38 percent of the votes cast in November.[11]

There are of course differences between the Republican coalition of the 1980s and its most recent manifestation. Today's Republican Party is influenced much more by the powerful and well-organized political presence of the religious right, both within and outside of

Washington. Although the new Republican coalition shares many of their economic concerns, it is not clear how long the economic agenda of traditional Republican elites will occupy center stage. The social, family-values agenda of the religious right — fighting against gays, abortion, sex education, and affirmative action, and fighting for gun control, prayer in public schools, and the right to teach creationism — is becoming ever more important and visible.

How tensions get played out between economic elites and family-values crusaders is uncertain. What is clear is that we are now and into the foreseeable future will be faced with a mean politics of scapegoating as women, homosexuals, blacks, and the poor are blamed overtly or subtly for the nation's family and social crises.

There may be good reasons to allow states, under guidelines established at the federal level to insure fairness and standards, more flexibility in administering programs. However, behind the Contract with America's emphasis on downsizing the federal government, giving more power to the states, and consolidating program funding into block grants is a desire to undermine federally financed or mandated social programs that benefit the poor throughout our society. "Historically the term *states' rights*," an NAACP member in Minnesota says, "has meant the right to discriminate against black folks."[12]

The consequences of current governmental priorities for the poor and ultimately for the country are sobering. "For people who are concerned primarily about the productivity of the workforce and the competitiveness of the U.S. economy," says Larry Brown, director of the Center on Hunger, Poverty and Nutrition Policy at Tufts University, "making more poor children hungry is not the way to go, which is what the block grants would do."[13] Republican attacks on affirmative action further exemplify punitive policies likely to hurt the poor. Tom Teepen notes how "affirmative-action policies that hold once-closed doors open to capable minority businesses, students and job applicants" are threatened by a "P.O.'d White Guys agenda." The likely result, he says, is to "make the nation's already dangerous racial tensions even more explosive."[14]

The fact that many discontented whites are pursuing punitive policies against the poor, particularly poor people of color, points to the need to address issues of race and poverty. But how are we to do that? How can we respond to white fears without scapegoating blacks and other people of color?

Chapter 16

The Politics of Poverty

Blaming the poor and powerless for America's social and economic problems is far more comforting and acceptable than blaming the rich and powerful. Blaming the poor upholds a fundamental tenet of the American Dream: that individuals can dramatically alter the course of their own lives, that they can rise in the class hierarchy on their own initiative. To maintain our own dreams of success we must blame the poor for their failure; if their failure is due to flaws in the structure of society, these same societal limitations could thwart our dreams of success. The notion that the failure of the poor is due to their character weaknesses enables others to blame the impoverished for their own poverty while simultaneously preserving the faith of the nonpoor in the possibility of success.

— RUTH SIDEL, *Keeping Women and Children Last*

Our propensity to focus on problem peoples rather than on problems is rooted in a historical amnesia that denies the past, reinforces injustice in the present, and therefore distorts the future. "The typical White Guy's response" to disproportionate black poverty rooted in a cumulative history of "350 years of slavery, segregation and systematic discrimination," Tom Teepen writes, "is to draw himself up in indignation, . . . [say] that he never enslaved or discriminated against anyone, isn't guilty for the past and isn't responsible for it. OK," he continues, "but we're all responsible for the future, and if we don't keep working" to narrow racial disparities, "we will leave our children with all the consequences of a widening injustice."[1]

For historical, political, and economic reasons, poverty in the

United States is *disproportionately but by no means exclusively* a problem of blacks and other people of color. We shouldn't be afraid to say this, and it shouldn't surprise us any more than it is "surprising" that blacks in post-apartheid South Africa are disproportionately poorer than whites. In our society, given the history of slavery and discrimination and the relationship between poverty and race, it is predictable that although a roughly equal number of black and white households receive welfare, a higher *percentage* of blacks do so. Of all black households, 15.5 percent receive welfare compared to 2 percent of white households. For food stamps the percentages are 26 and 4.6 percent respectively.[2]

The Edsalls, in *Chain Reaction,* note that these percentages help explain white resentment against blacks. In my view they also explain black resentment against whites. White elites benefit disproportionately from a white-dominated system and then deflect attention from themselves by pitting middle-class and lower-income whites against people of color. They define blacks with problems as a problem people and allow inadequate social programs, including welfare, to lock them into situations of oppressive poverty. Even when welfare is recognized as a deficient system, as it is in the Contract with America, it is the poor and not the system who are blamed.

Hostile whites who criticize welfare and scapegoat recipients might be surprised to discover not only that about equal numbers of black and white families receive welfare but that many African-American leaders and many welfare recipients themselves have a profound dislike for the system. As Salim Muwakkil, who covers issues central to the African-American community for *In These Times,* writes: "The Gingrichian argument that welfare is dangerous because it encourages dependency is one that has widespread support. Some of the most withering condemnations of welfare have come from black radical organizations."[3]

Few would argue against the need to reform or do away with welfare. The welfare debate underscores, however, the importance of focusing on the problems people face and their causes rather than on problem peoples. If the focus is on the problems faced by welfare recipients and others living in poverty, then our attention will center *on breaking the cycle of poverty.* Breaking poverty's cycle will necessarily require confronting powerful political and economic groups that dominate American life. It will require pursuing alternative policies that within the framework of welfare reform must include adequate support levels, decent jobs and training, housing, child care, and health care. If the focus is on problem peoples, however, then the likely result and intended purpose of "welfare reform" becomes punitive, pushing people off welfare into an unknown abyss. Welfare recipient and single mother Jodeen Wink, writing in response to the Contract with America, says:

> If we expect people to get off welfare we won't force them to work 35 hours per week to earn a grossly inadequate AFDC grant....At AFDC grant wages people will still need housing, energy, food and medical assistance. So much for welfare reform. If we want women off welfare it's common sense to wait until their children are in school before forcing them into the labor market. No one can get off welfare when they have the enormous cost of child care hanging over high-school-kid wages. And like it or not, taking care of preschool aged children is work: not just for day care centers and not just for the wealthy, but for poor people too.[4]

Punitive welfare reform is fueled not only by racism but by a series of questionable, wrong-headed, and self-serving assumptions. Many of the same people who brought us tax breaks in the 1980s, which resulted in the largest upward distribution of wealth in the history of our country along with astronomical debts, are portraying welfare as a budget-busting program. The notion that costly assistance provided to the unworthy poor is bankrupting the country, a belief held by many voters and many personalists, obscures class divisions that are tearing apart the social fabric of the country.

Writing in *Harper's Magazine*, Michael Lind notes how within the major news media it is "against the rules to talk about a rapacious American oligarchy, and the suggestion that the small group of people with most of the money and power in the United States just *might* be responsible to some degree for what has been happening to the country over the last twenty years invariably invites the mass media to expressions of wrath and denial." "The most remarkable thing about our own American oligarchy," he observes, "is the pretense that it doesn't constitute anything as definite as a social class." The strategy of what Lind refers to as America's "overclass" is not surprisingly to focus attention away from themselves when it comes to assessing our national crisis:

> Not only do the comfortable members of the overclass single out the weakest and least influential of their fellow citizens as the cause of all their sorrows but they routinely, and preposterously, treat the genuine pathologies of the ghetto — high levels of violence and illegitimacy — as the major problems facing a country with uncontrollable trade and fiscal deficits, a low savings rate, an obsolete military strategy, an anachronistic and corrupt electoral system, the worst system of primary education in the First World, and the bulk of its population facing long-term economic decline.[5]

A mean and distorted politics is fed by hate radio. According to Rush Limbaugh the "poor in this country are the biggest piglets at the mother pig and her nipples. The poor.... give nothing back. Nothing."[6] "Corporate welfare" recipients, high-income beneficiaries of changes in the tax code, and the military-related complex are by far and away the "biggest piglets," but anger against the poor, fueled by Limbaugh's ignorance and distortions, is reflected at the ballot box. Hobart Rowen writing in the *Washington Post* notes that according to a survey sponsored by the Harvard School of Public Health, in the 1994 mid-term elections "almost half the voters (46 percent) think either welfare or foreign aid is the biggest item in the federal budget." Reality is quite different. Federal expenditures for foreign aid in 1994 were $12.3 billion, less than 1 percent of the federal budget. AFDC, which Rowan notes has been "transformed into some kind of demon by [Newt] Gingrich for supporting teenage mothers on welfare," makes up a little more *than 1 percent of the federal budget, while welfare and food stamps together account for 2.8 percent.* By contrast, spending for Social Security at $321 billion was about 22 percent of federal expenditures; military spending cost $277 billion, and interest on the debt another $212 billion.[7]

❖

Blaming the poor for our nation's fiscal crisis conveniently masks the ways in which poor and middle-class Americans are hurt by the priorities of the wealthy who dominate political and economic life. Between 1980 and 1990, the after-tax income *gains* of the wealthiest 1 percent, a total of 2.5 million people, equalled the *total income* of the poorest 20 percent of our citizens, a total of 50 million people.[8] During the same time period the purchasing power of the minimum wage fell 22 percent.[9] In this light it should not surprise us that between 1985 and 1990 the number of people in the United States who lacked sufficient food to eat each month increased by 50 percent.[10] Ironically, a *Business Week* cover story, "Inequality: How the Gap between Rich and Poor Hurts the Economy," notes that the wide gap between rich and poor not only hurts skills but that an "expanding cadre of economists argues" that "lower U.S. growth [is] fueled by inequality." A "half-dozen economic theorists...show how income gaps hurt gross domestic product by lowering efficiency."[11]

Many middle-class whites may have good reasons for feeling insecure about jobs and frustrated over rising taxes, but making the poor the targets of their anger is both wrong and counterproductive. Only one in five Americans, for example, generally those with higher incomes, itemize deductions. According to the Congressional Budget Office our government's failure to limit itemized deductions to 15 percent of incomes will mean lost tax revenues totalling $247 billion over the next five years.[12]

The federal deduction of home-mortgage interest payments costs the U.S. Treasury approximately $51 billion a year. This loss in revenue is more than four times the annual cost of welfare ($12.6 billion for 1995) and nearly twice the yearly expenditure for food stamps ($28 billion for 1995).[13] A portion of this subsidy seems justified if it aids working families who might not otherwise afford a home. Although 65 percent of U.S. households make $40,000 a year or less, however, they receive only 6 percent of the government's house-tax subsidy. By contrast, about 2 percent of U.S. households earn between $100,000 and $200,000 a year, but they receive 28 percent of all mortgage deductions.[14] Overall, the richest 5 percent of U.S. taxpayers receive 44 percent of the homeowner's subsidy,[15] with 80 percent of the benefits going to the upper fifth of income earners — all of whom could afford a house, with or without the deduction, and many of whom use tax-deductible home equity loans for other purposes.[16] If we eliminated the home-mortgage deduction *only for the top fifth of U.S. income earners,* we could pay the annual federal costs of welfare and food stamps combined. Merely capping the home-interest deduction at $20,000, which would be the interest payment on a $250,000 to $300,000 home, would save $23.5 billion![17]

Excessively generous military pensions, which cost the federal treasury twice as much as AFDC, provide a similar contrast. The federal government spends twice as much on military bands as it does for public television,[18] and spends $193 million a year on military bands compared to just $21 million for kindergarten-through-twelfth-grade arts education. The Coast Guard, Army, Marine, and Air Force music budgets together total $25 million *more* than the entire budget for the National Endowment for the Arts! That $193 million expenditure makes the Pentagon the world's largest employer of musicians (more than eight thousand on the payroll),[19] with eighty-five active military bands and another eighty-five bands with reserve units.[20] It is noteworthy that the architects of the Contract with America are increasing military spending while cutting and seeking to do away with federal funding for the Corporation for Public Broadcasting.

Let us also remember that what a *New York Times* editorial calls "corporate welfare" and what Labor Secretary Robert Reich refers to as "Aid to Dependent Corporations" costs the federal treasury plenty — somewhere between $40 billion and $75 billion per year, according to the *Times.*[21] There are also excesses like the bailout of Wall Street investors who flocked to the high interest rates offered by a Mexican government that fell into financial crisis in 1995. "Junk bonds, in effect," one banker who wished to be anonymous said. "But the guys who run the mutual funds and pension funds couldn't resist, so they took huge risks with the money of people who didn't really get what was at stake. It comes close," he continued, "to violating fiduciary responsibility in some cases, and when the balloon went up, all they could do was run to Washington for help."[22]

The true cost of corporate welfare may be higher than the *New York Times* estimate. The Progressive Policy Institute, a public policy think-tank associated with the Democratic Leadership Council, recently identified 120 programs and tax subsidies to "powerful industry groups" that if eliminated or reduced could save the federal treasury $265 billion over five years.[23] Senator Paul Wellstone has decried the fact that congressional budget hawks find it easy to target social programs for cuts while large corporations, wealthy Americans, and other interests receive $420 billion in special tax breaks annually.[24] Simply restoring corporate tax rates to their 1953 level would bring an additional $53 billion into the federal treasury each year,[25] more than enough to offset current federal expenditures for both welfare and food stamps.

Cost is not the only deception concerning welfare. John T. Cook and J. Larry Brown from the Center on Hunger, Poverty and Nutrition Policy at Tufts University describe and then counter the perspective that is fueling punitive welfare reform. They note that the conservative argument (the personalist perspective) says that welfare (AFDC) causes increases in out-of-wedlock births and single-parent families, which in turn cause poverty and related social problems. Therefore, eliminating welfare will reduce poverty and related social problems. According to Cook and Brown these definitions of both problem and solution are wrong because:

- From 1970 to 1990, a time in which single-parent families and out-of-wedlock births *increased by 65.9 percent,* the value of welfare benefits *decreased 35.2 percent,* as the average monthly AFDC benefit per family fell from $644 per month to $417. Within the logic of the conservative position, reduced welfare benefits should translate into fewer out-of-wedlock births.

- Nearly two-thirds of the increase in female-headed households over the past several decades were among the nonpoor.

The "growth in out-of-wedlock births occurred among never-married women at all income levels, not primarily among the poor."

- Recent research demonstrates that the existence of welfare benefits "has little if any effect on out-of-wedlock births."

- Other "western industrial nations provide more welfare benefits, but have much smaller proportions of births out of wedlock than the U.S."

According to Cook and Brown, the empirical evidence shows that out-of-wedlock births and single-parent families are caused primarily by

- A decline in the "availability of viable educational or employment prospects... for poor young people, especially young low-income residents of central cities."

- A trend toward nonmarital childbearing in practically all western industrial countries that crosses all income and educational levels. For more affluent single women, "growing economic independence" has made child rearing apart from marriage economically viable.

- Decreases in men's earning power, "which has made it harder for some men to begin and maintain families."

Rather than blaming poor single mothers, the authors note that the "real causes of poverty" are declining real wages and earnings, structural changes in the U.S. economy, demographic changes that put downward pressures on wages, limits on asset accumulation by welfare recipients, weakening of the safety net, worsening distribution of income, and changes in trade, technology, and competitiveness in an increasingly integrated world economy. In conclusion the writers say:

The argument that welfare causes out-of-wedlock births and single-parent families, and that these in turn cause poverty, is not supported by the empirical evidence. The evidence overwhelmingly contradicts this position. Out-of-wedlock births

and single-parent families arise due to economic and social factors, largely driven by employment-related changes in
the economy. Moreover, the evidence shows that poverty in
the U.S. is not caused by out-of-wedlock births nor single-
parent families, but by a much broader set of economic and
demographic factors.[26]

The perspective of Cook and Brown is a helpful corrective to the
nasty nature of much of the welfare debate, but it should not obscure
the need to reform welfare. On the positive side, AFDC, in spite of
being a deeply flawed program, has helped millions of families to
mitigate the pangs of hunger, to escape abusive relationships, and
to avoid homelessness and despair. Advocates of punitive welfare reform, who vilify recipients, often downplay both these successes and
the impact of dismantling present programs. On the other hand,
the present welfare system can legitimately be judged a failure. It
more often than not helps people to cope with poverty rather than
to break out of the devastating cycles of poverty, powerlessness, and
dependency.

Many advocates of a social approach to understanding the crisis
of families in our society may soften their criticism of the present
welfare system because they understand that punitive welfare reform, which makes the poor even more vulnerable, is far worse
than the flawed system it seeks to replace. Jim Wallis in *The Soul
of Politics* summarizes the strengths and weaknesses that liberals and
conservatives bring to public debate:

> Liberalism's best impulse is to care about the disenfranchised
> and insist that a society is responsible for its people. But liberal-
> ism became captive to large distant institutions and impersonal
> bureaucracies that are more concerned with control than caring,
> and the result became more dependency than empowerment.
>
> Conservatism's best impulse is to stress the need for indi-
> vidual initiative and moral responsibility. But because of its
> attachment to institutions of wealth and power, preference for
> the status quo, and the lack of a strong ethic of social respon-
> sibility, conservatism has virtually abandoned the poor and the
> dispossessed.[27]

❖

Donald Fraser, a former U.S. congressperson from Minnesota and a longtime mayor of Minneapolis, is a progressive voice who defies traditional political categories and believes it is time to do away with the welfare system. Unlike many Democrats who defend a flawed system and many Republicans whose approach to welfare reform promises to deepen inequalities and poverty, Fraser wants to insure that the needs of children in our society are met.

Fraser was alarmed that the number of families headed by single-parent households increased dramatically during his tenure as mayor of Minneapolis. In 1980 27 percent of births in Minneapolis were to unmarried parents. Thirteen years later this figure had risen to approximately 50 percent. The problem of single parenthood, he noted, was most pronounced within communities of color, but the fastest growth rate of such households was among whites. The welfare system, he said, encouraged the breakup of families because AFDC benefits were available only to one-parent households. Like sociologist William Julius Wilson, cited earlier, Fraser underscored that marriage rates are higher among men who earn higher wages and that increases in single parenthood are linked to worsening jobs in terms of pay and benefits. Minimum-wage earnings by a second parent, he said, are worse than no earnings because they cannot make up for lost AFDC benefits and lost medical care. Fraser, like single-mother Jodeen Wink cited earlier, saw that efforts to reform welfare by forcing AFDC recipients into minimum-wage jobs were counterproductive. He worried also that welfare reforms with two-year-and-out provisions would place burdens on cities. With few good jobs available, the cities would have to create and fund jobs for which there were few public monies. Even training of single parents was not without pitfalls. Welfare reforms that limit training to single parents might end up encouraging a further erosion of two-parent households, he said, because single parenthood might be seen as a ticket to training.

The solution to many of these problems, Fraser said, is to eliminate AFDC as we know it and replace it with a federally funded entitlement program to support children in lower-income families. All low-income families, one- or two-parent, would receive a monthly cash grant from the federal government for each child. The amount of this entitlement would be carefully crafted in order to target support levels to the actual costs of caring for children. The goal, he said, would be to design a system in which a single parent is neither better nor worse off for having a child. States could provide additional help needed by some families.

Fraser noted that one way that such a program could function would be to integrate federal support for children into the Earned Income Tax Credit (EITC) program. The EITC is a refundable tax credit that supplements the incomes of working families living with the limitations of low wages. Working families with low incomes and at least one child at home could receive monthly cash grants in the form of advances on the EITC, lump-sum payments at the end of the tax year, or they could have their withholding adjusted by their employer to increase monthly income in anticipation of no tax liability. Fraser also proposed sliding-fee child care as an additional federal entitlement for all parents who are unable to pay full costs. This would help overburdened parents and financially and emotionally needy children and have the additional benefit of raising the wages of child-care workers. A long-term goal, Fraser said, would be to offer a child-care payment to a mother or father who chose to stay at home and raise a child during early years of life.[28] This hoped-for goal of paying a parent to stay at home with young children is already public policy in Sweden. In many cases, as Penelope Leach argues persuasively, support for stay-at-home care offers advantages over public day care, which is inappropriate for infants and oftentimes less than ideal for small children as well.[29]

Fraser's proposals are open to legitimate criticism. He may overstate, for example, the degree to which the availability of welfare payments serves as a draw to young motherhood. Penelope Leach notes that much is made, both in the United States and the United Kingdom, "of the risk of women having more and more children because welfare or benefit payments are increased as the number of children increases."

Only prejudice, ignorance or both can sustain a belief that the extra sums constitute extra "income" or "profit" for the mother. Under AFDC, for example, a second child brings an extra $30 per month in Alabama, $40 in Florida. Which of us would like to attempt the impossible task of maintaining a child on less than $10 per week? Which of us would actually plan a pregnancy to obtain such a sum? The evidence is that nobody does.[30]

Fraser's proposals suffer also from the fact that although they acknowledge the importance of jobs and respond to their absence, they fail to address the fundamental issue of creating jobs that offer wages sufficient to support the needs of families. This said, his suggestions are constructive because they offer alternatives to punitive welfare reform while acknowledging the inadequacy of AFDC. They balance issues of personal and social responsibility, acknowledge the importance of jobs and income, health care and child care, and outline steps that move in the direction of breaking the cycles of poverty. Most important, they offer a way out of the double jeopardy of poverty and the absence of nurturing experienced by many children who are the products of the old welfare system and the likely victims of Contract with America–type solutions. I believe that a logical extension of Fraser's concerns and proposals would be for the United States to replace welfare with family policies similar to those in place in many European countries. Family policies in Europe generally involve universal access to health care and child care, subsidized housing, and a cash payment to all families with children to help meet essential needs.

Strategies that ignore fundamental causes of poverty while punishing the poor exact enormous human costs. "Welfare reforms which focus primarily on elimination of benefits for single parents and their children," Cook and Brown conclude in their paper on the welfare reform debate, "will not lead to increased economic self-sufficiency. Such reforms are likely, however, to inflict harm on a large number of American families and their children, and diminish their productive capacity."[31] Equally important, such strategies divert attention from systemic forces.

Poverty is widespread within the United States. Ignoring the causes of extensive poverty while scapegoating a segment of the poor, as in the case of inflating the financial costs of welfare, is both self-serving and rooted in questionable assumptions. Stereotypes make scapegoating possible. However, if we are to tame the mean politics that rises out of white fears like ash from an angry volcano, then advocates of a social perspective must acknowledge that stereotypes, though always dangerous, are *sometimes* founded in reality.

Kenneth S. Tollett, a black professor of education at Howard University's Graduate School of Arts and Sciences, says that the "stereotype is not a stereotype any more." "The behavior of black males [in the underclass]," he says, "is now beginning to look like the black stereotype. The statements we have called stereotypes in the past have become true."[32] In other words, fears about crime and about the dysfunctional behavior of a significant segment of the impoverished black community are not irrational. They are based at least partially on real behaviors in which stereotypical ideas are confirmed by the actions of many black men in the so-called underclass.

When the leading cause of death among young African-American men is gun violence and when two-thirds of black babies are born to unwed mothers, then stereotypes have "come true." The problem is that a stereotype, even a reasonably accurate one for a certain segment of the "black underclass," is now the basis of an even broader stereotype that casts blacks generically, and sometimes even genetically, as a problem people. It prevents many of us from seeing achievements by blacks. Equally important, the broad stereotype prevents many whites from examining either the roots of disproportionate black poverty or the causes of extensive poverty in our society.

The broad stereotype, for example, leads many to believe that poor people are all on welfare when in fact many poor people in our country are full-time workers or their dependents. It would have us believe that poverty is a problem principally for blacks and other people of color, whereas 62 percent of all poor children in America are white.[33] The broad stereotype suggests that the growth in single-parent families is primarily among poor blacks, whereas between

1970 and 1990 nearly two-thirds of the increase in female-headed households with no spouse present was in nonpoor households.[34]

The stereotype projects the typical AFDC recipient as a teenage mother, whereas current teenage mothers comprise only 13 percent of all recipients.[35] Or it pictures her as a baby-making machine with numerous children, whereas the average family receiving AFDC has 1.9 kids. Or it would show her getting rich on welfare, whereas accounting for inflation, the average monthly AFDC benefit per family was $676 in 1970 and $373 in 1993, a 45 percent decrease. The average yearly AFDC benefit of $4,476 per family during 1993 was 38.3 percent of the federal poverty threshold for a family of three.[36]

The stereotype suggests that welfare recipients are lazy freeloaders who don't want to work, whereas the fact is that few decent jobs are available, and for parents to take low-paying jobs without benefits would put many families at risk. The emphasis of the corporate community on downsizing and of the U.S. Federal Reserve policy on raising interest rates if unemployment falls to near 6 percent insures that the entry of welfare recipients into the labor pool will either drive wages down further or result in an interest-rate hike that will throw additional people out of work.

Jacqueline Jones notes how a "focus on the urban 'underclass' diverts attention from the real sources of poverty."[37] Citing data from the Department of Commerce, she dethrones much of the broad stereotype that would have us believe that only blacks are poor. According to the data:

- Whites outnumber blacks living in poverty more than two to one — 23.7 million to 10.2 million.

- Even in urban inner cities, more whites live below the poverty line (8.3 million) than blacks (6.1 million).

- Nonurban poverty is greater than urban poverty. In nonmetropolitan areas approximately 20 million people are poor compared to 15 million people of all races in inner cities.

- The highest rates of black poverty are found outside the ghetto.[38]

These statistics should not take attention away from the fact that blacks and other people of color are disproportionately poor when compared to whites. They suggest, however, that poverty in the United States is widespread. Concern about extensive poverty should challenge stereotypes of all kinds and lead us toward a more careful analysis of the corporate-led forces that drive both society and families in the direction of breakdown and that feed our insecurities. David C. Korten, in *When Corporations Rule the World,* writes:

> Governments seem wholly incapable of responding [to pressing problems], and public frustration is turning to rage. It is more than a failure of government bureaucracies, however. It is a crisis of governance born of a convergence of ideological, political and technological forces behind a process of economic globalization that is shifting power away from governments responsible for the public good and toward a handful of corporations and financial institutions driven by a single imperative — the quest for short-term financial gain. This has concentrated massive economic and political power in the hands of an elite few whose absolute share of the products of a declining pool of natural wealth continues to increase at a substantial rate....
>
> These forces have transformed once beneficial corporations and financial institutions into instruments of a market tyranny that is extending its reach across the planet like a cancer, colonizing ever more of the planet's living spaces, destroying livelihoods, displacing people, rendering democratic institutions impotent, and feeding on life in an insatiable quest for money.[39]

Ignoring the root causes of poverty ironically allows the insecurities felt by many to become major problems in themselves. Insecurities, after all, propel people in the direction of scapegoating and away from solutions to real and deep problems. An example of this phenomenon is this nation's near obsession with crime. Let me be clear: As a parent living in a city whose murder rate increased dramatically in 1995, whose child by age three had had her tricycle trashed, and who lives with the awareness that unprovoked attacks at the neighborhood park, day or night, are too common, I am concerned about crime. However, preoccupation with and even distortion of crime is fueling a political backlash, particularly among fearful whites. One statistic can help put the relationship between crime and a "problem people" in perspective: According to the Justice Department the annual cost of street crime, the stuff of our nightly newscasts, is approximately $19 billion. The cost of white-collar, corporate crimes is between $130–$470 billion a year.[40]

Although white-collar, corporate crime should receive far greater attention, we can't ignore the reality of street crime and the fact that it arouses public concern. Just as we should not shy away from the relationship between race and poverty, we also should not ignore the links between poverty, race, and destructive behavior, whether it be crime, teenage pregnancy, or violence. This was the bold message of the black theater company who put on *Josie Josie*.

During the euphoria of apartheid's fall, *Josie Josie* was an honest and sobering reminder that the apartheid system left blacks with many scars. The terrible legacy of apartheid was both socially rooted and deeply internalized. In America, at a neighborhood level where passions are ignited, poverty correlates with race, and both poverty and race correlate with problematic personal and social behaviors. Just as black women in Soweto experienced in their daily lives the projected "worst fears" of my white South African theater companions, so too in the United States, where fear of crime feeds a political and social backlash among whites, it is African-American households that are most likely to be burglarized.[41]

Crime is a legitimate concern for many parents and others throughout our society. However, I suspect inflated fear of crime is rooted in profound economic insecurities felt by many Americans after a decade of "casino capitalism" and in the context of ongoing changes in the global economy. A deepening sense of economic insecurity may help explain why fear of crime, and broadcast time devoted to coverage of crime, are escalating at a time when crime itself is not. The FBI reports that, despite increased killing by teens, both violent and nonviolent crime reported to police dipped in 1994 for the third straight year.[42] "Behind hype, this truth: Crime is not going up," the *Milwaukee Journal* reports in an article entitled "Distortions Feed Our Fears." In fact, according to the article, the national murder rate has fallen, property crimes including robbery have decreased, rapes have declined, the number of officers killed in the line of duty has fallen (farmers are more likely to die on the job than police officers), air pollution is more deadly than guns, corporate crime costs more than street crime, blacks are more likely to be burglarized than whites, and alcohol kills more than cocaine.[43]

Whether by design or not, distorted fears about crime blind us to broader economic and social forces that both encourage criminal behavior and feed our economic insecurities. Preoccupations with crime, like broader stereotypes about race and poverty, blur our vision. A focus on widespread poverty and the political and economic forces that lie behind our insecurities, on the other hand, would help us focus attention on corporations and financial institutions that have become instruments of a "market tyranny" that is destabilizing community life throughout the world. It would also enable us to focus attention on how the United States has among all major industrial countries the greatest inequality of both wealth and income. The gap that separates the rich from the shrinking middle class and the poor is widening at a faster rate here than anywhere else. Looking beyond stereotypes might also enable us to see the need for a family policy that would benefit all families.

There is one other important problem with seeing the world through stereotypes. Jody Kretzmann of the Center for Urban Affairs and Policy Research at Northwestern University points out that universities, funders, politicians, social service providers, the media, and many poor people themselves have come to view troubled neighborhoods almost solely through the lens of problems. Assessing neighborhoods in this predominantly negative light, Kretzmann says, results in drawing a map of our neighborhood that centers on deficits and needs, what he calls a "needs map." A neighborhood "needs map" catalogs a long list of problems: unemployment, truancy, gangs, broken families, slum housing, crime, child abuse, illiteracy, high drop-out rates, lead poisoning, and drugs. The problem with this map, Kretzmann says, is not that it is false but that it tells only part of a complex story. He proposes an alternative map, an "assets map," which identifies the many rich and diverse resources that exist, even in the poorest of neighborhoods: local institutions, citizen associations, gifted individuals, churches and synagogues, block clubs, youth and senior citizen groups, hospitals, parks, libraries, educational institutions, and businesses. Even this partial list based on an "assets map," Kretzmann says, provides evidence of a hopeful base from which communities can be transformed by building on their strengths. He does not suggest denying the validity of the "needs map," which identifies real problems, but he suggests we can no longer allow such a map to determine our actions, erode our hope, and block possibilities for renewal.[44]

Poor, lower-to-middle-class whites and blacks have good reasons to feel insecure, angry, or frustrated. Wages and benefits are falling. The average CEO in the United States receives 149 times the average factory worker's pay. For many workers there is no such thing as job security, taxes are rising while in many cases the quality of services declines, and many families are a health emergency away from falling into a major crisis. Unfortunately, as was the case during the Reagan-Bush years, fearful whites, especially white men, are embracing a reactionary economic and social agenda whose most recent manifestations are linked to the destructive economic and social policies growing out of the Contract with America.

Fort Worth Star-Telegram writer Molly Ivans has grown tired of the holier-than-thou attitude of the architects of the Contract with America, who blame the poor for all that is wrong with America. Ivans, who refers to Newt Gingrich as "the draft-dodging, dope-smoking, dead-beat dad, wife-divorcing Newt Gingrich," writes:

> There's a lot wrong with this country. But welfare mothers had nothing to do with the savings and loan disaster. Illegal workers aren't moving their factories to Taiwan. The homeless don't keep raising interest rates.... But all this anger is being aimed at the wrong people, 180 degrees in the wrong direction — against those who are the most powerless, the most helpless among us. It is not only cruel and vulgar, but stupid.[45]

Ironically, scapegoating the poor will not only hurt targeted groups but will also victimize lower- or middle-class whites whose prejudices and fears block understanding of how their insecurities are linked to the globalization of the economy and to the interests and priorities of the architects of that system. The politics of poverty, as writer Jacqueline Jones notes, are not local but transnational. The "inexorable workings of the global market economy force American companies to consolidate or streamline their operations and to cut costs with innovative technologies or by moving to locations, in the United States or elsewhere, where labor is cheap; workers of all races pay the price."[46]

Personalists blame poverty and social breakdown on racial flaws, dysfunctional personal behaviors, and ill-advised government social programs, while ignoring the causes of expansive poverty. Advocates of the social roots of family disruption retreat from discussions about values in the context of race and poverty. The consequence in the first instance is that whites and others who ignore social causes and pursue punitive policies put families at risk and insure their own continued slide into the ranks of the economically marginalized. The result of the second is to encourage unwittingly the formation of political coalitions whose agenda includes divisive and at times hate-filled social policies aimed at gays, immigrants, blacks, and other people of color as well as social cutbacks, regressive tax policies, and corporate initiatives that undermine the economic well-being of many families.

Unfortunate as it may be, unless we are willing to face openly how poverty often distorts personal behaviors and values, we will be unable to focus attention where it's needed: on systemic injustice. It is tempting, wrong, and politically expedient to blame the poor for poverty. It is equally tempting and wrong to ignore the problematic behavior of the poor and downplay the importance of personal responsibility because we are afraid that raising these issues will feed a politics of blame. As Jim Wallis writes, to "speak only of moral behavior, apart from oppressive social realities, just blames the victim; and to talk only about social conditions, apart from moral choices, is to keep treating people only as victims."[47]

What should be clear is that silence about moral behavior *is* feeding a mean politics that helps cover up an essential truth: in our society poverty is ugly and crippling, and it is rooted in class divisions and a corporate-dominated system that distorts political and economic life. The huge and widening gap in income, wealth, political power, opportunity, and privilege that separates a prospering minority from the vast majority of U.S. citizens is at the heart of the family and social crises gripping our nation. This deep chasm has become an ugly, festering wound that can be healed only if it is exposed to the light of day.

Chapter 17

Market and Nonmarket Values

A market culture [with] a market morality builds a market mentality. ... That makes it difficult for non-market values to gain a foothold.

— CORNEL WEST

Those of us who look at the crises of family and society through social lenses not only have shied away from discussions about race, poverty, and crime; we have also been reluctant to talk about values. By ceding the arena of values to the religious right, advocates of a social approach have failed to articulate an alternative vision that is compelling for individuals, families, and society.

Personalists say criminal behavior, absent fathers, teenage mothers, and divorce are problems rooted in values. They are right. They are concerned about violence, sexual images, and other values communicated through TV, music, and movies, and these concerns are justified. Personalists say they believe in teaching abstinence, in committed marital relationships, in taking responsibility for the children we bring into the world, in fidelity, in delayed gratification, and I agree with them. They want to strengthen families. I concur.

I think many of these personal values are important to a broad range of people in our society, including many social progressives. By not championing these and other important values, those of us who see social change as vital to helping children and families are actually stimulating interest in the political and social agendas of members of the religious right, agendas that are disastrous for children and society as a whole.

This does not mean that my personal values coincide with those

172

of the religious right. I believe parents must play vital roles in children's lives, but I reject the attack by members of the religious right against women who work, and I reject the strict gender roles they advocate within and outside the family. I believe in teaching abstinence to my children and other children, but I would like those who fail to heed this instruction (and there will be many), including teens who are emotionally and financially unprepared for either sexual intimacy or the responsibilities of parenting, to know about birth control, the challenges of caring for a child, and the reality of AIDS. I believe, along with proponents of the religious right, that committed, covenantal, marital relations are vital to the well-being of families, neighborhoods, and society. Unlike them, however, I see a relationship between family disruption and distorted economic priorities that add dramatically to family stress. I also think covenantal relationships and commitments are so important to individuals, children, and society that it is vital to affirm them for same-sex couples who are presently denied social support for and the legal option of marriage, and then are condemned for their aberrant lifestyles.

Those of us who believe that families will not be valued in our society without significant social changes must talk openly about values. It is important for us to do so, because personal values and conduct are vital in and of themselves, and because our silence about values pushes people in the political direction of the religious right. Our failure to be clear about and model personal values is not only harmful to our own families; it can erode or undermine the possibility of a healthy social agenda on which the well-being of children depends.

Examination of values offers many benefits. It reveals similarities and differences between the values of the religious right and those of other more progressive social voices. It subjects proponents of family values to greater scrutiny and points out contradictions between stated values and conflicting outcomes due to personal biases and punitive social policies. It encourages those of us who are advocates of a social approach to examine more critically the personal dimensions of the family crisis while pushing us toward a more radical assessment of the gulf that exists between children's needs and the present economic and political direction of our country.

In a society coming apart at the seams, we would all do well to assess our conduct in relation to values. If we did so honestly, I think it would become apparent that in our society things are more valued than relationships; money beyond essential needs is valued more than time with our children; ideological certainty more than diversity; individualism more than community; career more than family time; distorted masculinity more than peace in our homes and in our society; bombs more than schools; affluence isolated amid suburbs, gated communities, and guard dogs more than shared wealth and safer cities; and, perhaps most important, excessive consumption for some of our citizens is cherished more than social equality, the health of the environment, or the well-being of future generations.

Discussion of values must include assessment of both personal and social values and choices and their relationship to each other. Nonmarket values — love, commitment, sharing, compassion, joy, hope, fairness, care, concern, service to others, community, justice, fidelity, trust, truth, and spirituality have little in common with market morality. Market values, which dominate American life and the global economy, inundate us with violence, sex, and models of affluence in an effort to sell. Richard Barnet writes:

> These packaged dreams of life in America — fast, violent, opulent — exert a powerful influence on literally billions of people on the planet, challenging values and customs and promoting the credo of individualism: The goal of life is personal pleasure. The prime source of pleasure is the acquisition of personal riches, power, and fame. The business of living is getting and spending. Security, happiness, and self-fulfillment depend on having enough money, and there is always a reason to need more. These are the prime values of the industrial economy dependent on mass consumption. This credo is now broadcast to the farthest reaches of the globe every day in thousands of ways.[1]

Market values offer us degraded images of ourselves and false promises of redemption through consumption. "It is our job to make people unhappy with what they have," says B. Earl Pucket, the former president of Allied Stores.[2] Being "unhappy with what we have" and attempting to fill the void through possessions are apt descriptions of life in America. On mean streets without hope, in a gun culture marred by deprivation, these dissatisfactions and false promises are dangerous. Violence, at least the kind of violence we see on mean streets where morality has died, is a consequence not only of poverty but of utter despair. It is a consequence of the enormous disparity between the promised good life and the indignities of daily life, and of the sense of utter hopelessness and meaninglessness that ensues.

But mean streets filled with corpses, drugs, and despair are only the most visible signs of the failure of market values to satisfy. The crowded corridors of suburban shopping malls are another painful reminder of a fruitless search for meaning in possessions, signs of deep emotional holes and spiritual voids that deepen chasms with each unnecessary purchase.

"The conditions of life which really make a difference to happiness are those covered by three sources," Michael Argyle writes in *The Psychology of Happiness*, "social relations, work and leisure. And...a satisfying state of affairs in these spheres does not depend much on wealth, either absolute or relative."[3] Unfortunately the social forces dominating economic life distort definitions of life's meaning and conspire to steal happiness from our lives. They erode the relational foundations on which both happiness and the well-being of children depend.

If work is important to happiness, then what of the unemployed who are denied this aspect of meaning and then stigmatized as "lazy"? And what of those for whom work has become one or more low-wage jobs of desperation? Or what of those for whom work has become a dogged climb up a corporate ladder, bringing high income but relational loss and disconnection at home and at work? If happiness is relational, then we might wish to challenge the decision to spend excessive hours at malls, in long commutes to work, and at work itself. If happiness is relational, then we might ask ourselves whether meaningful ties can be maintained where job choices narrow to fast-food chains or the local drug trade or where there are no jobs at all. If work is important for our emotional as well as material well-being, then "welfare reform" that pushes people into jobs that offer poverty wages with limited or no benefits will be rejected. We might also consider whether our leisure time builds or undermines relationships, whether our fears of material losses that feed the political meanness in the land are worth the relational destruction they cause, and whether elevating the global market economy to a godlike status will bring satisfaction or insecurity as communities unravel. In *How Much Is Enough?* Alan Durning writes:

> Mutual dependence for day-to-day sustenance...bonds people as proximity never can. Yet those bonds have severed with the sweeping advance of the commercial mass market....Members of the consumer class enjoy a degree of personal independence unprecedented in human history, yet hand in hand comes a decline in our attachments to each other. Informal visits between neighbors and friends, family conversation, and time spent at family meals have all diminished in the United States since mid-century.[4]

Many problems addressed in this book, including crime, violence, and the deterioration of the family, will not be solved without wide adoption of personal and social values and policies that strengthen families, communities, and neighborhoods both economically and relationally. The consumer society, our confusion of the "good life" with material goods, and the economic determinism at the heart of the global economy undermine efforts to do so. Durning writes:

> Like the household, the community economy has atrophied — or been dismembered — under the blind force of the money economy. Shopping malls, superhighways, and "strips" have replaced corner stores, local restaurants, and neighborhood theaters — the things that help create a sense of common identity and community in an area. Traditional communities are all but extinct in some nations. In the United States, where the demise of local economies is furthest advanced, many neighborhoods are little more than a place to sleep, where neighbors share only

a video franchise and a convenience store. Americans move, on average, every five years, and develop little attachment to those who live near them. The transformation of retailing is a leading cause of the decline of traditional community in the global consumer society.[5]

When it comes to understanding social issues, including race, homosexuality, abortion, poverty, and politics, there is a wide gulf separating people on the political right and those on the political left, personalists and advocates of a social approach. This may surprise no one. What I do find surprising, and disconcerting, is that with some important and notable exceptions, they do share a broad-based commitment to the values of the market, including definitions of the good life, meaning rooted in consumption, and traditional measures of success and power. Personalists, by and large, explain the failure of people to achieve the good life by sighting personal shortcomings, while social advocates stress societal factors that serve as roadblocks. But both define the good life in largely material terms and see it as a noble goal.

The crisis of our children cries out for new definitions of meaning, hope, and purpose. It is here that voices of the religious right get closer to a meaningful critique than many social advocates might wish to acknowledge. They sense, correctly I think, that something is *fundamentally* wrong. This is what leads them to talk about nonmaterial issues such as families, values, and culture. Their sense of fundamental discord in American life, however, leads them in the direction of punitive economic policies, intolerant fundamentalism, and a politics of blame. Their personal and public priorities reflect social intolerance. Their preferred public policies aggravate economic inequalities and feed insecurities, which in a vicious cycle becomes fertile ground for greater intolerance and fear.

The crisis of children and families requires more fundamental shifts in values and priorities. Ghetto violence is a product of hopelessness and not poverty alone. Empty lives amid material abundance speak of needs that are profoundly spiritual and relational. Both signify the absence of community, and both demand profound changes in personal behavior and values as well as deep social transformation.

The complex web of forces that results in the erosion of families and communities is captured well by Donald Fraser, former mayor of Minneapolis:

> Children are the future of our nation. With the fortunes of children in America in continuing decline, a wake-up call is needed to rouse local communities.... In the last 30 years families have faced new problems. The restructuring in our economy has resulted in declining wage opportunities and deepening poverty even among working families. With more adults in the workforce and fewer at home, the fabric that supports families and communities has weakened. Parents experience more stress and have less time for the children. An aging population, later marriage and many childless couples contribute to this dilemma. The dramatic growth in single-parent households has meant more families living in poverty with less internal support. This combination of events has eroded community support and shortchanges children. Communities today offer less support for children's successful growth and development.
>
> As a result, more children experience problems, beginning with poorer school performance, and ranging from abuse to being involved in violence. Youth face an economy that provides fewer decent jobs, some are joining gangs, and at an ever younger age some are becoming parents. These are symptoms of a deepening social disorder, one that many observers link to weakened community and family roles.[6]

In an effort to build community, my family has moved with others into a neighborhood in south Minneapolis. About fifty of us, all members of the Community of St. Martin, live within a mile of one another. Our proximity, and our common desire for community, lead us to share tools, skills, child care, meals, problems, worship, play, and conversation. We join hands in various kinds of social justice work, run an alternative book store and restaurant, celebrate joys, and offer support to one another in times of need. Some of our children attend the same public schools, we shop together at local markets and co-ops, and many of us support a local farm from which we receive seasonal produce from June through October. My involvement in the Community of St. Martin, the local school, neighborhood, and church is for me an attempt to rebuild a sense of community and neighborhood, which the consumer culture and global economy tear down.

A desire for community resides deep within the human spirit. Much of our dysfunctional behavior as children, parents, and society reflects its absence. Gangs are an expression of the need for community where families and neighborhoods have broken down. Others, ironically it seems to me, seek community through networks made possible by personal computers. In our society, however, many of us are looking for community, or substituting for its absence, through our frequent visits to shopping malls, which have become the shrines of our modern-day religion.

What "bonds" people together in our culture is often not relationships but consumption, or our desire to consume. We often express love by giving material gifts rather than gifts of time. We show our children, through constant advertisements and our own conduct, that possessions matter more to us than time spent with them. Unfortunately, but not surprisingly, our children have gotten the message, which may not be good news for the next generation. The "present generation of young Americans," Alan Durning writes, "believes that being good parents is equivalent to providing lots of goodies. Raising a family," he says, "remains an important life goal for them, but spending time with their children does not."[7]

Our children need our time. They need to see positive personal values modeled in the family where the foundations of community are laid. They need neighborhoods that are more than places to sleep and where sleep isn't interrupted with gunfire. They need vital neighborhoods where a strong web of formal and informal networks and institutions thrive. Community is the basis of a healthy society. Families, neighborhoods, and the society as a whole are in trouble and largely unfriendly to children because problems in each domain feed — and are fed by — problems in the other. Present economic and social policies and priorities shred the social fabric of our neighborhoods and nation. Our children, our neighborhoods, and our society falter because of the triumph of market values. The bad news is that our failure is more colossal than either the personalists or many advocates of the social approach imagine. The good news...well, the good news depends on us.

Chapter 18

Luxury Hotel

In this world of betrayal there is nothing true nor false. Everything depends on the color of the crystal through which one gazes.
— Salvadoran poet Ramón del Campoamor

It is 1972 and I am in India, riding on a bus from the airport to Bombay, a half-hour trip. For me it is a journey into hell. The pitch-black of the late hour is interrupted by occasional campfires, which appear like cats' eyes on the land along the roadway. The dark night is mirrored within my soul as I peer out the bus window searching for glimpses of the life of the people and for remnants of meaning in my own. I see families huddled together. Most are living in the open air. The lucky ones are sheltered in cement culverts that line the highway.

I am a twenty-one-year-old college senior participating in the "global studies" program of St. Olaf College, a small Lutheran college in Minnesota about an hour south of the Twin Cities. My world has unraveled over the past month and a half. I feel betrayed by my parents, who tried to isolate me in the suburbs, and by my church, which never related the gospel to a world of hunger, poverty, and inequality. As I see people dying of hunger, I feel my world dying from the cancer of deception and lies.

My father didn't want me to take this trip. He had suffered several heart attacks from the sheer stress and exhaustion of hundred-hour work weeks at a small printing company outside Minneapolis and was, I think, afraid not only for my safety, but that he might die before I got home. So convinced was my father that he was dying that he sold the family cabin, which he and my grandfather had

181

built, for a fraction of its value in order to make final payment on our family home.

Health and safety were not my father's only concerns. His only experience outside the United States was during World War II on a navy battleship. My first and middle name commemorated the man who saved his life during the war. I've heard others relive their war experiences with fondness, even delight, but not my father. Any mention of the war left him visibly distressed. He had seen so much death, and missed my mother so intensely, that the war left him with deep emotional scars and an unconscious desire to be anchored near home.

My father hated the war, but he was proud that the United States had helped defeat Japan and Nazi Germany. World War II became a lens through which he, and many others who lived during this time, viewed the world and judged U.S. foreign policies and intentions. Vietnam was the sharply contrasting lens of my generation. When we disagree strongly with another, we would do well to try on each other's glasses. My father, to his and perhaps to my credit, was convinced, slowly and reluctantly, of the folly of U.S. involvement in Vietnam. He had a hard time, at least initially, with my involvement in anti-war protests or in understanding my commitment to non-violence, but before he died he understood that my passion for peace was rooted ultimately in his and my mother's abhorrence of war.

My father asked me why I wanted to spend five months of my college time in Ethiopia, India, Israel, Taiwan, and Japan (the proposed itinerary of the program). His question communicated honest confusion. He had never been to college, and it was a source of great pride for my parents that each of their children attended. Whatever my father's image of college, it did not include foreign travel. Given his experience during World War II, it was nearly incomprehensible to him that anyone would choose to be far away from home.

My college major was political science. I tried to explain to my father that the Vietnam War had made me suspicious of U.S. foreign policy, and I wanted to see more of the world for myself. The previous year I had spent a semester in Chicago on an urban studies program, which made me think that waging war overseas was costly, not only on the battlefield, but at home in the form of unmet needs.

Chicago's Mayor Richard Daley and President Richard Nixon didn't seem to model the textbook democracy I had studied, and I thought the world would be filled with similar surprises. I was not disappointed. As a Christian I found that my church's love for me and hatred for any challenge I brought to them about the Vietnam War left me confused and angry. I was struggling to find my way in a world that had been kept invisible to me throughout my youth.

Whatever my explanation for wanting to study abroad, my father accepted it with a nod. Riding the bus into Bombay, I wish he had convinced me to stay home. In Ethiopia I (and the students with whom I was traveling) received contempt from Ethiopians simply for being American. It shocked and confused me. The mythology of U.S. support for "freedom and democracy," already frayed by Vietnam, unraveled further with the discovery that my country was supporting a brutal dictatorship headed by Haile Selassie. Ethiopian students who approached us in an effort to explain both the nature of the Selassie government and the disastrous consequences of U.S. aid were arrested for their trouble. I alternated between the jail (trying to get these students out) and the nearest bathroom (I lost thirty pounds in as many days with nonstop diarrhea).

One diversionary highlight for our group in Ethiopia was playing the Ethiopian national team in an informal basketball game. The game was played at the outdoor court at the YMCA where we were staying. We called ourselves the "global trotters," often changing players on the fly. The term "fast break" took on new meaning as player after player sprinted from the court on behalf of a more important and more basic calling.

My dysentery seemed symbolic of the political disorientation that began with Vietnam and Chicago and deepened in Ethiopia. I was like a boat severed from its moorings, drifting in an unknown sea. The sense that my political foundations were set in quicksand was further reinforced by the Indian government's decision to deny our student group permission to stay for the month we had planned. As I ride the bus into Bombay, I am unaware that the U.S. is backing a brutal dictator in Pakistan, General Khan, in a dispute with India.

I know only that days before our scheduled arrival the Indian government expelled the U.S. Peace Corps because of infiltration by the U.S. Central Intelligence Agency (CIA).

Bombay is a one-night stopover on our way to Sri Lanka, a last-minute replacement for India as a site for our itinerary. Dropping from 165 to 135 pounds in a month leaves me physically weak and adds to my emotional vulnerability. The trip through Bombay pushes me near an edge I prefer not to travel. It is a place that borders on insanity, where a willingness to let the pain of the world judge deeply held convictions threatens to become a one-way street into despair.

This experience of walking on a precipice where honesty, hope, cynicism, and insanity compete with each other like battered prize-fighters gave me a certain respect for many of the disoriented "bag ladies" I met years later during my nearly eight years of living in Manhattan. It also continues to feed both my commitment and my caution as I try to expose my children to difficult local and global realities.

As the private bus makes its way toward the city, some of the other students are laughing. Laughter is perhaps a sound defense against being overwhelmed, but I am far too serious to see it. I reject their laughter as a form of emotional cowardice. "Close your mouths," I shout above the bus's laboring engine, "and open your eyes." There is silence, interrupted only by the continuing rumblings of the old bus as it moves in the direction of our hotel.

We arrive in the city about nine o'clock. Many of the million or so residents without housing are preparing for "bedtime." Some lay out a thin blanket on the sidewalk, others cardboard, others nothing at all. Our bus travels slowly through the traffic and crowds, adding to my discomfort. Everything seems out of sequence. It is as if our bus is in slow motion, like an old 78-rpm record played on the 33 setting, driving through the fast-paced disarray of people's lives.

An uninvited guest riding through the bedrooms of an entire city, I long to be out of the chaos, away from the poverty and beggars. Our snail-paced journey is interrupted by a religious festival. The bus stops for what seems an eternity as people carrying statues claim right-of-way. To my right, lying on the sidewalk, is a dead woman, probably not much older than I am. I want only for the bus to move, but it sits motionless like a beached whale. The lifeless woman is surrounded by coins. Her gaunt, twisted face makes her look fifty. Sitting next to her is a young child, perhaps a year old, screaming uncontrollably. Each scream echoes inside, filling the empty spaces of my soul until there is no room left for compassion.

The bus lurches forward in time to save me. A few minutes later we arrive at our hotel. It is a nice hotel, luxurious in the context of the squalor that surrounds it. Several armed guards greet our bus and escort us in. Once inside they resume their positions at the door, and we proceed to a monstrous dining hall, complete with chandeliers, red tablecloths and napkins, fine china, and two forks at each setting. There is also an orchestra. Performers who thought they were finished for the day move abruptly back into position. We dine to the pleasures of classical music.

I am not sure whether it is the legacy of my dysentery, or the still-vivid image of a child whose screams could not revive her dead mother, that squelches my appetite. The truth is I am tired and overwhelmed. I want only to sleep.

I finish a soda, find my room, enter, use the bathroom, and plop down on a bed by the window. I choose poorly. As I lie in the air-conditioned comfort of a luxury room, I want only to forget what is outside. But from my bed I can see the bedrooms of the poor outside as the sidewalks grow crowded with people who have no other place to sleep.

I see something else. Rats. Rats moving along the sidewalks. And roaches. Roaches big enough to be seen at night from a second-floor hotel room. I close my eyes, but the damage is done. The image of what is outside will not go away, will not let me sleep.

I cannot stay here. I take my key and leave the room. The armed guards are puzzled as I walk past them, out of the hotel, onto the sidewalk. I walk for hours, stepping around people, rats, and roaches. I pay a dollar to a driver of a horse-drawn carriage to take me around the city.

Being outside the hotel on the street this night is for me part of a powerful struggle on which hinges the very direction of my life. I feel that if I let all the pain of Bombay into my heart that it will change me. I realize during this dark and stormy night that this luxury hotel—surrounded by misery and protected by armed guards—is the world itself. The first world and the third world, the rich and the poor, the suburb and the inner city, Winnetka and Cabrini Green, Edina and the Phillips neighborhood, Westwood and Watts, the United States and Haiti—and my country's relationship with poor countries throughout the world.

I was born in this hotel. I received my life within it as an unnamed entitlement, a hidden inheritance of race and class, circumstance and luck. Life within seems natural enough until I look outside. The Vietnam War opens the curtain a crack, letting a little light pass through the exposed window, forcing me to squint, still preventing an unencumbered view. Inner-city Chicago pulls the curtain open a bit wider. But in Ethiopia, and now here at a luxury hotel in Bombay, surrounded by misery, I feel for the first time how the chasm separating the rich man and poor Lazarus is my chasm, too. The world is broken by a deadly and deep divide between peoples and nations.

My departure from the hotel, my walk through the bedrooms of the sidewalk inn, are for me the beginnings of an exodus journey. Unlike the Israelites, however, I am not fleeing slavery. I am trying to remove myself voluntarily from Pharaoh's court.

After four or five hours on the street I am physically and emotionally exhausted. I realize that I could not make it on the sidewalks where people, rats, and roaches share a miserable existence. No one should have to. But I realize something else. I don't want to insulate myself within the hotel, either. I don't want to live in a world of luxury, of armed guards and nuclear umbrellas. I don't want to live in either world, luxury hotel or sidewalk, because each is morally repugnant. These worlds, separate yet connected, are pushing humanity in the direction of mutual destruction.

There are only a few hours before our early-morning departure. I sleep soundly knowing that I am not at home in either world, but with the curtain open completely now I see both the imperative and the possibility of something new.

Chapter 19

Interests

═══════════════════════════════════

As the leading "have" power, we may expect to have to fight to protect our national valuables against envious "have nots."
— U.S. Army General Maxwell Taylor

Smoking cigarettes is the dumbest thing I've ever heard.
— Lyrics from a song by Hannah Pallmeyer

Children are often brutally frank. They learn only gradually to nuance their clear perception of people and the world in ways that are pleasing to adults. When Hannah was five she made up a song. We had spoken to her about misleading advertising, and she knew that my father had smoked and died of lung cancer. Perhaps it was this combination that led to the above lyrics, which she sang whenever she passed a billboard advertising cigarettes or whenever she encountered a smoker! As adults we tend to be more cautious, more self-censoring.

Perhaps most infuriating and ultimately costly to the well-being of children is that representatives of government and business often make public statements with the full intent of deceiving us from a truth they utter among themselves. Oliver North lied to Congress in service to what in his estimation was a more important cause. "Operation Desert Shield," in which President Bush ordered the movement of hundreds of thousands of U.S. troops into the Middle East prior to actual hostilities between Iraq and the U.S., was known within the Pentagon as "Budget Shield" because the conflict with Iraq meant foreclosure on a peace dividend anticipated in the aftermath of the Cold War. In the 1980s the largest transfer of wealth in the history of our country from poor and working-class citizens to the upper 1 to 5 percent of the population was sold as a middle-class tax cut. In a similar vein, prior to the mid-term 1994 elections public perceptions of crime and welfare costs were grossly inflated by politicians and others in ways that took attention away from structural causes and issues.

Uncensored "truth" is rare in public discourse. This is particularly true when it comes to assessment of the relationship between wealth and poverty. The commonly held image of our country throughout the Cold War, for example, was that of a benevolent superpower seeking the welfare of all peoples against the maniacal, international communist menace. This image served powerful interests well, but it was less than forthcoming. George Kennan, at the time the most influential U.S. foreign-policy planner in the post–World War II period, wrote in 1948:

> We have about 50 percent of the world's wealth, but only 6.3 percent of its populations. . . . In this situation, we cannot fail to be the object of envy and resentment. *Our real task in the coming period is to devise a pattern of relationships which will permit us to maintain this position of disparity without positive detriment to our national security.* To do so we have to dispense with all sentimentality and day-dreaming; and our attention will have to be concentrated everywhere on our immediate national objectives. We need not deceive ourselves that we can afford today the luxury of altruism and world-benefaction. . . . We should cease to talk about vague and . . . unreal objectives such as human rights, the raising of the living standards and democratization. The day is not far off when we are going to have to deal in straight power concepts. The less we are hampered by idealistic slogans, the better.[1]

The document that contained these remarks was for many years secret, thus denying us a more honest assessment of the relationship between wealth and poverty, corporate interests and U.S. foreign policy.

The myth that the poor benefit whenever the rich prosper is widespread in and outside our country. It shapes U.S. domestic and foreign policy debates, and it is a hidden foundation underlying much of the discussion about children, family values, welfare reform, and the Contract with America. Despite widespread official observance the mythmakers suffer occasional lapses. "As the leading 'have' power, we may expect to have to fight to protect our national valuables against envious 'have nots.'"

It's 1982 and I am about to meet an old man who along with the children provide me with my earliest images and long-lasting impressions of Nicaragua. Perhaps eighty, he is sitting in a park next to his Eskimo Pie vending cart. Between sales he picks something up and then sets it down as another customer approaches. I am interested enough, in both ice cream and what he is doing, to walk across the street. I buy an Eskimo Pie and ask, "¿Qué hace?" (What are you doing?) His face erupts into a toothless grin as with great pride he shows me the letters he is writing on a crude chalkboard between sales. He tells me he learned to read and write during Nicaragua's literacy crusade and that he practices his letters whenever he can.

It is clear to me from this and many similar encounters that literacy among the poor is a source of hope, inspiration, and dignity. Many of Nicaragua's oldest and youngest citizens are attending school for the first time. If they who have been "blind" can learn to read and write, there is no telling what they might be capable of accomplishing. Tragically, the hope of the poor is a source of fear for others.

Two years later I am back in Nicaragua. On this trip I am helping Minneapolis-based Augsburg College purchase a house from a Nicaraguan doctor who is leaving for Miami. His former residence is well suited for a House of Studies, which the college is opening in Nicaragua through the Center for Global Education.[2] Like many members of the Reagan administration, this Miami-bound doctor doesn't like the direction of the revolutionary government, which ousted a U.S.–backed dictator in July of 1979.

The new government is setting out to improve the lives of Nicaragua's poor majority. It is redistributing wealth from the rich to the poor; subsidizing a basic package of foods and other necessities; expanding the number of schools and teachers; following up the literacy crusade with adult-education programs; making land and credit available to the poor; and nationalizing the export/import trade, which effectively, and in many cases for the first time, forces the rich to pay taxes.

Giving priority to the needs of the poor majority is a source of fear for the doctor. Like many other wealthy Nicaraguans, he finds literacy and similar programs upsetting. He worries that the awakening of the poor might be a nightmare for him. He is selling his house because the Nicaraguan government has made health care a right, and he fears that this could affect his work as a physician. The government is training basic health promoters to carry out vaccination campaigns and other preventive measures and is greatly expanding the number of simple rural clinics. These priorities are reflected in the health budget.

What is striking to me about my brief encounter with this wealthy doctor is that, apart from his abstract fears about them, Nicaragua's poor seem invisible to him. He is a pediatrician, and yet the woman who lives in his home and cooks for him is six months pregnant and has never had a prenatal visit. She is isolated within this household and largely unaffected by the revolution. She and her sister sleep on the floor, a cement slab in the laundry room. Each day the doctor and his wife send them to buy meat and ice cream for the family dog, food that is never shared with them and that they can't afford to purchase with their meager earnings.

In the spring of 1991, nearly seven years after my original encounter with the doctor, I am back in Managua leading a delegation of U.S. citizens for the Center for Global Education. Despite some impressive gains in the early years of the Nicaraguan revolution, including significant improvements in literacy and health care and a rapid decline in infant mortality (Nicaragua received awards from UNESCO and the World Health Organization for its literacy and health programs), the Nicaraguan revolution couldn't stand up to U.S. efforts, working in concert with Nicaragua's economic elites, to undermine it.

After a decade of U.S.–sponsored warfare, the people exhausted, the economy collapsed, the gains of the revolution more a memory than a reality, a U.S.–backed coalition returned to power in the 1990 election. The election, according to most observers, was fair and free. Technically speaking this is true. The election, however, was carried out after a decade of death and intimidation in which a weary populace had little choice but to elect the U.S.-approved candidate or live with the specter of an unending war. Conservative theologian Richard John Neuhaus, who supported U.S. efforts in Nicaragua, describes the logic of U.S. policy: "Washington believes that Nicaragua must serve as a warning to the rest of Central America to never again challenge U.S. hegemony because of the enormous economic and political costs. It's too bad that the poor have to suffer," he adds, "but historically the poor have always suffered. Nicaragua must be a lesson to the others."[3]

This morning we will meet some of Nicaragua's richest business people who are organized into an association known as COSEP, the Supreme Council of Private Enterprise. Some have returned recently from Miami. On the way to the COSEP office we pass numerous squatter settlements, where single-room hovels constructed of tin, cardboard, and wood scraps mar the landscape like chicken pox. There are child-beggars at every stoplight as well as child-vendors selling mangos, Coca Cola, water, and antennas for color television sets. Other signs of changes that followed the election are visible, including more Mercedes Benz cars and numerous luxury-goods outlets, all open in the past several months.

Seated in an air-conditioned office, our hosts are congenial. They are thrilled with the electoral ouster of the revolutionary government, but they are troubled nonetheless. There is a striking change between our conversation today and my conversation with the doctor seven years before. Seven years ago the poor were an abstraction. Poor people were outside the emotional parameters of rich Nicaraguans, who had no frame of reference from which to identify with a revolution committed to the poor. Their bewilderment turned to hostility when it became clear that the fall of the dictator had not meant their own rise to power.

Today these rich men, restored to prominence, are puzzled, not because the poor are invisible or an abstraction, but because poverty and poor people are seemingly everywhere. Nicaragua's impressive reductions in infant mortality and illiteracy have been reversed. Nicaragua now has the highest infant-mortality rate, the highest levels of illiteracy, the highest birthrate, and the highest level of child malnutrition in Central America. The numbers of slums, squatters, beggars, needy children, and crime seem to be expanding exponentially. Over the past few years, the geographical buffers that once separated the rich from the poor have crumbled as thousands upon thousands of people fleeing the war-torn countryside came to the cities. Rural poverty, a byproduct of both war and the economic policies of the new government, continues to fuel the exodus.

Listening to these wealthy and powerful men and their growing hostility toward the poor, I am reminded of a conversation I once had with a conservative Norwegian parliamentarian (a relative of a former professor of mine at St. Olaf College). We were both official observers of Nicaragua's first presidential elections in 1984. He explained to me why he, along with the governments of Sweden and Norway, supported the Nicaraguan revolution and why they were deeply troubled by U.S. policy.

"As we look around the world," he said, "we see a number of countries that no matter what they do will always need international assistance in order to survive. Nicaragua is potentially self-sustaining. It has a government committed to reforms that move the country in that direction. We are here helping," he continued, "but, we are frustrated. What is built with our aid is destroyed by your country's support for the *contras*."

For the business elites with whom I am speaking there is a bitter irony in their return to prominence. They regained what they consider their rightful place as political and economic masters of

Nicaragua by collaborating with a U.S. warfare strategy known as "low-intensity conflict."[4] At the heart of this strategy is the desire and means to emotionally and physically exhaust a country and its populace.

"Low-intensity conflict" proved successful, but it effectively destroyed their country. Now they are faced with poverty. Deep. Entrenched. Ugly. They don't know what to do about it and have stopped searching for answers. In fact they have never been willing to ask themselves or others how to get rid of poverty, because they have no solutions that would not conflict dramatically with their "interests." No, they are asking themselves, in our presence, another, more troubling question: "How do we get rid of the poor?"

I leave the meeting, stunned by the implications of a genocidal impulse lurking in the shadows of their question. If I were their teacher I would give them an "A" for honesty and an "F" for morality. *How do we get rid of the poor?* The question screams out at me. I try to think of its meaning in relation to the children I saw at the street corners and in the squatter settlements earlier in the morning. Equally troubling, I find myself thinking that the impulse to get rid of the poor is percolating within the United States, in debates about "welfare reform" and what lies behind "trashed tricycles," and in the hidden heart of the global economy.

Chapter 20

Values, Debt, and the Environment

Quite simply, our business practices are destroying the life on earth. Given current corporate practices, not one wildlife reserve, wilderness, or indigenous culture will survive the global market economy. We know that every natural system on the planet is disintegrating. The land, water, air, and sea have been functionally transformed from life-supporting systems into repositories for waste. There is no polite way to say that business is destroying the world.... How do we imagine a future when our commercial systems conflict with everything nature teaches us?

— BUSINESSMAN PAUL HAWKEN, *The Ecology of Commerce*

Increasingly, it is the corporate interest more than the human interest that defines the policy agendas of states and international bodies.

— DAVID C. KORTEN, *When Corporations Rule the World*

Children learn from our actions more than our words. Despite what we might say, our behaviors as individuals and as a society indicate clearly the triumph of market values over nonmarket ones. "For our societies," Penelope Leach writes in *Children First*, "money is a god, the marketplace is its temple and mass communications — from TV advertising to motivational speakers — ensure that its creed is an inescapable driving force not just in corporate lives but in the lives of every one of us."[1] Our captivity to the money god and to the market blinds us to the ways in which market morality excludes the poor, destroys families and communities, and undermines other values we say we hold dear. As Richard Barnet reminds us, questions of politics and economics "involve choices among competing values." Although we "celebrate the rhetoric of family, home, and hearth ... we worship the Free Market that is destroying the family."[2]

This chapter and chapter 21 examine how present patterns of buying and selling threaten to leave future generations economically, environmentally, and socially impoverished. What will our children say to us when they discover the full weight of the legacy we leave behind? It is a question that haunts me and one that demands our immediate attention.

Three issues can illustrate the problematic legacy we are offering our children: the relationship between taxes, debt, and consumption; environmental destruction; and the absence of social vision reflected in growing inequalities and prisons. In each case irresponsible behavior today impedes the prospects for a healthy future. This could reasonably make our children angry, depressed, or despondent. Each issue, therefore, amounts to a child's plea for parental and social conversion. This chapter examines the first two issues. Chapter 21 looks at the third.

Relationships between taxes, debt, and consumption have profound implications for present and future generations. The 1980s was a decade that got as close to the folly of the "roaring twenties" as any in my lifetime. It was marked by dramatic increases in wealth, poverty, and debt, a combined legacy that not only feeds present-day anxieties but hangs like an albatross around the necks of our children and future generations.

Federal programs of special significance to children were cut significantly during the 1980s. At the same time, huge tax breaks for the richest Americans and dramatic increases in military spending robbed the treasury of potential funds. As a nation we were in effect using materials from the dismantled homes of the poor to expand and then build fences around the property of the rich.

The problem lies both in our priorities and our choice of payment. Tax breaks for the rich and military expenditures were paid in part with dollars cut from social programs, but the bulk of the money came from borrowing. As a result the national debt more than quadrupled during the Reagan–Bush years, from $1 trillion to more than $4.4 trillion.[3] At the same time, huge deficits with our trading partners leave the U.S, once a leading creditor nation, the world's most indebted country. Consumers who spent and continue to spend well beyond their means are also deeply in debt, as are many corporations who pursue or fight against leveraged buy-outs.

Living excessively off reckless borrowing is in essence a theft from our children and their children and their children's children into the future as far as we can see or imagine. Taxes not paid or levied reflect a decision in favor of current consumption. A borrowed dollar not paid in taxes is available for some immediate use: consumption of new cars for the middle class, new weapons for the military-industrial complex, and casino capitalism and corporate raids for the wealthy. At the other extreme, a regressive system that puts a greater burden of taxes on the poor means that each dollar the poor pay in taxes is a dollar that isn't available for food, housing, or other vital needs. It is an appropriate symbol of folly that the 1980s, a decade of unimaginable tax breaks for the richest Americans, was a time in which the White House led an effort to redefine ketchup as a vegetable in our nation's school-lunch program.

Our children's anger will undoubtedly increase when they discover that until recently we robbed, or in the current vernacular "borrowed," billions of dollars from the Social Security Trust Fund in order to pay current government expenditures and that our leaders continue to use Social Security funds to mask the true size of the yearly federal budget deficit. Nor will they be pleased to find out that the national debt is not only tied to the greed of the very rich who benefitted most from tax changes, but that it is the top 1 percent who hold 79 percent of all public and private bonded debt assets.[4] In other words, the very rich purchase government bonds, which are used to finance the debt, and thereby grow richer from the deficit, which is a consequence of their own tax breaks.

If I were wealthy and found the means to buy a new Porsche and several thousand assault rifles but failed to feed my children, then you rightfully could consider me an irresponsible parent. You are likely to be even less generous when you discover that I "found the means" for doing so by borrowing money with the full intent of having future generations of my children pay it back. And when you discovered that government policies encouraged and rewarded me for doing all the above, you will hopefully be angry and determined to change course. If we are not careful, however, "changing course" could mean another boondoggle for the rich, an additional squeeze on those with modest incomes, and a further curse for the poor.

It is sobering to consider that President Ronald Reagan and Vice President George Bush went to Washington in 1981 calling for a balanced budget, increased military spending, and tax cuts. When they arrived the debt was $1 trillion. By the time George Bush left the presidency, the national debt had mushroomed to $4.4 trillion. In their Contract with America, the centerpiece of the 1994 mid-term elections, Republicans made the same claims. They promised to balance the budget, lower taxes, and increase military spending. I'm not sure which is more astounding, that Republicans, whose policies in the 1980s mortgaged the country's future while seriously eroding the health of children, are making similar claims to the ones they made in '81, or the fact that they achieved major electoral gains based on these promises that are either illusionary or if implemented will be achieved at the expense of the poor.

Proponents of a balanced budget are right when they say that the U.S. must get its financial house in order and that growing deficits have grave implications for children. "If we can balance the budget and reduce the debt, we can do a heck of a lot for our kids," a spokesman for Republican Senator Rod Grams says. "Senator Grams is concerned about children, about what the budget deficit means to their future."[5] It is clear from actual policy options that "our kids" refers to children from privileged families, and that the intent is to balance the budget on the backs of the poor. The exclusion or targeting of the poor is made explicit in Senator Grams' proposal to offer $500-per-child tax breaks. This tax cut would reduce federal revenues by $141 billion over seven years, would be available to families with yearly incomes up to $250,000, and would exclude one third of American children living in poverty, whose families are too poor to pay taxes.

Congress also proposed cutting the Earned Income Tax Credit, a program designed to reward low-income workers. Proposed cuts would reduce the income of 13 million families by $43 billion over seven years, in essence a $43 billion tax hike on the working poor.[6] At the same time, reductions in capital gains taxes would save our richest citizens approximately $40 billion. In a similar vein, the plan to balance the budget, increase military spending, and offer tax breaks to the rich is based on cutting food stamps and child-nutrition programs and restricting access to other programs used primarily by the poor. Not surprisingly, helping "our kids" does not include realistic means-testing for Social Security, home-mortgage deductions, and other programs that provide unneeded resources to the already well endowed.

In the first version of the Contract with America passed by the U.S. House of Representatives, two thirds of the spending cuts came from programs for low-income families. Roughly half of the money available through these cuts would go to the wealthiest 10 percent of U.S. households, with one fifth going to the wealthiest 1 percent of families![7] U.S. Senator Paul Wellstone calls the Republican plan a "shell game." Citing Republican promises and figures from the Congressional Budget Office, Wellstone estimates that the GOP's plan will slash at least $1.2 trillion from federal programs that benefit mostly low- and middle-income people while providing tax breaks of about $712 billion over ten years that will disproportionately benefit wealthy citizens.[8]

Reflecting on GOP plans to cut the Earned Income Credit, *Washington Post* columnist David Broder notes that "the evidence points clearly to the conclusion that Republicans, who love to accuse opponents of practicing 'class warfare,' are really sticking it to the economically struggling families of America." "The Republicans' economics," he said, "sure don't jibe with their family values."[9]

It is particularly ironic that a significant factor that restricted the response of the Clinton administration to pressing social problems was the debt he inherited from previous Republican administrations. In *The Agenda*, Bob Woodward describes how President Clinton came to Washington with a vision for the country that included a middle-class tax cut, more federal spending on children, investment in infrastructure, and social spending for education and training, health and welfare reform, environmental concerns, and a revitalized economy. This agenda was undermined, according to Woodward's portrayal, by the reality of the budget deficit, the power of the Federal Reserve to determine the parameters of economic debate, and the interests of the bond market. Early on President Clinton is quoted as saying, "Roosevelt was trying to help people. Here we help the bond market, and we hurt the people who voted us in." Later, after compromising many of his principles in an effort to get a budget passed, Clinton fumed: "Where are all the Democrats?.... We're Eisenhower Republicans here, and we are fighting the Reagan Republicans. We stand for lower deficits and free trade and the bond market. Isn't that great?"[10]

A second devastating legacy to our children is the environment. It is the fall of 1993 and a new school year has just begun. Hannah arrives home from school, excited, carrying a Gold C Coupon book. If you are connected to public education you probably have something similar to the Gold C as underfunded schools engage in fund-raisers in an effort to pay for needed programs. She is excited, because included in the Gold C is a coupon for Camp Snoopy at the Mall of America, the largest mall in the world, better known as the Megamall. "Anyone who thinks the Mall of America is just a big mall," a Mall of America advertisement says, "probably also thinks the Grand Canyon is just a big hole in the ground."[11] Ricki Thompson, a member of the Community of St. Martin, describes the Megamall in a special issue on economics produced by the editors of *Sojourners* magazine:

> The Megamall is big. Overwhelmingly big. 4.2 million square feet big. In comparison, South Coast Plaza, a large mall in California, is 2.85 million square feet. The Megamall includes more than 40 women's apparel shops, nine night clubs, 14 movie screens, and more than 40 restaurants. In the center of the mall is Knott's Camp Snoopy, the world's largest indoor amusement park. This 7-acre park features more than two dozen rides and attractions, including a roller coaster and flume.[12]

Hannah isn't old enough and hasn't been exposed to enough commercials to have much interest in the mall itself, but she has heard of Camp Snoopy. Trying to be respectful of her excitement, I tell Hannah that Camp Snoopy is probably a fun place. I ask if she knows why we don't take her there. She hasn't thought about it until today, but she is clearly interested in both the coupon and what I have to say.

For the next ten minutes Hannah and I have a wonderful conversation. We have talked many times before about how our family tries not to buy lots of things we don't need. She understands through these prior conversations that her parents stress the value of time over money or the things that money can buy, that we think sharing with the poor is important, and that we are concerned about the environment. The coupon for Camp Snoopy makes these issues real for her and gives us another chance to talk about them.

I tell Hannah that Camp Snoopy is located in a gigantic store called the Mall of America, which opened at the same time leaders from around the world were in Brazil for a meeting about environmental issues. At this "earth summit" people were concerned because the earth's land, water, and air are sick. They also talked about what we and others can do to help heal the earth instead of hurt it.

One of the reasons the earth is sick, I say, is because companies make things we don't need and then convince us through slick advertising that we must have them in order to be happy. All these things take resources to make, including energy. Most of them don't make us all that much happier, and almost all eventually end up as garbage.

I explain that when we buy things we don't need, it in some small way makes the earth sicker instead of healthier. The problem is that people who want us to buy things we don't really need are very smart and put places like Camp Snoopy near stores that sell things we don't need. The last thing I tell Hannah is that I want her to know why our family doesn't go there but that one day she will be old enough to make decisions for herself about whether to buy things, go to Camp Snoopy, or shop at the Megamall.

The next day I overhear Hannah telling a neighbor, who is holding a Gold C book open to the coupon on Camp Snoopy, about why our family doesn't go to the Mall of America. "The earth is sick," she says, and then continues on in the full detail of our prior conversation.

I know what many of you are thinking: "She's not a teenager yet." You may be right, and I know already how humbling it is to be a parent and how unpredictable parenting and raising children can be. My conversation with Hannah, however, reinforces two important things: we must monitor carefully what we say and do because our children are listening, watching, and, learning; and children can understand important issues that many of us are reluctant to broach with them.

The sad state of the environment may be the most tragic legacy we leave our kids. Our children are victims of an unregulated marketplace and a consumer culture that together threaten the foundations of life itself. Several years ago, Worldwatch Institute, a highly respected environmental organization, estimated that we had forty years to make a transition to sustainable societies. "If we have not succeeded by then," Worldwatch warned, "environmental deterioration and economic decline are likely to be feeding on each other, pulling us into a downward spiral of social disintegration."[13]

More recent reports from Worldwatch paint a sobering picture of environmental decline, including falling per-capita availability of crop land, food crops, seafood, cattle, and material from forests.[14] Sandra Postel writes:

> As a result of our population size, consumption patterns, and technology choices, we have surpassed the planet's carrying capacity. This is plainly evident by the extent to which we are damaging and depleting natural capital. The earth's environmental assets are now insufficient to sustain both our present patterns of economic activity and the life-support systems we depend on.[15]

Businessman Paul Hawken, one of a few business people who pays serious attention to the full depth of the environmental crisis, believes business is responsible for destroying the world. Only a monumental transformation of business itself can save us from the environmental abyss:

In order for free-market capitalism to transform itself in the century to come, it must fully acknowledge that the brilliant monuments of its triumph cast the darkest of shadows. Whatever possibilities business once represented, whatever dreams and glories corporate success once offered, the time has come to acknowledge that business as we know it is over. Over because it failed in one critical and thoughtless way: It did not honor the myriad forms of life that secure and connect its own breath and skin and heart to the breath and skin and heart of our earth.[16]

More practically, Hawken says that business takes too much from the environment and in a harmful way, that the products produced waste energy and generate excessive amounts of toxins and pollutants, and that the method of manufacture as well as the products made "produce extraordinary waste and cause harm to present and future generations of all species including humans."[17]

The transition to sustainable societies is a monumental undertaking that, for all practical purposes, is just beginning. Worldwatch identifies five issues that are key to a successful transition.

First is ending poverty. Environmentally speaking, the world is one. At present the rich not only do disproportionate harm to the global environmental commons; they also force the poor to degrade their environment in order to survive. Poor countries are forced by the International Monetary Fund to destroy tropical forests at a rapid pace in order to expand export earnings that are used to make interest payments on foreign debt; and rich landowners push landless peasants onto marginal lands, where they deplete fragile soils or clear-cut forests.

The environmental degradation that results from such actions threatens the well-being of rich and poor alike. Ending poverty, therefore, has become an environmental necessity as well as a moral imperative. As Sandra Postel writes, "the future of both rich and poor alike hinges on reducing poverty and thereby eliminating this driving force of global environmental decline."[18]

Ending poverty is also a central component in any effective strategy to reduce population growth rates. At the United Nations

Population Conference in Egypt in 1994 and a year later at the U.N. International Conference on Women in China, it was repeatedly stressed that ending poverty and reducing birth rates depend on greater justice, empowerment, and participation of women. Not surprisingly, when women within or outside the United States are treated as second-class citizens, when their human rights are denied, when violence pervades their homes and their lives, when their voices and insights are not valued, when they do not actively participate in determining economic and social policies, and when the parameters of their lives are determined by men, the negative results are manifested within the family and throughout society.

Second, Worldwatch says, sustainability requires a shift to renewable energy resources and away from our dependency on fossil fuels and nuclear power.[19]

Third, according to Worldwatch, the road to sustainability leads toward new definitions of meaning and away from present patterns of production and consumption.[20] Following World War II, retailing analyst Victor Lebow laid out the foundational values of a society determined by market morality:

> Our enormously productive economy... demands that we make consumption our way of life, that we convert the buying and use of goods into rituals, that we seek our spiritual satisfaction, our ego satisfaction, in consumption.... We need things consumed, burned up, worn out, replaced, and discarded at an ever increasing rate.[21]

With 5 percent of the world's population, the United States generates 50 percent of the world's solid waste.[22] Paul Hawken insists on a redefinition of value and prosperity that will be possible only if we "forget the standard economic indices and reconsider everything we make and how we make it."[23] A consumer corollary to this wisdom is that we consider carefully every purchase from the vantage point of both the environment and actual need.

It is tempting to blame business and government for our plight, but our children could rightfully see many of us as willing accomplices. They also are likely to hold us accountable for drawing them into an environmentally destructive system through advertising and programming. "However destructive may be the policies of government and the methods and products of the corporation," writes Wendell Berry in a way that balances properly the weight of both personal and social responsibility, "the root of the problem is always to be found in private life.... It always leads straight to the question of how we live. The world is being destroyed," Berry says, "no doubt about it — by the greed of the rich and powerful. It is also being destroyed by popular demand."[24]

Whatever our position in life, our children may one day blame us for the environmental crisis. Poor people, however, can rightfully claim that the environment is another case of their victimization. They are forced to live near toxic waste sites, and the rich often push them onto marginal lands in which destruction of the environment is a predictable consequence of their efforts to survive. Those of us who are affluent, even relatively speaking, have fewer excuses. Not only do we deplete environmental accounts that belong to future generations, we do so in pursuit of a nonrelational path to satisfaction and life's meaning. As Alan Durning notes, in our consumeristic culture "we have been fruitlessly attempting to satisfy with material things what are essentially social, psychological, and spiritual needs."[25]

Among the souvenirs at the Mall of America is a sweatshirt. On the front is written, "Shut Up and Shop"; on the back is a consumeristic revision of Psalm 23:

> Yea, though I shop the Mall of America with great anticipation and no idea of what lies beyond the next corner, I shall fear no evil because with over 4,000,000 square feet to cover and serious plastic in my pocket, there isn't enough time to understand fear.

Fourth, Worldwatch says sustainability will mean significant changes in our understanding and use of technology.

As a society, we have failed to discriminate between technologies that meet our needs in a sustainable way and those that harm the earth. We have let the market largely dictate which technologies move forward, without adjusting for its failure to take proper account of environmental damages.[26]

David C. Korten makes a slightly different point when he notes that technological priorities don't necessarily reflect human needs:

The leaders and institutions that promised a golden age are not delivering. They assail us with visions of wondrous new technological gadgets, such as airplane seats with individual television monitors, and an information highway that will make it possible to fax messages while we sun ourselves on the beach. Yet the things that most of us really want — a secure means of livelihood, a decent place to live, healthy and uncontaminated food to eat, good education and health care for our children, a clean and vital natural environment — seem to slip further from the grasp of most of the world's people with each passing day.

Fewer and fewer people believe that they face a secure economic future. Family and community units and the security they once provided are disintegrating. The natural environment on which we depend for our material needs is under deepening stress.[27]

Current trends in both technology and the globalization of the economy damage our social ecology as well as the physical environment. Behind globalization and much of the technological imperative is a desire to improve "efficiency" or one's "competitive position" by reducing wages and the number of workers. "Technological improvements," therefore, can hurt families, neighborhoods, and whole societies. They reinforce a work structure that rewards managers and technicians at the top of the global economy and punishes many other workers. Job insecurity and reduced wages are common for those in the middle, while unemployment or low wages victimize growing numbers at the bottom. Overcoming poverty, a prerequisite to sustainability, will likely prove impossible without a reassessment of both the environmental and social consequences of technology.

Finally, Worldwatch says, the transition we need requires new definitions of security, new methods of conflict resolution, alternatives to war, and massive conversion of materials and human talent away from weapons production into active efforts on behalf of peace and environmental integrity. In 1990, by way of example, the United States spent twenty-two times as much facing military threats real and imagined than it did on environmental threats to security.[28]

Redefining security is a sobering challenge. Our nation, despite an end to the Cold War and the collapse of our most formidable adversary, continues to devote more than 70 percent of federally funded research and development dollars to defense-related projects (in Japan the percentage is 5, in Germany, 15). Last year the United States sold weapons to 146 countries. In order to move away from militarism and successfully confront the other challenges posed by Worldwatch, we will need to examine a range of issues including traditional definitions of masculinity, corporate profits, and the power of the military-industrial complex.

Strengthening neighborhoods and building healthy communities will necessarily challenge the present architects of the global economy who have no answers to pressing issues of poverty and environmental degradation. A spokesperson for a major global economic enterprise told me recently that the insecurity that feeds a mean politics throughout our society dominates life within corporate boardrooms where fear of the future due to a changing global economy is pronounced. Within boardrooms dominated by fear, this spokesperson said, issues of poverty and sustainability never come up. They simply have no place.

What is needed is grass-roots action. "If there is to be an ecologically sound society," Paul Hawken writes, "it will have to come from the grass roots up, not from the top down. We have spent too much time and money making the world safe for upper-middle-class white men. 'Environmentalism,'" he continues, "cannot be the sole province of the 'socially responsible' or the highly educated."[29]

Among the rights of children living during the final years of the twentieth century should be a reasonable expectation of parental involvement in efforts to end poverty in our neighborhoods, nation,

and world and in endeavors to inspire hope and establish environmentally and socially sustainable societies. "We have little real choice
other than to give the highest priority to efforts to simultaneously
end overconsumption, population growth, and inequality," David C.
Korten writes. "They are inextricably linked, and no one, rich or
poor, could possibly want the consequences that we will all bear if
we do not achieve each of these outcomes in the very near future."[30]

Chapter 21

Values, Prisons, and Poverty

[*Between 1982 and 1990 the International Monetary Fund's (IMF) structural adjustment programs (SAPs)*] *led directly to the deaths of some 70 million children under five years of age and to the destitution and impoverishment of several hundred millions more. Not only children under five, but tens of millions of children above five, and an undetermined number of adults... have died or been put into destitution and absolute poverty by the forced operation of SAPs.*

— Former IMF economist Davison Budhoo

Children one day will demand a full accounting of our personal and social priorities. We owe them a meaningful present that isn't based on a theft from the future. Sustainability itself must be redefined to include both environmental and social aspects, and it must be understood in the context of a need to *restore* the environment, our communities, and our families. Paul Hawken writes:

"Restore" has many definitions, all with one theme. The act of restoration involves recognizing that something has been lost, used up, or removed. To restore is to bring back or return something to its original state. This can involve rebuilding, repairing, removing corruptions and mistakes; it allows for the idea of bringing a person or place or group back to health and equilibrium; it can mean returning something that originally belonged to someone else, whether it is returning lands taken from other cultures, or dignity stolen by bureaucratic regulations and officialdom; it encompasses the idea of reviving and rejuvenating connections, relationships, and responsibilities....

Above all it means to heal, to make whole, to reweave broken strands and threads into a social fabric that honors and nurtures life around it. To restore is to make something well again. It is mending the world. People have to believe there will be a future in order to look forward.[1]

In my search to understand Audrey's trashed tricycle, I have concluded that the well-being of my children is dependent upon greater social justice, which must extend from my household to my neighborhood, into my city, state, and nation and ultimately throughout the world. My children will not be safe in an unsafe neighborhood. My neighborhood will not be safe until my city is a good place to live for all its citizens. The argument extends further, touching national and global realities. Ending poverty, Worldwatch argues, is an environmental necessity. It is also a social necessity. The alternative to greater justice is a punitive social policy that springs from and reinforces a fortress mentality. The likely outcome of such a policy is social breakdown.

How we prioritize social problems and the resources to solve them determines, to a large degree, the legacy we leave our children. This is abundantly illustrated in the ways we approach and address two of the pressing issues of our time: global poverty, and crime and imprisonment.

Global Poverty

In the aftermath of the Cold War, our nation's leaders said that the war was over and we won. This is a dubious claim for a nation in which one of four children is born into poverty. Domestic policies in the 1980s resulted in huge transfers of wealth within the United States to the richest of our citizens. International policies during the same period facilitated the largest transfer of wealth in human history from the world's poorest peoples to the world's richest, largely through interest payments on debt.[2]

Theologian Pablo Richard challenged the triumphalism of the Cold War victors after the fall of the Berlin Wall:

The world changed abruptly in the last months of 1989....But has the life-death situation of the poor and oppressed masses of the Third World really changed? The Berlin Wall fell, and the rich world trembled with joy. In reality, the fall of the wall was very positive. But we are aware that another gigantic wall is being constructed in the Third World, to hide the reality of the poor majorities. A wall between the rich and the poor is being built, so that poverty does not annoy the powerful and the poor are obliged to die in the silence of history....A wall of disinformation... is being built to casually pervert the reality of the Third World.[3]

Through the lens of the victors, however, an international market economy not only proved itself; it became the only game in town. What followed were more austerity measures imposed on poor countries through the International Monetary Fund (IMF), the World Bank, and the U.S. Agency for International Development (AID). Imposed austerity emptied the treasuries of poor countries and forced them to play by certain rules in the international market economy handbook for appropriate behavior: control wages, privatize, reduce internal consumption and increase exports, promote free movement of capital, reduce government expenditures, and encourage foreign investment.

In Nicaragua, following my conversation with business leaders who were asking how to get rid of the poor, I spoke with the U.S. government official most responsible for implementing U.S. development programs in that country. This official told me that Nicaragua's development hinged on its willingness to cut wages in half and to replace its police and military with forces willing to impose those conditions. Not too hidden in this "advice" is the threat that if Nicaragua is unwilling to live by these rules, it will be abandoned altogether.[4] This is not an empty threat. As Richard Barnet and John Cavanagh write, for multinational companies "'going global' is a strategy for picking and choosing from a global menu. Vast areas of the world and the people who live there are written off."[5]

The Cold War triumphalism trumpeted by many personalists stands in sharp contrast to the dead or impoverished children in and outside the United States for whom there is no place at the table. The "victors," are arrogant, confident, and without rival. They are pursuing business as usual as if environmental constraints, poverty, and other social problems are mythical abstractions or unrelated to their own conduct. They are busily building on the logic of their prejudices through the North American Free Trade Agreement (NAFTA) and the General Agreements on Tariffs and Trade (GATT). These international agreements, in the name of a globalized economy, solidify alliances among elites, foster insecurity among disappearing middle classes, abandon the poor, and turn a blind eye to environmental destruction.

The architects of these policies, both Democrats and Republicans, have little to offer to address pressing environmental and social problems. They have no plan that includes a partnership with the poor or with future generations. Issues like ending poverty or environmental and social sustainability are well beyond the parameters of their vision. Jesuit economist Xabier Gorostiaga notes that the "world has become a 'champagne glass'" in which "the richest 20 percent of humanity hoards 83 percent of the world's wealth, while the poorest 60 percent of humanity subsists on 6 percent of the wealth." Citing United Nations statistics, Gorostiaga says that "the accumulated personal wealth of 358 billionaires is $762 billion," more than the combined per capita income of 45 percent of the world's population.[6]

Where are the architects of the global economy leading us? Gorostiaga says that "globalization will fill it [the champagne glass] fuller for the wealthy few" while defining many peoples and nations as the "disposable population." "Frankly," Gorostiaga writes, "in the eyes of many, the world would be a better place if these surplus human beings simply did not exist. Worse yet, whole countries are now considered disposable nations because they have no place in the international market system."[7]

Richard Barnet and John Cavanagh make a similar point:

> As economies are drawn closer, nations, cities, and neighborhoods are being pulled apart. The processes of global economic integration are stimulating political and social disintegration.

Family ties are severed, established authority is undermined, and the bonds of local community are strained. Like cells, nations are multiplying by dividing....

...A huge and increasing proportion of human beings are not needed and will never be needed to make goods or to provide services because too many people in the world are too poor to buy them.[8]

Alan Durning takes the logic of these divisions between rich and poor and looks ahead. "Following a business-as-usual course into the future," he writes, "could doom half of humanity to absolute poverty by sometime between 2050 and 2075."[9] Durning defines absolute poverty as "the lack of sufficient income in cash or kind to meet the most basic biological needs for food, clothing, and shelter."[10] Ironically, the cost of a livable future may not be as high as some might think. The United Nations Children's Fund (UNICEF) stated in its report *The State of the World's Children 1993:*

Amid all the problems of a world bleeding from continuing wars and environmental wounds, it is nonetheless becoming clear that one of the greatest of all human aspirations is now within reach. Within a decade, it should be possible to bring to an end the age-old evils of child malnutrition, preventable disease, and widespread illiteracy.

As an indication of how close that goal might be, the financial cost can be put at about $25 billion a year. That is UNICEF's estimate of the extra resources required to put into practice today's low-cost strategies for protecting the world's children. Specifically, it is an estimate of the cost of controlling the major childhood diseases, halving the rate of child malnutrition, bringing clean water and safe sanitation to all communities, making family planning services universally available, and providing almost every child with at least a basic education.[11]

By way of comparison, this $25 billion price tag is $11 billion *less* than the $36 billion in new arms export deals signed by U.S. weapons manufacturers in 1993 following the Gulf War.

Our children are likely to ask us as we should ourselves: What kind of world can we expect if we cordon off the poor and fail to make needed investments in the world's children? It could well be the world of anarchy described by Robert Kaplan in chapter 1.

Crime and Punishment

Our impoverished social vision is equally evident (and equally disturbing) in our obsession with prisons as the solution to problems of crime. Citizens are concerned about crime. This legitimate issue, regrettably, has become both an object of media distortion and a political football. Politicians are tripping over each other trying to demonstrate who can be tougher on crime, by which they mean, who can fund the most prisons and mandate the longest sentences for criminals. But how many prisons can we build? How many prisoners are enough? Coleman McCarthy, in an article aptly titled "'War on Crime,' in Operation, Becomes War on Blacks and Poor," notes that the U.S. prison population has tripled since 1973.[12] We have already more prisoners per capita than any other nation and, sometime in the latter half of the next century, if recent increases in incarceration rates continue, half of the U.S. population will be locked up.[13]

Our children may ask us, and we should ask ourselves: What kind of nation and world will this be? By the year 2050 half the world's people could be living in absolute poverty while half our nation's people live in prisons!

If building more prisons and mandating stiffer sentences are effective crime fighters, then why does the problem of crime continue to plague our society? Why does Australia have four murders with violent hand guns in a year and the United States more than twenty thousand? Why is our risk of being robbed more than two hundred times greater than that of our Japanese counterparts? Why do we persist with the illusion that we can solve the crime problem by locking people up and putting more police on our streets?

Daniel D. Polsby writes:

The problem is not simply that criminals pay little attention to the punishments in the books. Nor is it even that they also know that for the majority of crimes, their chances of being arrested are small. The most important reason for criminal behavior is this: the income that offenders can earn in the world of crime, as compared with the world of work, all too often makes crime appear a better choice. Thus the crime bill,... which provides for more prisons and police officers, should be of only very limited help.... One more criminal locked up does not necessarily mean one less criminal on the street. The situation is very like one that conservationists and hunters have always understood. Populations of game animals readily recover from hunting seasons but not from loss of habitat. Mean streets, when there are few legitimate entry-level opportunities for young men, are a criminal habitat, so to speak, in the social ecology of modern American cities. Cull however much one will, the habitat will be reoccupied promptly after its previous occupant is sent away. So social science has found.[14]

Jonathan Kozol offers compelling testimony to the social roots of crime when he points out that nearly three-quarters of the inmates in New York State prisons come from the same seven neighborhoods in New York City. He also notes that in 1990 only 23,000 black men earned degrees from colleges and universities in the United States while that same year 2.3 million black men and black juveniles passed through the nation's jail and prison systems.[15]

So long as the most vulnerable people in our population are consigned to places that the rest of us will always shun and flee and view with fear, I am afraid that educational denial, medical and economic devastation, and aesthetic degradation will be virtually inevitable.... So long as there are ghetto neighborhoods and ghetto hospitals and ghetto schools, I am convinced there will be ghetto desperation, ghetto violence, and ghetto fear because a ghetto is itself an evil and unnatural construction.[16]

Attacking the social roots of poverty and crime would cost money, but so do traditional approaches. The National Council on Crime and Delinquency estimates the cost of federal and state spending to build and operate new prisons over the next ten years will reach $351 billion.[17] Citizens in the U.S. spend more than $5 billion yearly on home security systems, and the cost of prisons nationwide is nearly double expenditures for welfare.[18] A Minnesota state planning agency report, "Within Our Means: Tough Choices for Government Spending," estimates daily per-person costs for different forms of sentencing: prison, $72; local jail, $56; intensive supervision, $13; electronic monitoring, $8; standard probation, $3; and unsupervised probation, 67 cents. Social investments that help prevent crime may be the best investment of all. According to the report, "preventing only five individuals from committing crimes that would send them to prison for 30 years would save [the state] nearly $4 million in prison costs."[19] Commenting on the report, Leonard Inskip writes:

> Diverting nonviolent offenders to alternative programs would permit state prisons to focus on violent criminals. Savings could be directed to such prevention programs as intervention in abusive homes, help for unmarried teen mothers, early identification of children with anger and control problems.[20]

Except in cases of violent crimes, a more-prisons, longer-sentences approach to crime is both ineffective and costly. As Reverend Gregory J. Boyle writes, "The measure of success in any crime bill is the reduction of crime, not the proliferation of prisons. Jobs, education, opportunity, and attentive adults give an injection of hope to youth who have ceased to care. Hope is the only antidote there is to crime."[21]

As more prisons are built, as hope diminishes and crime escalates, our society may well move further in the direction of punitive approaches. A symbol of the mean-spirited if not downright stupid politics of the present moment is a Republican-sponsored bill to reform the 1994 Crime Law. Among its provisions are the banning of weight-lifting and removal of all exercise training equipment from federal prisons. Instead of infusing our streets with hope by investing in our communities, and in place of meaningful gun control, our leaders will instead restrict a prisoner's ability to exercise. This is the stuff out of which tragic comedies are born.

❖

There is a meanness in the land, and our children are victimized by the social policies it implies. This meanness is present in debates about crime, prisons, and punitive welfare reform, in immigration policies that attempt to build walls between the rich and the poor, in debates about family values that don't value families but that do scapegoat women, homosexuals, and people of color. It is present when we define people with problems as problem peoples, when architects of the global economy are indifferent to the poverty and environmental destruction they cause, when Nicaraguan elites ask aloud how to get rid of the poor, and when U.S. officials promote lower wages and military repression as keys to development.

It is ironic that political apartheid fell in South Africa at the same time a global apartheid economy became firmly entrenched. Economic, racial, and geographic divisions are pronounced. As economic divisions widen within and between nations, as racism festering within becomes an open sore, as suburbanization gives way to gated communities and decayed central cities, as prisons fill and social tensions mount, as global integration feeds local and regional insecurities, I wonder if we are close to embracing the option of "social cleansing" to defend a way of life many see slipping away.

Social cleansing refers to the murder of those in society who are defined as undesirable, including street children, the unemployed, vagrants, homosexuals, and prostitutes. It is especially common in Colombia and Brazil, where vigilante groups have close ties with state security forces. In response to a claim against the state seeking compensation for one such murder, Colombia's Ministry of Defense responded in a way that would make Rush Limbaugh, Charles Murray, and the authors of the Republicans' Contract with America proud: "There is no case for the payment of any compensation by the nation, particularly for an individual who was neither useful nor productive, either to society or to his family."[22] Perhaps the black-on-black violence in our nation's urban mean streets, the causes of which we seem to tolerate if not eagerly embrace, is a form of social cleansing already in place. There is little doubt that the mean-spirited assault against the poor throughout our society reflects deep hostility.

Those who think I am overstating the case of meanness in the land might wish to consider that in a nation of immigrant peoples, hostility toward immigrants is building. In the mid-term elections of November 1994, voters in California approved Proposition 187, which denies welfare services, nonemergency medical treatment, and public schooling to foreigners living in the state illegally. Republicans won stunning political victories throughout the country based in part on their Contract with America, which includes punitive provisions such as "The Taking Back Our Streets Act," which calls for "effective death penalty provisions and cuts in social spending from the crime bill of the Summer of 1994 to fund prison construction," and the "Personal Responsibility Act," which would "discourage illegitimacy and teen pregnancy by prohibiting welfare to minor mothers and denying increased AFDC for [mothers having] additional children while on welfare, cut spending for welfare programs and enact a tough two-years-and-out provision with work requirements to promote individual responsibility."[23]

Skeptics should ponder the words of television evangelist James Robison, who predicts that God will one day lift up a tyrannical leader to protect the American way of life. According to Robison, God will send us a tyrant in order to confront the "communist propaganda and infiltration" that are linked to "satanic forces" attacking the United States. "Let me tell you something about the character of God," Robison told a group of pastors at a training session on how to mobilize congregations for conservative political causes. "If necessary, God would raise up a tyrant, a man who might not have the best ethics, to protect the freedom interests of the ethical and the godly."[24] I know people in the religious right who are willing to sacrifice democracy in their efforts to end abortion.

The counterbalance to the meanness and the inevitable despair that it encourages is to elevate nonmarket values over those of the marketplace. Cornel West says:

There is no radical democratic tradition, there is no struggle against white supremacy, against male supremacy, against

vast economic inequality, against homophobia, against structures of domination as it affects disabled, without non-market
values: love, care, concern, service to others, community, justice, fidelity, trust, commitment... truth telling and promise
keeping.[25]

Chapter 22

Are You a Good Parent?

I can teach you things,
  but I cannot make you learn.
I can allow you freedom,
  but I. cannot be responsible for it.
I can offer you advice,
  but I cannot decide for you.
I can teach you to share,
  but I cannot make you unselfish.
I can advise you about the facts of life,
  but I cannot build your reputation.
I can tell you about drinks and drugs,
  but I cannot say "no" for you.
I can teach you about kindness,
  but I cannot make you gracious.
I can model values for you,
  but I cannot make you moral.
I can teach you self-respect,
  but I cannot make you honorable.
I can give you love,
  but I cannot make you beautiful inside.
I can give you life,
  but I cannot live it for you.

FROM A POSTER AT A SOUTH AFRICAN
COMMUNITY ACTION CENTER

Parenting relatively privileged children in a world marred by hunger, poverty, inequality,and war is filled with challenges and pitfalls. Sara and I are aware first of all that, like all children, our children have needs that in an ideal world would be met. They need a safe and secure environment within which to grow, including physical and emotional nurturing. They need to be held. They need clothing, shelter, health care, books, and nutritious food. They need schools that not only challenge them intellectually but that are safe, that allow them to develop social skills, and that help them to discover richness in diversity and learn to resolve conflicts peacefully. They need to be exposed to different cultures, perspectives, and ideas, and to have their own concerns be heard and respected.

Children need time and space to play. They need meaningful friendships and affirmation that makes self-respect and respect for others possible. They need time together with extended families, time within the immediate family unit, time alone, and one-on-one time with Mom and with Dad. They need time for silence or prayer and for cultivation of their seemingly innate awe for the majesty of trees, birds, and butterflies, and space to explore spiritual dimensions of their everyday lives. They need to feel valued for who they are and valuable to the family and community of which they are a part. They need to have limits set for them and with them and freedom, with reasonable consequences, to test them. They need safe places to ask disturbing questions and to feel loved, secure, and challenged.

I think children also benefit from seeing the humanity and fallibility of their parents. They need to see us showing affection to each other and to them. It is even healthy for our children to see us angry at injustice, even at each other, so long as we seek to resolve conflicts peacefully. This helps them understand our justified and unjustified anger as well as their own. Children need to see our tears and our laughter, our profound concerns, disappointments, fears, and hopes. And they, who experience our imperfections more directly than most, have a right to hear our apologies when we wrong them.

However reasonable this partial list of needs may be for children, it presents a daunting task for parents. We try to meet at least some of these needs by providing our children with a loving, safe, and secure home. We also believe the African proverb that says "it takes a community to raise a child." The Community of St. Martin, of which we are members, is important in our children's lives. Neighborhood-based, the community worships, plays, and acts together. Our children's lives are intertwined with other parents, children, and single adults who share similar concerns about parenting, peace, nonviolence, and economic justice.

A stable base provided in our home and within the community, we hope, makes it possible for our children and for us to learn about and respond to an unstable world. We want our children to experience our constant love, see us and others engaged in the world, and see themselves as capable people, valued in and of themselves and valuable to the broader community and world in which they live.

Life with children is a balancing act. Responding to our children's daily needs, the routine tasks of cooking, cleaning, and home maintenance, the regularity of necessary work, the inevitability of occasional illnesses, all place demands on our time and limited emotional reserves. Despite the advantages of co-parenting and relative economic security, we feel stretched much of the time. When our youngest daughter was about eighteen months old, she had pinworms. For nearly a week, she woke up in the middle of the night screaming, grabbing her crotch, inconsolable. By the time we found the tiny worms and got the medication we needed, the entire family was exhausted from sleep deprivation. The medicine quickly rid her body of pinworms, but the following night the stomach flu made its way through the household. Several weeks later the pinworms returned along with the exhaustion.

In times like these I find myself not only wondering how single or impoverished parents make it, but also understanding the tragedy of child abuse. And given pressures of time and money, it is understandable and yet lamentable that few parents have sufficient time or energy to involve themselves in their children's school or other community concerns, in politics, or in broader peace and justice issues. To concern oneself with poverty in one's community, U.S. foreign policy, the intricacies of "free trade" agreements, or the global environmental crisis is a luxury that many parents can't afford. However, to ignore these broader issues may be disastrous for our children and ourselves.

I confess that although I have devoted most of my work life over the past twenty years to wrestling with issues of hunger, poverty, and U.S. foreign policy, and although through teaching, writing, and public speaking I make a case that children's needs and environmental realities require fundamental shifts in personal, social, and economic priorities, my full commitment to addressing these concerns is compromised by the immediacy of daily tasks, including the daily responsibilities of parenting. It's as if my family is living in a house that seems reasonably safe but whose foundation is slowly being eaten away by termites. The termites are a concern to me, but the full damage of their appetite lies somewhere in the future. Naomi's pinworms demand and receive immediate attention.

Ironically, my children add dramatically to my concern about the world even as they divert some of my attention away from important issues outside the home. They inspire me and give me tangible reasons for wanting to work for greater justice. The immediacy of their needs and the intensity of their joy is an antidote to my temptation to despair over mean politics, the depleting ozone layer, and other larger issues.

I know that the tension between the immediate needs of children and broader needs of our world is a necessary one. Etched in my mind is a memory that illustrates how if we neglect our children while caring for the world, we are likely to lose our children along the way.

Many years ago, long before the birth of my children, I was working for Clergy and Laity Concerned (CALC), an organization based in New York City. Martin Luther King Jr. and Abraham Heschel were among its founders. CALC, through local branches around the country, played an important role in mobilizing religious opposition to the war in Vietnam. Among my co-workers at that time was a woman in her late fifties. She and her husband, who was a pastor, devoted their lives to ending U.S. involvement in that ill-fated war. They worked tirelessly for years. She often seemed sad and anxious. When I met her husband he seemed much the same.

I knew their commitment to peace had been costly. He paid a price for alienating conservative church members, and both he and his wife were arrested during nonviolent protests against the war.

I learned later that the source of their anxiety and pain was much deeper and the costs associated with their commitments more profound. They had two sons. As they labored to end U.S. involvement in Vietnam, one committed suicide. The other abused drugs to the point of doing permanent damage to his emotional health and mental capabilities. I didn't know this family well, but judging from the guilt they carried in their body language and on their faces, it seems likely that in an effort to end U.S. participation in an ugly war, these fine people failed to nurture their own children.

I saw similar tragedies unfold within the peace movement: many times leaders, usually men, saw relationships as unaffordable luxuries, distractions from the real struggles for justice. I was in some measure among them. Consumed by my commitment to justice, I was oblivious to the injustice of my own humorless obsession. I thought anyone who laughed didn't know what was going on in the world, and it was my mission to set them straight. Somewhere along the way I learned the painful lesson that it wasn't good for me, others, or the causes I cared about to make other people as miserable as I was. While some activists suggested that the key to ending the war was for more people to get arrested, a friend of mine offered a different critique. The problem, he said, was that he knew more people willing to risk arrest than were willing to talk to their neighbors.

I don't mean to downplay decisions to go to jail or the tension between pressing social issues and family responsibilities. Tension over the balance between personal and social duties or imperatives is unavoidable and in some ways unresolvable.

The work I did in Central America was always an emotionally wrenching experience. Seeing children victimized by war, walking through squatter settlements and listening to screaming children within small tin structures baking in the oppressive sun, talking with representatives of the "Mothers of the Disappeared," and meeting priests from the Catholic university in El Salvador who warned of the travesty of U.S. foreign policy and who would later be brutally murdered at the hands of U.S.–trained forces, challenged me deeply.

The "Mothers" in particular ripped open my heart. They organized together after consulting with Archbishop Oscar Romero, who suggested that the government's wave of terror against the civilian population would not be halted through personal grief but through collective action. Each woman had a graphic story to tell of a son or daughter taken by "death squads." These squads, made up of men from paramilitary and military groups, were aligned with the U.S.–trained security forces. At the hands of the death squads, the children of some of these women were "disappeared" and never seen again. Others were found dead, disfigured, and brutally tortured (they showed graphic pictures). Thousands of recently declassified State Department, Defense Department, and CIA documents confirm much of what the "Mothers" told me, as well as my own suspicions, including the charge of U.S. involvement and complicity with the death squads. According to an article in the *National Catholic Reporter*, the documents show "that the Reagan White House was fully aware of who ran, funded and protected the El Salvador death squads of the 1980s, and planned the 1980 death of San Salvador Archbishop Oscar Arnulfo Romero."[1]

This brief background provides a partial sense of my mental space when I landed in Texas from El Salvador and boarded a U.S. carrier for the final leg of the trip to Minneapolis. Coming home, always difficult, this time involved a great deal of soul searching. I felt challenged and exhausted. The stories of the "Mothers," as well as my time with numerous other people and groups in El Salvador, presented me with a dual challenge: work to change U.S. foreign policy and reassess personal priorities. On this particular occasion, however, I was emotionally overloaded. Unable to absorb one more gruesome story or sort through another aspect of U.S. foreign policy, I picked up the airline magazine from the pocket of the seat in front of me. Much to my surprise one of the articles grabbed my attention. I can't remember which carrier I was on or the exact title of the article, but it posed the question: Are you a good parent? This question is of keen interest to me, and one way or another I ask it of myself often.

Throughout years of living and working in Central America, I saw that people who understood their encounters in light of the love they felt for their own children had the most profound, life-changing experiences. To listen to the "Mothers" tell their stories may be of interest to many people. But hearing them while thinking of one's own children added a hundredfold to the impact. The love I feel for Hannah, Audrey, and Naomi, for example, became a lens through which I saw a Salvadoran mother's pain, felt her torment, understood her plea for me to do what I could to change the U.S. policies she held responsible for the ugly fate of her children and her country.

The question "Are you a good parent?," therefore, is one that takes on a certain urgency depending on the context in which it is asked. Should the stories of these mothers and their precious, tortured children influence how I parent? I believe the answer is yes, but the basic premise of the magazine article had a far different frame of reference. The article made it clear that I was a bad parent. If I were a good parent, it said, I would stash away $300 a month for each of my children from their first birthday onward. It was a simple definition. Simple, deficient, and troubling.

Sara and I set modest income goals, which keep our earnings below a federally taxable level. This particular income, neither rigid nor arbitrary, provides the parameters within which we live. It reflects the value we place on both time and money. Work provides us with sufficient financial resources to meet our family's needs, but by working less than full time we free precious hours that can be used in a variety of ways. More time can be spent with children, building community, or working for social change.

Our choices about work, income, and lifestyle are linked to issues beyond our stewardship of time. We believe the global environmental crisis is fueled by excessive lifestyles and consumption made possible by "excessive earnings," which are seductive.

The income goal we set is also a form of tax protest. When President Clinton warns that our children are less safe than children in any other advanced country, he should add that throughout Europe taxes provide a wide range of universally available benefits, including health care, whereas our regressive tax system encourages wasteful military spending and favors the richest of our citizens.

We understand that choosing an alternative lifestyle is a privilege. It doesn't mean being poor and isn't anything like it. If people hear that as a family we limit our income willingly, they sometimes think we are foolish or wonder about all the things we must be giving up. It doesn't feel as if we're sacrificing anything. Our lives are richer and fuller because of the choices we make in which our lifestyle is in some measure a reflection of our values, our vision, and our hope for the future. Our lifestyle choice is precisely that, a choice we are making. There is power in the choosing. For the most part choosing to live differently feels more like a gift than a sacrifice.

This doesn't mean there are no tensions. We believe that those of us with the power to choose should do so "wisely." But discerning what this means is sometimes agonizing. Once again we are wrestling with the issue of relative privilege. The way we have structured our lives and our priorities has given our children time with both Mom and Dad, adequate food, health care, clothing, a house to live in, and more. Isn't it reasonable to think that beyond what we are doing already for our children that the needs of children in El Salvador or Rwanda or inner-city Minneapolis or Chicago have greater claim on our resources? Should we use our time to bank resources so *our* kids can go to college? Or should we work less and use some of the time we have freed up to work for social changes in the hopes of building a society in which educating *all* our youth will be a national priority? On the other hand, given the political direction of the country and the difficulty of effecting social change, is it fair to our children that our choices mean they will be unable to attend the colleges we did, or perhaps any college at all? These are hard questions that defy easy answers.

We live in a world of massive inequality, hunger, poverty, and environmental decay. One of four of our nation's children is born into poverty. It seems important to draw a line, neither an arbitrary nor a fixed line, but a line that makes clear our responsibility to our children and that doesn't put their every desire or even their every need ahead of the needs of others.

We are searching for alternatives in which we neither sacrifice our children in our efforts to "save the world" nor isolate them from the world that we and they must live in responsibly and with hope. If we ignore our kids while attempting to "save the world," we may lose our children. If we focus solely on our children and ignore the world, we risk alienating our kids who, upon discovering the world outside their overprotected home, are likely to be resentful. As I was.

What are we going to tell our children when they discover that our present personal, social, and economic priorities have undermined their future and that of their children? Ignoring the world more or less guarantees that our children will face graver social problems than need be the case. To focus on our children apart from a profound concern for the health of our communities and our world is about as foolish as seeing air-conditioning as an appropriate solution to the problem of global warming. To focus solely on our children is like a father and daughter so absorbed by their game of chess around the dining room table that they fail to notice that the house is on fire.

It's also important not to build an artificial wedge between parental responsibilities and peacemaking. Changing diapers and reading books to children (sometimes the same book over and over) may seem like meaningless diversions to those of us who want to "save the world," but within them are contained seeds of the world's healing. As a father I am learning that to parent well involves cultivating our best impulses, including nurturing, compassion, selflessness, generosity, sharing, and humility. These are values our nonpeaceful world needs desperately, values I affirm and yet often fail to model fully in my own parenting and life.

The family is also a place where children and parents experience and practice democracy or dictatorship, where conflicts get resolved or fester, where power is abused or used respectfully. Even our failings, and there are many, can teach us the much-needed values of patience and forgiveness.

We want our children to see themselves as capable of shaping the world they live in. Involving our children in specific acts of caring is therefore important. From nightly "Penny and Ralph" stories, which cast our children as characters helping find solutions to "real problems," to "Lemonade Stands for Rwanda," we hope to teach our children that it is possible to live in the world without being overwhelmed by it. It is a lesson we also need to learn as parents.

❖

It is a warm July day, perfect for a cold glass of lemonade. Rwanda is in the news. Big time. Half a million Rwandans have died in several months of bloody civil war. Gruesome stories and pictures fill the front pages of local papers and occupy lead stories on the network news. Naomi, not yet two years old, has no sense of what is happening in Rwanda as she tries to pronounce the name of this faraway country. She is eager, however, to help with the "Lemonade for Rwanda" stand, which we and other friends from our faith community are setting up outside the local market.

Audrey, now four, and Hannah, who is six and an avid reader, understand more. We have shared our home with Central American refugees, and they know something about the tragedy of war. We also pray regularly for the poor and collect food that we donate to a local food shelf at various points throughout the year. A portion of our children's small allowance is designated for giving, and our family is part of both a local Lutheran church and an ecumenical faith community that demonstrate concern for the poor in a variety of ways. Our children also know that their parents' "work" is in some way connected to issues of peace and justice.

Today's lemonade stand is a success on many counts. Most people who pass by give more than the 25 cents we are requesting, and many give money and don't drink any lemonade at all. At day's end we are pleasantly surprised with the total: $132.12 to be sent to an agency working to help victims of war in Rwanda.

In addition to selling lemonade, we hand out literature about the Rwandan crisis to our customers, stating these basic themes:

In Rwanda, beginning in 1919 the white Belgian colonial bureaucracy distributed identity cards that arbitrarily classified some people as Hutu, others as Tutsi, based on physical appearances or their places in the social structure. They, and later the French, played Hutu and Tutsi peoples against each other in pursuit of their own colonial ambitions, setting the stage for the recent tragedy. Despite ample evidence of human-rights abuses, the Bush administration was eager to train Rwandan military leaders. So it turned a blind eye to earlier atrocities, telling members of Congress that "there is no evidence of any systematic human-rights abuses by the military or any other element of the government of Rwanda."[2] The civil war was triggered in April 1994 by the death of the Rwandan president, a Hutu, who was killed in a plane crash on his way home from a peace conference. Following his death armed Hutu forces began slaughtering Tutsi peoples as well as Hutu who had supported the peace process. Despite evidence of mass slaughter, the Clinton administration withdrew support for an international peacekeeping initiative in May, which prolonged the slaughter.[3]

This brief description of what lies behind the visible crisis in Rwanda is discouraging for sure, but more empowering than the common view that Rwanda represents another case of random violence. It helps our children and others see the war as a consequence of policies pursued in and since colonial times, including the policies of our own government.

Perhaps most important, through the lemonade stand our children take action for the benefit of others in need. They make a small difference in relation to a big problem, and throughout the day as people give quarters or dollars, sometimes without drinking lemonade, our children see that other people care, too. Injustice is part of life, from trashed tricycles to war. Bad things happen in the world, but our children have a basic sense of fairness that we hope to reinforce. They are learning that people who care are not alone, that we can do something, and that through our action we can help others express their concern as well.

Our children must see us caring for them and engaged in the world. Secure in the love we have as a family and rooted in our faith community, we hope to teach our children, and to learn ourselves, that the world is full of beauty and pain, how to live in it, and how to change it. In a nutshell our challenge as parents is that our children see us actively engaged for greater justice in the world while they experience their own household as essentially just. In this way our children learn that they are central to our lives, not the center of the universe, and that we and they together have a central role to play in making the world a better place.

Chapter 23

Toward a Better World for Children

My heart is moved by all I cannot save; so much has been destroyed.
I have to cast my lot with those who age after age, perversely with
no extraordinary power, reconstitute the world.
—ADRIENNE RICH

*The problems the United States should be addressing as we move
into the next century are widespread poverty amidst incredible affluence, massive hopelessness and alienation among those who feel
outside of the boundaries of the society, and a deeply felt despair
among the poor and the working class that is increasingly expressed
through violence. There is no question that the welfare system in
particular and the society in general have not addressed these issues and, in fact, have exacerbated them — not through generosity
but through miserliness, not through the coddling of recipients but
through their humiliation, not through making poor people dependent on a panoply of services but rather by not providing the
essential education, job training, child care, health care, and, perhaps most important, jobs by which families can support themselves
at a decent standard of living. The central problem American society
must deal with is not the character of poor women and the structure
of the welfare system; the central problem is poverty, the multiplic-
ity of ways that it is embedded in the structure of American society,
and the need to find real ways of altering that fundamental structure in order to truly help people move into mainstream society. We
must recognize that people are not poor due to character defects but
rather that the poverty that plagues so many Americans has been*

230

socially constructed and therefore must be dealt with by fundamental economic and social change.
— SOCIOLOGIST RUTH SIDEL, *Keeping Women and Children Last*

Mahatma Gandhi suggested that we should evaluate the merits of our actions and social policies based on their likely impact on the most vulnerable people in society. If we translate his counsel into today's world, then the focus of our concern should arguably be children. If we listen carefully, then the lives and needs of our children challenge both personal and social priorities. Here are some ways that we can (and, I believe, we must) respond:

Increase Funding for Programs That Work

Our children will be the first to tell us that problems in our families and our society will not be solved through increases in government spending alone. But they will defend the need for more money and make a case for how it can best be spent. They might wonder aloud, for example, about our failure to invest in programs that we know are working and that save money. The Supplemental Food Program for Women, Infants, and Children (WIC) improves the health of mothers and children and saves the federal treasury about $3 for every dollar spent (healthy mothers are more likely to give birth to healthy babies, thereby eliminating federal dollars spent for the care of premature, low-weight babies born to impoverished mothers). WIC reaches only 60 percent of those eligible. Similar benefits come from investments in Head Start, a program reaching only 25 percent of eligible youngsters. It could serve all who need it for an additional yearly investment of $1.2 billion dollars, money that would be available if we eliminated even one of the thirteen unneeded weapons systems cited earlier.[1] In the present political climate symbolized by the Contract with America, however, WIC remains underfunded, and programs like Head Start are being cut as military spending increases.

Support Organizations That Advocate for Children

For those of you who are concerned about the issues raised in this book, I encourage participation in the Families Against Violence Advocacy Network, and in groups like Bread for the World and the Children's Defense Fund that work within the legislative arena promoting programs that respond to children's needs.[2]

Bread for the World, in the context of the 1996 election and future elections, encourages candidates to make a "commitment to end childhood hunger." Voters are asked to consider a candidate's stance in relation to, and candidates are asked to affirm and recognize, the following facts or principles:

- "Childhood hunger in the United States is preventable and unacceptable."

- "More than one in four children under age twelve is hungry or at risk of hunger."

- "Good nutrition in childhood saves money by preventing nutrition-related medical, education, and future welfare costs."

- "The nation's nutrition programs, including the Special Supplemental Nutrition Program for Women, Infants and Children (WIC), school lunch and breakfast, summer and child care meals, and food stamps, have significantly improved children's nutrition, have bipartisan support, and will continue to undergo change to make them more effective."

- "Churches and charities...do not have the capacity to replace public programs."

- "The federal government has a legitimate and necessary role in setting nutrition standards and providing resources to assure that all children in the United States have access to a nutritionally adequate diet."

Replace Welfare with a National Family Policy

A child-friendly social agenda would include efforts to reform or replace the present welfare system with the specific goals of breaking the cycles of oppression and lifting families out of poverty. The United States needs what most other advanced industrial countries already have: a national family policy. Replacing welfare with a national family policy would involve:

- A national commitment to universal health care.

- Universal or sliding-scale-fee day-care options or public support for in-home care.

- Adequate funding for job training programs.

- Promotion of programs and policies to increase the cash income of families in order to insure adequate financial resources to meet essential needs. The minimum wage, by example, should be increased significantly. I would like to see the United States provide a family allowance to all families with children, regardless of income. This would be of great help to many families and would also be a powerful symbol that our nation values all of its children.

- The government serving as employer of last resort. If we value work, as I believe we should, and the economy isn't generating enough "living wage" jobs, then government must step in to provide decent-paying jobs that address pressing national problems.

In the present political climate a family allowance may be unrealistic. It should remain a future goal while we work to expand the Earned Income Credit, which supplements the incomes of the working poor. In a similar way, if we are unable to replace welfare, then it becomes important that we standardize welfare payments and eligibility requirements among the states. It should be possible to offer states flexible options in designing and implementing programs, but without federal standards, states are likely to compete with each other in a race to lowest-common-denominator programs in which both the poor and more progressive states are penalized.

It is essential that efforts to reform welfare be delinked from efforts to balance the budget because, as we have seen, present efforts seek to balance the budget on the backs of the poor. Breaking the cycles of poverty will cost money, but the benefits to families, children, and society would make it well worth the cost. There is much to be done, other countries do a better job than ours of achieving social equity. It is not so much a question of money — remember those unneeded weapons systems, tax breaks for the rich, high prison costs, and huge corporate advertising budgets — as it is a matter of priorities. In fact, if we got our values and our personal and social priorities straight I think it would be relatively easy to get our nation's financial house in order and provide benefits and opportunities to all of our citizens.

Penelope Leach suggests that "child-impact statements," similar to environmental-impact statements, "should be required with any planning or licensing application, any policy proposal, any new regulation or addition to case law. Children's interests," she notes, "would not always override other interests...but they should always be recognized, assessed and weighed with the rest."[3]

A national family policy like the one just described would help children and families. So too would better, more equitable opportunities for education. The U.S., as a consequence of poverty, family breakdown, and unequal funding for schools, ranks forty-ninth among all nations in terms of the proportion of its population that is literate.[4] Most state funding for education is dependent on local property taxes, which guarantees that students living in affluent school districts receive better educational opportunities than those living in poor ones. School funding should come from progressive income taxes on the general populace, not geographically based property taxes.

Parenting classes should become a mandatory feature of U.S. education, beginning in kindergarten and continuing through high school, and should be widely available to prospective parents. Elevating concerns about parenting to the classroom is likely to improve the well-being of children and to strengthen families far more than reestablishing orphanages (as the Republican's Contract with America advocates) or requiring parents to be licensed before bearing a child, advocated by a number of university professors as an appropriate response to neglected children.[5]

Bring Back the Progressive Income Tax

I believe it is essential to re-establish progressivity in the U.S. tax system. If as a society we are unwilling to establish a *maximum* wage to serve as a counterpart to a minimum wage, we can at least tax high incomes at a significantly higher rate. Progressive taxation was considered normal in our country from the 1930s until 1980. In 1964 there was a 91 percent tax rate on taxable income in excess of $400,000 a year.[6] Rich Americans who fleeced the country in the 1980s and continue doing so today should pay dramatically higher taxes, both to pay back the debt the nation incurred while lining their pockets and to support other socially vital programs such as universal health care, education, and expanded day-care options.

If I see a clear relationship between higher taxes and the well-being of children and society, then I for one am willing to pay more. If higher taxes result in adequate funding for WIC, make health care available to all, reduce crime and lead to safer neighborhoods, if taxes help bring an end to welfare, not punitively but by breaking the cycle of poverty, then taxes and government programs become investments instead of a burden. Federal and state programs should be funded sufficiently to insure that the basic needs of all citizens are met. This means universal access to quality health care and education as well as means-testing rather than automatic entitlements for many other programs.

Make Social Security Taxes and Benefits Reflect Income

One measure that could raise billions of dollars to improve the social welfare of children would require rich citizens to pay Social Security taxes on all of their income and subject benefit recipients to means-testing. The Social Security tax is now one of our most regressive taxes. In 1993 a median-income family earning $37,800 paid 7.65 percent of its income in Social Security taxes; a family earning $378,000 paid at a rate of 1.46 percent, and a rich family earning a hundred times the median family income, $3.78 million, paid Social Security taxes at the rate of one-tenth of 1 percent.[7] Collecting Social Security taxes on all income would create a sizable pool of funds that could be used to enhance the social welfare of our communities. Means-testing benefits would free up additional resources. One suggestion would be to eliminate Social Security payments to citizens earning $25,000 a year from other sources while targeting payments to others based on income so that Social Security payments would stop whenever the combined income from other sources and Social Security exceeded $30,000.

Revenues from Social Security taxes should be kept in a separate trust fund. This will prevent politicians from concealing the actual size of the budget deficit and help to safeguard the retirement income of workers. Surplus revenues from Social Security taxes should be invested in small and medium-sized companies that pay living wages and address pressing social needs. The goal of such investments should be to generate a reasonable return on investment while promoting businesses that create jobs, regenerate local economies, and develop and use environmentally appropriate technologies. In this way, social security funds can help renew our neighborhoods and our ecological and social environment.

Fund Public TV and Regulate Advertisers

We need to confront the destructive role television plays in the education of our children. Parents must monitor their children's viewing, but that isn't enough. Expanded public funding for appropriate children's programming and increased regulation of advertisers are urgently needed.

It is important to underscore that we could do everything described above and still fail our children. More social programs and better ones are necessary, but they are not enough. Children's needs are being denied and dismissed by poverty and the pursuit of affluence in the midst of the so-called culture of poverty and within a broader material culture that idolizes "success." In my view, children's needs aren't being met because current social arrangements and economic priorities make good choices difficult if not impossible for many parents, and because those of us with power to make good choices — those with a reasonably healthy base of economic and social security — often make poor ones.

Our children need our time as well as our money. They and we also need new definitions of life's meaning. We need to affirm non-market values and make commitments at all levels to change the direction of economics and society in order to end poverty and to establish socially and environmentally regenerative societies that move in the direction of sustainability for all peoples on earth.

Unmet children's needs and the environmental crisis have profound and common links to economic forces. It is not enough for companies to provide family-friendly work options for a shrinking pool of workers when at the same time they pursue policies and technologies that eliminate jobs, drive wages down, and harm the environment. At present any semblance of a progressive social vision is being crushed by economic policies that foster gross inequalities, threaten environmental catastrophe, and undermine democracy. It is ultimately self-defeating for the federal government to expand the Earned Income Credit (it is currently being cut) or offer a $500-per-child tax credit (which excludes many of our poorest families) while facilitating the interests of corporations who use their economic power and political influence in socially and environmentally destructive ways. The cumulative outcome of corporate priorities is to subvert authentic health-care reform, to block efforts to redesign production systems that could dramatically reduce the generation of hazardous and biologically useless waste, and to undermine the well-being of workers and communities through trade agreements such as GATT and NAFTA. David C. Korten writes:

No sane person seeks a world divided between billions of excluded people living in absolute deprivation and a tiny elite guarding their wealth and luxury behind fortress walls. No one rejoices at the prospect of life in a world of collapsing social and ecological systems. Yet we continue to place human civilization and even the survival of our species at risk mainly to allow a million or so people to accumulate money beyond any conceivable need.... We are now coming to see that economic globalization has come at a heavy price. In the name of modernity we are creating dysfunctional societies that are breeding pathological behavior — violence, extreme competitiveness, suicide, drug abuse, greed, and environmental degradation — at every hand. Such behavior is an inevitable consequence when a society fails to meet the needs of its members for social bonding, trust, affection, and a shared sacred meaning. The threefold crisis of deepening poverty, environmental destruction, and social disintegration is a manifestation of this dysfunction."[8]

Citing the imperatives of the global economy, U.S. businesses — along with their political allies and their international counterparts — are eroding the economic, ecological, and political foundations of life. These foundations are the basis of community, global peace, vigorous democracy, vibrant communities, sustainable economies, and, ultimately, of healthy families and children. *Their erosion casts doubt over the future and should be seen as a key parenting issue of the 1990s and beyond.* Perhaps hope resides in the fact that the powerful architects of the global economy have troubled children, too.

Nobody knows with precision what a "just and regenerative economy" will look like. What I can say with certainty is that environmental realities and growing inequalities will necessitate profound changes. We are on a pathway that leads to destruction and yet it is important to stress that disintegration and dysfunction are not inevitable. Certainly creative, community-based approaches to development that empower local residents and give them a concrete stake in their neighborhoods are vital. Local empowerment will be an important corrective to both distant bureaucracies and mammoth corporations. Reestablishing *national* control over a *domestic* economy will be an essential step back from current efforts toward globalization dominated by a small, international economic and political elite.

David C. Korten offers a number of helpful insights and clues about how to counter "the corrosive effects of globalization." He writes:

Market mechanisms are essential to modern societies. We must learn to use them in ways that recognize self-interest as an important and enduring human motivation and put it to work with maximum constructive benefit. At a minimum, this requires that business recognize and accept the need for effective action from agencies external to the market — usually government — to provide a context for the market.... It must also be accepted by both business and the public that when government intervenes to this end it may reduce corporate profits, limit the freedom of corporate action, and increase the prices of some consumer goods. The potential payoffs include good jobs that pay a living wage and protect the health and safety of workers and the community, a clean environment, economic stability, job security, and strong and secure families and communities.

There will also be cases of government inefficiency, just as there are cases of corporate inefficiency. It is appropriate to reduce the costs of such inefficiency both to taxpayers and to business.... To play its essential role in relation to the market, a government must have jurisdiction over the economy within the borders of its territory. It must be able to set the rules for the domestic economy without having to prove to foreign governments and corporations that such rules are not barriers to international trade and investment. A government must be able to assess taxes and regulate the affairs of corporations that conduct business within its jurisdiction without being subject to corporate threats to withhold critical technologies or transfer jobs to foreign facilities. For such jurisdiction to be maintained, economic boundaries must coincide with political boundaries. If not, government becomes impotent, and democracy becomes a hollow facade. When the economy is global and governments are national, global corporations and financial institutions function largely beyond reach of public accountability, governments become more vulnerable to inappropriate corporate influence, and citizenship is reduced to making consumer choices among the products corporations find it profitable to sell.

Domestic economies that favor locally owned businesses that serve community interests in ways that foreign producers and footloose investors cannot need not exclude imported goods and outside investors.... But the people and their government have both the right and the need to be in control of their own economic lives. And they have every moral right to build economic speed bumps on their borders to create advantage for local investment..... It is a much sounder framework than corporate libertarianism offers.[9]

We live in a country and a world in which divisions between rich and poor are becoming an unbreachable chasm and where middle-income Americans feel vulnerable and squeezed. Social programs can never fully compensate for personal neglect, and excellent parenting coupled with fine social programs cannot undo the fact that business, with our complicity, is destroying the world.

There is an eerie parallel between violence on the mean streets of our cities, which grows out of neglect and despair, and the pervasive violence of warfare, which percolates in environments where economic inequalities are as stark as the resulting social breakdown. We must choose, both at home and abroad, between responses that seek greater justice and those that seek foolishly to insulate a privileged minority from the poor. In the end, living in walled cities or "luxury hotels" guarded by nuclear missiles will prove not only morally repugnant but practically impossible.

Seymour Melman notes that the sum of United States military budgets from 1947 to 1991 exceeded the total value of U.S. industry and infrastructure. In other words, during "the Cold War the U.S. military used up more than enough resources to rebuild nearly all of its civilian asset base."[10] In the aftermath of the Cold War, dramatic reductions in military spending and new definitions of security are desperately needed. The combined military budgets of Russia,

China, Iraq, North Korea, Iran, Libya, and Cuba total approximately $90 billion, less than 35 percent of the 1994 U.S. military budget. U.S. taxpayers are spending approximately $140 billion yearly to "defend" Germany, Japan, and South Korea.[11]

Lawrence Korb, Assistant Secretary of Defense in the Reagan administration, writing in *Foreign Affairs* magazine in 1995 noted that a "few sensible cuts could save $40 billion a year" from inflated defense spending.[12] Randall Forsberg has detailed cooperative approaches to security that would have enabled the U.S. to make far deeper cuts in military spending, as much as an 80 percent reduction between 1992 and 2000.[13]

Forsberg's vision contrasts sharply with "the national security restoration act," named by Republicans in their Contract with America, which says: "No U.S. troops under U.N. command and restoration of the essential parts of our national security funding to strengthen our national defense and maintain our credibility worldwide."[14] As Lawrence Korb points out, under "the terms of the joint budget resolution Congress adopted in June [1995], between 1995 and 2002 domestic discretionary funding will fall from $248 billion to $218 billion while military expenditures will rise from $262 billion to $281 billion."[15] Our children's needs cry out for new priorities including a redirection of research and development funds *away* from the military *toward* technologies that both create jobs and move in the direction of renewable energy resources and regenerative economies.

As we approach a new century still strapped with the baggage of the old, it is increasingly clear that peace is essential to the well-being of children and that parenting is an essential aspect of peacemaking. The problems of our children are linked to the problem of war through distorted definitions of masculinity that are reinforced through TV and music, within families, on our mean streets, and in the foreign policies of the nation. The links in these chains are strong and will not be broken without dealing with violence as a men's issue, without modeling nonviolent behavior, without teaching conflict resolution in our homes and in our schools, without increasing the time that men spend nurturing children, and without new definitions of both masculinity and national security.

One of the most serious issues raised by our children may be that the reckless living of the affluent is at the expense of the unmet needs of today's children as well as the needs of future generations. Unless we alter in a radical manner our living styles, economic and technological priorities, methods of conflict resolution, and patterns of production and consumption, our children and grandchildren will be subjected to many unwanted bill collectors. A gross but accurate symbol of the global economy is that of low-wage Asian workers making toys for violent play for the U.S. marketplace, earning $5 a day, unable to afford the products they make, and unable to buy food without working overtime. As one worker making "power rangers" for U.S. children says of her assembly-line job: "It's too much, but I can do it if I don't stop. I cannot smile, I cannot talk, I cannot make a sound."[16]

Ironically, as U.S. corporations spend nearly $125 billion each year to fuel our consumer desires many people cannot afford basic necessities. Even more paradoxical, the more we consume things we don't need the more empty our lives become and the faster we accelerate depletion of the earth's resources and its ability to recycle our waste. Citing Harvard University economist Juliet Schor's book *The Overworked American,* Linda Starke of Worldwatch Institute writes:

> [Schor] points out that since mid-century, when given the choice, we have consistently opted for more money over more time for leisure and family. Yet has this made Americans any happier? Polls indicate the answer is no. We are trapped on a treadmill of more work, more consumer goods, and hence more destruction of the earth.[17]

If the world is our children's inheritance and that of future generations, then I consider it reasonable for children to expect parents to leave them with ozone sufficient to protect people and other living things; with a land, water, and resource base suitable for meaningful life; and with economic and social foundations for peace established in our local communities and in our world. Minimally, they must see us striving for such goals.

It is also important that we involve our children in these efforts. It is their world, too. We have created a mess for them and so must work hand in hand with them to heal our homes, our neighborhoods, and our world.

A few years ago I met Fernando Cardenal, a priest who had organized a successful literacy crusade in Nicaragua shortly after a popular rebellion led to the ouster of a U.S.–backed dictator. Cardenal, who at the time was Minister of Education, expressed concern that in revolutionary Nicaragua the youth were asked to do too much. It was young people who traveled to distant places to work side by side with *campesinos* by day and teach them to read at night. It was young men and women, boys and girls, who vaccinated poor children for the first time in the history of the country, eliminating polio in the process. It was young people who went to the coffee fields to help bring in the harvest on which foreign exchange earnings depended.

At the time we spoke, the U.S.–sponsored *contra* war was taking a toll on Nicaragua, and Cardenal knew that this too would affect the young as they were killed fighting and as the resources of a very poor country were stretched even thinner during wartime. Speaking to a delegation of U.S. citizens Cardenal said: "In my country we may ask too much of our young people. But in your country the problem is worse. You ask nothing of the young," he said. "You offer them no meaningful vision of life beyond themselves."

Earlier I wrote about an "assets" approach to community renewal that offered an important alternative to "needs-based" approaches. The idea was not to deny real problems but to recognize gifts and possibilities. In a similar way we need an "assets-based" approach to our children, whom we have allowed to become a source of our fears more than our hopes. We need to call forth the gifts of our children. In doing so we offer them and ourselves possibility for spiritual and social renewal.

❖

Children need our time, and enough material resources to meet essential needs. They need parents who are intimately involved in their care and they require evidence that society cares. They need social policies that strengthen families, neighborhoods, and society. They need encouragement to envision a future that offers more hope than violent neighborhoods or neighborhoods that are little more than places to sleep. They need visions more compelling than a society dominated by prisons and by market values, more encouraging than a world in which half of humanity lives in absolute poverty. They need visions that draw them into important tasks, including tasks that help to heal the wounds we have inflicted upon them. We must call forth the idealism of our young people in efforts to vaccinate children, improve literacy, heal the wounds of our cities, and move in the direction of social and environmental sustainability.

Chapter 24

Community

It has occurred to me throughout the course of this writing that children and families are in crisis because the many layers of community on which they depend have atrophied. In other words, troubled children and families both reflect and are consequences of an absence of community.

Children undoubtedly benefit from a nurturing parental presence. But healthy families and well-adjusted children are not the products of capable, committed parents alone. They depend on and are nurtured in the context of vital connections that bind families together with neighbors, neighborhood organizations, religious and civic groups, public institutions, and businesses. Relationships mold families and communities and hold them together. They form an intricate web woven from common threads that stretch from our homes and neighborhoods to political institutions and into the marketplace.

Relational threads, fragile and fraying, are under greater stress within an increasingly globalized economy. Our nation's democracy is in peril as powerful groups pursue narrow economic interests that fracture our common life. Multinational companies unofficially declare independence from any nation state, and most government officials are now beholden to these corporate interests rather than to common citizens. The content of democracy, therefore, is distorted and limited to consumer choices for the relatively affluent at the expense of meaningful participation in the body politic. Employers in search of lower taxes, higher profits, and lower wages for most of their workforce, play city against suburb, state against state, worker against worker, and U.S. "third world" constituencies against impoverished Mexican workers, who in turn must compete with their Chinese counterparts. Not surprisingly, as wages move in the direction of the lowest common denominator, as benefits and tax revenues decline, and as national income is further concentrated in the hands of those at the top, the quality of our community life deteriorates. In Brazil, during a period marked simultaneously by dramatic rises in both economic growth and poverty, it was said that Brazil was doing well but the people were not. The same is true for the United States. If we are to believe the stock market, where stock prices rise with each announcement of corporate layoffs, the country is doing well. The vast majority of citizens are not. And although many people lack basic necessities, the good life is defined as accumulating nonessentials, thereby eroding the self-esteem of the poor and undermining our relationships to one another and our fragile links to ecology.

The collective result of these trends is a huge emotional and spiritual vacuum created by the absence of community. When mega-farms produce the food that travels several thousand miles to our tables, when we purchase this food prepackaged at huge stores with distant corporate headquarters, when we prepare it in a hurry, when we eat it on the run rather than at table with family and friends, more than soil is eroded and more than nutrients are lost along the way. We lose a sense of connection to the earth and to one another. Rural communities fracture, profits from our food dollars are siphoned off, and our relationships to families and local businesses atrophy. When social inequalities widen and our neighborhoods fill with fear or become little more than places to sleep, then our neighborhoods are often marked more by anxiety than neighborliness or community. If the African proverb is correct that it takes a community to raise a child, then it is no wonder that the crisis of children and families in our society has closely paralleled this erosion of community.

The Worldwatch Institute reminds us that ecologically, despite illusions that are as strong as the walls enclosing the gated communities of the rich, we are one. The fate of the rich and the fate of the poor are linked together by the common environment we share, and the earth as we know it will not survive the present chasm that divides the prosperous from the destitute. We should not be surprised that the same holds true for our neighborhoods and our families. The "social ecology" of our families and our communities is healthy when wealth is shared and when basic material and emotional needs are met. In the absence of at least minimal justice our lives are distorted, our communities fractured, and our families stressed and vulnerable.

I have made the claim that many of our local, national, and international problems, including those that put serious strain on families, are consequences of the absence of community and further aggravated by it. This leads to an additional insight that has profoundly influenced my life choices. In order to live in the world I have been describing and to find the courage and strength to change it, *I need to be part of an intentional community.* Let me explain.

My concern about such issues as hunger, poverty, and the environment date back to the early 1970s. For ten or twelve years my response to various social problems consisted overwhelmingly of saying "NO." "NO" to the U.S. involvement in Indochina. "NO" to U.S. support for repressive governments in Central America, South Africa, and elsewhere. "NO" to tax breaks for the rich. "NO" to social cutbacks. "NO" to reckless military spending.

There are still many ills that require us to organize a deafening and compelling response: "NO." However, somewhere along the way, at a point that corresponds at least in part to my becoming a parent, I began to feel a need for greater balance in my life. I realized that in order to have sufficient energy or courage or conviction or hope to say "no" to the things that required such a response, I need to say "yes" to some things, too. During much of my "no-saying" time I was single or married without children, a student, transient or working on a national program. Somewhere, somehow, I realized that I need roots in my neighborhood and meaningful relationships in my home, on my street, and within my city. It is still imperative to say "no" to some things, but building positive alternatives is essential as well.

People, myself included, cannot maintain a sustained commitment to anything by drawing solely on reservoirs of fear or on concerns about negative political, economic, and social trends. We need the strength and hope that can be fed only by positive visions and hopeful actions. I for one want to live in a manner that embodies or anticipates, at least partially, the future I long for. Realizing that it is in relationship with others in a specific place that hope and faith and commitment are bolstered, I have actively sought to nurture a sense of community with others. More specifically, our family is part of an intentional ecumenical Christian faith community, the Community of St. Martin (CSM). I would like to share a little more about CSM, not because it is perfect (it isn't) or because it is a model that others should emulate (it may or may not be), but because it is so important to my life and to all that I have written here. Further, my experience as a parent raising children in an increasingly unjust world is that being part of an intentional community has many advantages.

In order to introduce you to CSM it is important to make a subtle yet crucial distinction between a more generic longing for community (a desire to be connected to others in meaningful ways), and *the formation of an intentional community* (a group of people who consciously join together sharing common visions and goals). I believe that in our society there is a deep longing for community, that is, a profound desire to be connected to others in meaningful ways. The experience of CSM suggests that *one way* of satisfying this longing for community is through participation in an intentional community. I hope that by learning about the Community of St. Martin you might be inspired to create or deepen community in your own life in ways that make sense to you.

Many of the issues and trends discussed here conspire against community. Time pressures, job losses, pervasive violence, racism, mean politics, crime, corporate downsizing, poverty, growing inequalities, and faulty definitions of the "good life" undermine relationships and tend to fracture neighborhoods and communities. It is not surprising, then, that many people feel disconnected, alone, and isolated, and many parents feel overwhelmed. Despite numerous obstacles, however, or perhaps because of them, the desire for community runs deep. Many of us, in our search for community (meaningful relationships), find at least partial satisfaction in our marriages, through our extended families, in book clubs, at church or synagogue, in bowling leagues, or through important ties to people at work. In some ways, the Community of St. Martin evolved after people tasted and liked the fruits of certain aspects of community— of meaningful connection to others — and wanted more. More community, some of us decided, could be experienced only with greater intentionality. It would be created, not found. Therefore, we choose to be part of the Community of St. Martin.

CSM, now ten years old, began when about a dozen or so people decided to leave their work at a retreat center in the mountains of Washington State to locate together in Minneapolis, Minnesota. (Sara and I, living in Central America at the time, were not among the community's founders.) Several historic Martins inspired the community's name, which expresses a commitment to nonviolence. Martin of Tours walked between two warring armies and prevented a battle; Martin Niemoeller resisted Nazi occupation through creative, nonviolent resistance; and Martin Luther King, building on the life of Jesus and the nonviolent practice of Gandhi, challenged a nation marred by racism and inequality. Nonviolence and other important values that have guided CSM from the very beginning are reflected in our vision statement:

> We strive to be an ecumenical Christian community. Rooted in Scripture, sharing worship and ministry, we affirm active nonviolence, love of justice and peace, and the integrity of God's creation. Acknowledging our complicity in the materialism and oppression of the dominant culture, we seek to practice loving hospitality and care-filled stewardship of God's gifts of ourselves, land, time and possessions. Through an ongoing process of action and reflection we seek to shape our lives according to our faith and the urgings of the Spirit. We commit ourselves to one another and to the way of Jesus Christ. Our community is open to all who share these values.

Our vision and goals may seem odd to some and exciting to others. To us they make sense, and the challenge is how to live them out. In a city, country, and world seething with violence, we are committed to nonviolence in our parenting, politics, and programs. In a city and world marred by inequality and war, we seek to be builders of peace and justice. We want to make our neighborhoods and our world better places for ourselves and others. We know that we are part of the problems that concern us, and we long to discover and participate in creative solutions. We want to live in opposition to destructive aspects of our society by living differently here and now. But how?

An essential insight is that we need each other. Alone we feel disconnected, overwhelmed, fragmented, and sometimes powerless. We choose to be part of an intentional community because we offer one another encouragement and because our collective vision and our united action make us stronger and more effective. We worship together on Sunday evenings so that those of us who belong to local churches can participate in them as well. Our worship is ecumenical, open, diverse, and powerful. Drawing on music and liturgies from around the world, we affirm essential links between faith and justice, peacemaking and worship, spiritual wholeness and social change.

CSM is open and invitational. We are reasonably diverse, young and old, single and married, with and without children, gay and straight. We make decisions by consensus. We have a leadership council that is self-selecting and changes each year. We have regular community forums for discussion of key issues and committees that take special responsibility for coordinating worship, education, and other ministries of the community. We try to nurture and build upon the unique gifts of each member.

For many of us, one of the great strengths of CSM is that many members live in the same neighborhood. Sara and I moved four miles to live near other community members because doing so offers many advantages. We don't travel long distances to see each other. Meals, child care, health emergencies, and other crises and celebrations are readily shared. Intimate friends are to be found across the street, next door, and down the block. In addition to arranged meetings, our lives intersect naturally during walks, at schools and markets, or while playing in the yard or at local parks. It should be obvious from even this brief description that being connected to CSM offers benefits to its members, about fifty adults and thirty-five children. Yet we are part of CSM for other reasons as well.

Although there is an inevitable if sometimes overstated tension between meeting internal community needs and responding to external problems, it is clear that most if not all CSM members want the community to be an instrument for making our neighborhoods and our world better places to live for others and not just for ourselves.

Some members serve as block club organizers and others on neighborhood development or revitalization committees. Many are involved in local schools. Our commitment to nonviolent parenting and peacemaking spills over into the neighborhood through Peace Village, a program for neighborhood children that addresses issues such as conflict resolution, media literacy, and the environment. A bookstore–restaurant, St. Martin's Table, serves nutritious vegetarian meals and specializes in books and resources on peacemaking. During the 1980s, CSM members worked hard to change U.S. foreign policy in Central America while opening our homes and providing emotional, legal, and financial support to refugees. Through a "teaching ministry" we offer classes to people throughout the Twin Cities on U.S. foreign policy, spiritual direction, children in poverty, the latest Jesus scholarship, feminist theology, and numerous other topics. We have tried and failed to create jobs through a small business in the city's poorest neighborhood. Undoubtedly we will attempt to learn from our mistakes and try similar ventures again.

There is an additional benefit of being part of CSM that is particularly important to me as a parent. The prospect of standing alone against the values of the dominant culture is about as good as the chance of a house with a weak foundation being unscathed after taking a direct hit by a tornado. It is important in our own household to teach our children nonviolent forms of conflict resolution, to explain environmental concerns and why our family doesn't go to the Mall of America, to counter homophobia and demonstrate respect for diversity, to condemn racism, and to teach reading and the value of books rather than flip on the television. In isolation, however, over time my kids are likely to conclude that their parents are weird if not demented. Although there are no guarantees, I believe that participation in an intentional community increases the likelihood that the values we cherish will take hold. CSM, in its common life, worship, and action and through the living examples of many individual members, models important values. Our children see, hear, and taste these values in weekly worship, children's education, common meals, daily living, and common action. As parents we feel less alone, and so do our children.

I worry about children, including my own of course, about the world in which they live and about the future they are likely to have. I've seen too much evidence to be optimistic for them or other children, but I continue to have hope. To abandon hope would lead me into an abyss I would rather not enter. I know that hope depends on honesty; that it manifests whenever we are willing to change course as individuals and societies. Hope balances urgency with humor, patience with activism, personal with social responsibility. My hope is modest. Sometimes it is little more than an act of faith. Always it is rooted in community and, more specifically, with those with whom I am intimately bound within the Community of St. Martin.

As I tuck my children into bed on this snowy Minnesota night, listening to their rhythmic breathing as they drift off to sleep, I remember that children too, mine and others, are a source of hope. I thank God for them and pray that as parents and as a society we will nurture them, love them, learn from them, and hold them tightly in our arms, caressing and healing our wounded world together.

Epilogue

Penny and Ralph

Penny the squirrel and Ralph the bird are sitting on a branch of a tree in our backyard, resting after a long day of hard work. The bright, sunny days of fall, which start out and end cool but grow warm throughout the day, are coming to an end as autumn drifts into winter. Penny and Ralph know that birds and squirrels often have trouble finding food during the months of snow and cold that are part of a typical Minnesota winter. They spent today, like many recent days, gathering acorns, worms, insects, sunflower seeds, and other foods.

Tomorrow they will carry most of the food up the tree and place it carefully in their nests. They will also bury some food at the base of the tree, a reserve supply in case it is an unusually difficult winter. Penny and Ralph have gathered enough food to make it through the winter, provided they are careful to eat what they need and not stuff themselves. And they have collected a little extra too in case a neighbor gets sick or some other need arises. Several older birds and squirrels live nearby, and Penny and Ralph know winter is especially difficult for them. A light rain is falling and has been for hours. Ralph shivers as a gust of wind pushes against his feathers. Leaves, brown and brittle, rustle in the wind like paper chimes. Ralph wonders how they stay attached to the twigs and branches. As the temperature falls rain drops turn into snowflakes, which dance through the air like graceful butterflies. One, two, three flakes, then dozens, then hundreds and thousands of butterfly snowflakes fill the air and then disappear with a quiet splat as they hit the ground.

Penny and Ralph have lived in our backyard for many years. They are each other's best friends and good friends of our family, too. Sitting together on a branch in the tree is one of their favorite things to do. Ralph loves to sing and Penny, who listens for hours, thumps her tail like a drum. Sometimes they play tag, chasing each other from branch to branch. Ralph can fly and seems to have the advantage, but Penny sometimes surprises him.

One time as Penny was about to tag Ralph, he flew to a safe spot several branches below. He seemed well out of Penny's reach when all of a sudden Penny pushed up her tail and leaped from the branch. She was a flying squirrel. When she landed next to Ralph he was so surprised that he fell out of the tree. Just before hitting the ground he stretched out his wings and glided gracefully up to Penny, where the two of them sat laughing until their sides hurt.

Tonight they are perched on the branch, looking at the first snowflakes they have seen since a late storm last spring. It seems magical as the snow begins to cover the grass like a beautiful white blanket.

"Isn't it wonderful?" Penny says.

Ralph nods. It isn't that he doesn't want to speak, but the grass all white and the sky dancing with snowflakes is so beautiful it leaves him speechless.

The beauty quickly gives way to concern. The wind is blowing stronger now, and the size and number of the snowflakes has increased so much that Ralph sees almost nothing beyond his own beak.

"Penny," Ralph says, wanting to be sure that she is still beside him.

"Yes," Penny answers.

"Are you scared? I mean...I'm a little scared. The snow is falling so fast that it's covering all the food we left by the tree," Ralph says. "If the snow melts in a couple of days, we'll be fine," he continues, "but if it doesn't, we'll be in trouble."

"I see what you mean," Penny says. Her voice is calm, but if you listen carefully you can tell she thinks Ralph is right to be concerned and that it is okay to be scared. "I'll climb down and carry the food up to you, and you can put it in our nests," she says.

With great effort Penny walks over snow-covered branches to the tree trunk and starts down. It is slippery, and Penny nearly falls. When she reaches the base of the tree she is surprised that the snow is already deep. She tries walking, but after a step or two she can't move. Penny sinks so far that she finds herself looking up at walls of snow, much as a toddler looks at the knees of a grown-up.

Now Penny is scared. The falling snow threatens to bury her. She tries digging down to the ground, but as much as she digs, she finds snow and more snow. The food is out of her reach. She tries retracing her steps, but the snow blocks her way and she can't reach the trunk of the tree. If she could only reach the trunk, she could sink her claws into the bark. She is a good climber and knows she could pull herself up to safety.

"Are you okay?" Ralph yells. But Penny can't hear him. The wind whistles through the branches and the snow muffles the sound. "Are you okay?" he yells again, even louder.

Penny still cannot hear the voice of her friend. Ralph is worried now. He flies down to the base of the tree and lands softly in the deep snow. Frantically, he flaps his wings back and forth, trying to clear the snow away from Penny enough to free her. At the same time, Penny places her legs close to her body and packs the snow firmly beneath her feet. She takes a deep breath and with every ounce of her strength leaps toward the tree trunk. Her front paw reaches the tree. It hits an icy spot and begins to slip, but as it slides it catches on a dry piece of bark as Penny grabs hold. She makes her way carefully up the tree. Ralph flies up and lands on a snow-covered branch. Penny scrambles over beside him.

They are tired and sad. All the food they have gathered — food not just for today and not just for themselves but for the many days of the coming winter and for other needy birds and squirrels — is buried hopelessly.

"The snow's too deep," Penny says, panting.

"What can we do now?" Ralph asks. His voice is sad, too.

Penny and Ralph sit in silence for a long time. The snow doesn't seem beautiful anymore, and the wind feels colder.

"I have an idea," Penny says.

Ralph looks up suddenly. "What?"

"Let's talk to Hannah and Audrey," Penny says. "Maybe they can help."

"Great idea," Ralph agrees.

Ralph flies past the kitchen around to the front of the house to a second-story window outside the girls' bedroom. Hannah and Audrey are getting ready for bed. They are excited about the season's first snowfall, looking forward to the morning when they can play outside. Ralph raps his beak sharply against the window. Hannah and Audrey look at each other.

"What's that?" Audrey asks.

"I don't know," Hannah says.

Ralph bangs on the window again. This time they follow the sound to the window. Hannah and Audrey run over, see Ralph, and open the window. Ralph explains how the snow has buried the food they have gathered. He and Penny need their help.

Hannah and Audrey and Ralph sit for a long time thinking.

"I have an idea," Hannah says. "Let's ask Mom and Dad to help us get shovels from the garage."

"Then we can dig through the snow and reach your food," Audrey adds.

For the next hour Hannah and Audrey work alongside Penny and Ralph shoveling snow. With the snow removed, Penny and Ralph reach the food and carry it quickly up to their nests.

"I'll be right back," Audrey says.

"Me too," Ralph says. He flies away quickly in the opposite direction but returns a few minutes later looking concerned. "I've talked with other squirrels and birds in the neighborhood, and they all have the same problem."

"Not to worry," Audrey responds, returning from the house. "I called the neighbors, and they'll be out digging soon."

"Thanks for your help," Penny says to the girls.

"Yeah, thanks," Ralph adds. "Without your help. . . . " The weight of how serious the problem could have been leaves Ralph groping for words.

"We were glad to help," Hannah says.

Audrey just smiles.

Notes

Chapter 1: A Loss of Innocence

1. Jack Nelson, *Hunger for Justice: The Politics of Food and Faith* (Maryknoll, N.Y.: Orbis Books, 1980), 102.
2. Janine Jackson and Jim Naureckas, "Crime Contradictions: U.S. News Illustrates Flaws in Crime Coverage," *Extra*, May–June 1994, 10–11.
3. Walter Wink, *Engaging the Powers* (Minneapolis: Fortress Press, 1992), 13.
4. Jackson and Naureckas, "Crime Contradictions," 10.
5. Ibid.
6. Tracy Chapman, in her song "Why?" from Elektra/Asylum Records.
7. Jim Dawson, "Youth Homicide Reaching Grim Highs," *Star Tribune*, February 18, 1995.
8. Ibid.
9. Ibid.
10. Mike Males, "Bashing Youth: Media Myths about Teenagers," *Extra*, March–April 1994, 9.
11. Robert Kaplan, "The Coming Anarchy," *Atlantic Monthly* February 1994. All references to Kaplan are from this article.
12. President Bill Clinton as cited by Joel Bleifuss, "The Death of Nations," *In These Times*, June 27, 1994.

Chapter 2: An Honest Assessment

1. "U.S. Adolescents at Risk, Report Says," *Star Tribune*, October 12, 1995.
2. *On the Way: From Kairos to Jubilee*, 6; available from PAX Christi, 348 E. 10th St., Erie, PA 16503, 814-453-4955.
3. *Star Tribune*, March 14, 1995.
4. David C. Korten, *When Corporations Rule the World* (West Hartford, Conn.: Kumarian Press, and San Francisco: Berret-Koehler Publishers, 1995), 1–2.

Chapter 3: A Trial by Children

1. Paul Miller, "Hunger in Montana — Research Findings and Future Actions," address at a conference entitled "Hunger and Homelessness: A Call to Action," Great Falls, Montana, October 12, 1994.

2. "Limbaugh vs. Reality," *Extra,* July–August 1994, 12.

3. Penelope Leach, *Children First: What Our Society Must Do — and Is Not Doing — for Our Children Today* (New York: Alfred A. Knopf, 1994), 178.

4. Holly Sklar, "Washington D.C. Divide and Conquer," *Z Magazine,* March 1992, 15; emphasis added.

5. "U.S. Schools Need $112 Billion in Major Repairs, Says the GAO," *Star Tribune,* February 2, 1995.

6. President Clinton's First Military Budget: Billions for Cold War Weapons," *The Defense Monitor* 22, no. 4 (1993): 1–2.

7. *Hunger 1994: Transforming the Politics of Hunger* (a publication of Bread for the World Institute, 1100 Wayne Avenue, Suite 1000, Silver Spring, MD 20910), 73.

Chapter 4: Relative Privileges

1. Don Terry, "In an 11-Year-Old's Funeral, a Grim Lesson, *New York Times,* August 8, 1994.

2. "Mike Males, "Bashing Youth: Media Myths about Teenagers," *Extra,* March–April 1994, 10.

3. Penelope Leach, *Children First: What Our Society Must Do — and Is Not Doing — for Our Children Today* (New York: Alfred A. Knopf, 1994), 187.

Chapter 5: Failing Children

1. Myriam Miedzian, *Boys Will Be Boys: Breaking the Link between Masculinity and Violence* (New York: Anchor Books, Doubleday, 1991), xxiv.

2. David Walsh, *Selling Out America's Children* (Minneapolis: Deaconess Press, 1994), 2–4.

3. "Drug Use in the U.S.," *Star Tribune,* September 13, 1995.

4. Sylvia Ann Hewlett, *When the Bough Breaks: The High Cost of Neglecting Our Children* (New York: Harper Perennial, 1991), 14.

5. "Who We Are and What We Stand For," Focus on the Family, Colorado Springs, CO 80995.

6. Walsh, *Selling Out America's Children,* 22.

7. Barbara Dafoe Whitehead, "Dan Quayle Was Right," *Atlantic Monthly,* April 1993; emphasis added.

8. Ibid, 55.

9. Ibid., 48; emphasis added.

10. Judith Stacey, "Dan Quayle's Revenge: The New Family Values Crusaders," *The Nation,* July 25–August 1, 1994, 120–21.

11. Ibid, 119.

12. Ibid.

13. Ibid., 120.

14. Ibid., 121–22.

15. Ibid., 119.

16. Penelope Leach, *Children First: What Our Society Must Do — and Is Not Doing — for Our Children Today* (New York: Alfred A. Knopf, 1994), 187–89.

Chapter 7: The Axman

1. Sylvia Ann Hewlett, *When the Bough Breaks: The High Cost of Neglecting Our Children* (New York: Harper Perennial, 1991), 97.

Chapter 8: Poverty-fed Prejudices

1. Norman Draper, "Twin Cities' Core Has Worst Poverty Rate for Minorities," *Star Tribune*, December 13, 1993.
2. "80s a Grim Decade for State's Minorities," *Star Tribune*, July 24, 1992.
3. "Conrad deFlebre, "Minnesota's Arrest, Incarceration Numbers Are Nation's Highest in Racial Disproportion," *Star Tribune*, October 18, 1995.

Chapter 9: Poor Perceptions

1. Jack Nelson-Pallmeyer, *War against the Poor: Low-Intensity Conflict and Christian Faith* (Maryknoll, N.Y.: Orbis Books, 1986), 15.
2. Conclusions of William Julius Wilson cited by David Moberg, "Can We Save the Inner City?" *In These Times*, February 7, 1994, 23.
3. Ibid.
4. William Julius Wilson, *The Truly Disadvantaged: The Inner City, the Underclass, and Public Policy* (Chicago: University of Chicago Press, 1987), 84–89.
5. Sylvia Ann Hewlett, *When the Bough Breaks: The High Cost of Neglecting Our Children* (New York: Harper Perennial, 1991), 53.
6. Ibid.
7. "Racism Resurgent: How Media Let *The Bell Curve*'s Pseudo-Science Define the Agenda on Race," *Extra* (January–February 1995), 15.
8. Jonathan Kozol, *Amazing Grace: The Lives of Children and the Conscience of a Nation* (New York: Crown Publishers, 1995), 156.
9. "Racism Resurgent," 14.
10. Kozol, *Amazing Grace*, 180–81.
11. Gregory J. Boyle, *Star Tribune*, January 12, 1995.

Chapter 10: Conflicting Perspectives

1. "Who We Are and What We Stand For," Focus on the Family, 4.
2. *The Twin Cities Funny Pages*, January 1995.
3. Barbara Dafoe Whitehead, "Dan Quayle Was Right," *Atlantic Monthly*, April 1993, 52, 55.
4. David Walsh, *Selling Out America's Children* (Minneapolis: Deaconess Press, 1994), 43.

5. Ibid., 14.
6. Ibid, 43–44.
7. Myriam Miedzian, *Boys Will Be Boys: Breaking the Link between Masculinity and Violence* (New York: Anchor Books, Doubleday, 1991), 176.
8. Ibid., 179.
9. *Citizen,* a publication of Focus on the Family, September 19, 1994, 3.
10. Sylvia Ann Hewlett, *When the Bough Breaks: The High Cost of Neglecting Our Children* (New York: Harper Perennial, 1991), 16.
11. Walsh, *Selling Out America's Children,* 39.
12. Hewlett, *When the Bough Breaks,* 154, and Walsh, *Selling Out America's Children,* 43.
13. Hewlett, *When the Bough Breaks,* 150–51.
14. Ibid., 152–53.
15. Miedzian, *Boys Will Be Boys,* xxvii.
16. Walsh, *Selling Out America's Children,* 42; emphasis added.

Chapter 11: Men and Violence

1. Myriam Miedzian, *Boys Will Be Boys: Breaking the Link between Masculinity and Violence* (New York: Anchor Books, Doubleday, 1991), 5.
2. *The Seville Statement on Violence: Preparing the Ground for the Constructing of Peace,* disseminated by decision of the General Conference of UNESCO, edited with commentary by David Adams (UNESCO, 1991), 20, 22, 24.
3. Ibid., 10.
4. Miedzian, *Boys Will Be Boys,* 10, 12, 74–75.
5. Ibid., 247.
6. Ibid., 56.
7. Ibid., 15.
8. "Who We Are and What We Stand For," Focus on the Family, 5–6.
9. Ibid., 6.
10. Mike Males, "Bashing Youth: Media Myths about Teenagers," *Extra,* March–April 1994, 9.
11. Dorothee Soelle as cited in Elizabeth A. Johnson, *She Who Is: The Mystery of God in Feminist Theological Discourse* (New York: Crossroad, 1993), 253.
12. R. W. Apple Jr., "War: Bush's Presidential Rite of Passage," *New York Times,* December 21, 1989.
13. Ed Magnunson, "Passing the Manhood Test," *Time,* January 8, 1990.
14. Photo caption, *St. Paul Pioneer Press,* January 5, 1995.
15. Miedzian, *Boys Will Be Boys,* 117–32.
16. Quoted from the Family Pledge of Nonviolence. For more information write or call: Families Against Violence Advocacy Network, c/o Parenting for Peace and Justice Network, 4144 Lindell Blvd., #408, St. Louis, MO 63108, 314-533-4445.

Chapter 12: Public Policy

1. Jason DeParle, "Daring Research or 'Social Science Pornography'?" *New York Times Magazine*, October 9, 1994, 50.
2. Ibid.
3. David Boaz, "The Right Ought to Focus on Families and Not on Gay Rights," *Star Tribune*, September 13, 1994.
4. Ibid.
5. Mel White, *Stranger at the Gate: To Be Gay and Christian in America* (New York: Simon & Schuster, 1994), 220, 224–25.
6. Ibid., 294.
7. Kevin Phillips, *The Politics of Rich and Poor* (New York: Random House, 1990), 8; emphasis added.
8. Paul Hawken, *The Ecology of Commerce* (New York: Harper Business, 1993), 17.
9. "Limbaugh vs. Reality," *Extra*, July–August 1994, 12.
10. Representative Martin Sabo, "America's Growing Income Gap Is a Problem That Citizens No Longer Can Ignore," *Star Tribune*, October 26, 1995.
11. Ibid., 82.
12. Jack Nelson-Pallmeyer, *Brave New World Order* (Maryknoll, N.Y.: Orbis Books, 1992), 21; italics added.
13. Sylvia Ann Hewlett, *When the Bough Breaks: The High Cost of Neglecting Our Children* (New York: Harper Perennial, 1991), 48–49.
14. Ibid., 44, 45, and 47.
15. *Star Tribune*, August 27, 1995.
16. Hewlett, *When the Bough Breaks*, 48.
17. Cited by John Canham-Clyne, "When 'Both Sides' Aren't Enough: The Restricted Debate over Health Care Reform," *Extra*, January–February, 1994, 9.
18. *Hunger 1994: Transforming the Politics of Hunger* (a publication of Bread for the World Institute, 1100 Wayne Avenue, Suite 1000, Silver Spring, MD 20910), 11.
19. Ibid., 69.
20. "Minnesota Children's Well-being Declines in All 87 Counties, Says Recent Study," *Metro Lutheran*, October 1994, 12.
21. *Hunger 1994: Transforming the Politics of Hunger*, 69–70.
22. Hewlett, *When the Bough Breaks*, 58, 61, 187.
23. *Winners and Losers: Federal Spending from 1982–86*, pamphlet, Jobs with Peace Campaign, 76 Summer Street, Boston, MA 02110.
24. Hewlett, *When the Bough Breaks*, 56 and 45.
25. Ibid., 92, 98, 138, 112.
26. Cited by Charles Derber, "The Politics of Triage: The Contract with America's Surplus Populations," *Tikkun* (May–June 1995), 41.
27. *New York Times*, February 13, 1994.
28. Richard Barnet in *The Global War against the Poor*, a pamphlet published by Servant Leadership Press, 1640 Columbia Road NW, Washington, DC 20009.
29. Derber, "The Politics of Triage," 43.
30. *Star Tribune*, October 29, 1995.
31. Ibid., October 26, 1995.

32. Ibid., February 2, 1995.
33. Ibid., January 19, 1995.
34. Jodeen Wink, "Low Wages Are a Big Reason That Workfare's Not Working," *Star Tribune,* January 31, 1995.
35. Paul Miller, "Hunger in Montana — Research Findings and Future Actions," address at a conference entitled "Hunger and Homelessness: A Call to Action," Great Falls, Montana, October 12, 1994.
36. *Star Tribune,* editorial, February 5, 1995.
37. "Working Families on the Edge," a report to constituents from Minnesota Congressman Martin Olav Sabo, April 1995.
38. *Star Tribune,* October 26, 1995.
39. Ibid., October 28, 1995.
40. Westminster Town Hall Forum, Minneapolis, October 13, 1994.
41. Hewlett, *When the Bough Breaks,* 73–74.

Chapter 13: Buckle Up, Bake Bread

1. Sylvia Ann Hewlett, *When The Bough Breaks: The High Cost of Neglecting Our Children* (New York: Harper Perennial, 1991), 153, 154.
2. Penelope Leach, *Children First: What Our Society Must Do — and Is Not Doing — for Our Children Today* (New York: Alfred A. Knopf, 1994), xiii.

Chapter 14: Where Personal and Social Responsibility Meet

1. Westminster Town Hall Forum, October 13, 1994.
2. David Walsh, *Selling Out America's Children* (Minneapolis: Deaconess Press, 1994), 52–53.
3. Ibid.
4. Ibid., 54.
5. Ibid., 55.
6. Westminster Town Hall Forum, October 13, 1994.
7. Walsh, *Selling Out America's Children,* 19.
8. Myriam Miedzian, "'You Can't Trust Men with Kids' and Other Objections Answered," *Boys Will Be Boys: Breaking the Link between Masculinity and Violence* (New York: Anchor Books, Doubleday, 1991), 103–14.
9. Jesse Jackson, "The Role of Men in Children's Lives," keynote address, "Family Reunion III" conference, Nashville, July 11, 1994.
10. Ibid.
11. Sylvia Ann Hewlett, *When the Bough Breaks: The High Cost of Neglecting Our Children* (New York: Harper Perennial, 1991), 32–33; emphasis in original.
12. *On the Way: From Kairos to Jubilee,* 6; emphasis added. Available from PAX Christi, 348 E. 10th St., Erie, PA 16503, 814-453-4955.

Chapter 15: Race, Poverty, and Politics

1. *Star Tribune*, February 18, 1995.
2. Richard I. Kirkland Jr., "Today's GOP: The Party's Over for Big Business," *Fortune*, February 6, 1995, 56.
3. Ibid., 7.
4. Ibid., 6.
5. Westminster Town Hall Forum, October 13, 1994.
6. Ibid.
7. Donald L. Barlett and James B. Steele, *America: Who Really Pays the Taxes* (New York: Simon & Schuster, 1994), 104.
8. Michael Lind, "To Have and Have Not," *Harper's Magazine*, June 1995, 44.
9. "Women of the World: A Snapshot of the U.N. World Conference on Women," *Star Tribune*, September 9, 1995.
10. Lind, "To Have and Have Not."
11. *In These Times*, April 3, 1995.
12. Cited by Wayne Washington, "In Fear of a Step Back for Civil Rights," *Star Tribune*, February 3, 1995.
13. Ibid., January 18, 1995.
14. Tom Teepen, "The Gap on Affirmative Action Could Ignite Racial Tensions," *Star Tribune*, March 4, 1995.

Chapter 16: The Politics of Poverty

1. Tom Teepen, "The Gap on Affirmative Action Could Ignite Racial Tensions," *Star Tribune*, March 4, 1995.
2. Thomas Byrne Edsall with Mary D. Edsall, *Chain Reaction* (New York: W. W. Norton & Company, 1991), 162.
3. Salim Muwakkil, "Beyond Tough Love," *In These Times*, January 9, 1995.
4. Jodeen Wink, "Low Wages Are a Big Reason That Workfare's Not Working," *Star Tribune*, January 31, 1995.
5. Michael Lind, "To Have and Have Not," *Harper's Magazine*, June 1995, 36.
6. "The Politics of Triage," *Tikkun*, May–June 1995.
7. Hobart Rowan, "The Budget: Fact and Fiction," *Washington Post National Weekly Edition*, January 16–22, 1995.
8. *Hunger 1995: Causes of Hunger* (a publication of Bread for the World Institute, 1100 Wayne Avenue, Suite 1000, Silver Spring, MD 20910), 23.
9. *Star Tribune*, editorial, February 5, 1995.
10. *Hunger 1995: Causes of Hunger*, 16.
11. *Business Week*, August 15, 1994, 79.
12. Mike Meyers, "For the Middle Class: Many Happy Returns," *Star Tribune*, January 23, 1995.
13. These figures were provided over the phone by the Children's Defense Fund, Washington, D.C.
14. Jean Hopfensperger, "Federal Assistance: Is Everyone on the Dole?" *Star Tribune*, August 27, 1995.

15. Peter Dreier and John Atlas, "Mansions on the Hill," *In These Times*, June 26, 1995, 20.

16. Sylvia Ann Hewlett, *When the Bough Breaks: The High Cost of Neglecting Our Children* (New York: Harper Perennial, 1991), 316; and Chuck Matthei, "A Community to Which We Belong," in *Who Is My Neighbor?* a study guide from the editors of *Sojourners* magazine, 72.

17. Hopfensperger, "Federal Assistance."

18. Myriam Miedzian, *Boys Will Be Boys: Breaking the Link between Masculinity and Violence* (New York: Anchor Books, Doubleday, 1991), 186, 237.

19. *Star Tribune*, March 16, 1995.

20. Ibid., March 29, 1995.

21. Ibid., January 19, 1995.

22. Steven Pearlstein and John M. Berry, "Faster, More Flexible Peso Rescue Still Aims to Protect Big U.S. Investors," *Star Tribune*, February 1, 1995.

23. Kirk Victor, "Takin' on the Bacon," *National Journal*, May 6, 1995.

24. Greg Gordon, "Tax Breaks for Wealthy Targeted," *Star Tribune*, February 16, 1995.

25. "Harper's Index," *Harper's Magazine*, August 1995, 13.

26. John T. Cook and J. Larry Brown, *Summary of Key Issues in the Welfare-Reform Debate: Facts Versus Fiction* (Medford, Mass.: Center on Hunger, Poverty and Nutrition Policy, Tufts University, 1994), 6.

27. Jim Wallis, *The Soul of Politics* (New York: New Press, and Maryknoll, N.Y.: Orbis Books, 1994), 22.

28. Donald M. Fraser, "Get Tough," *In These Times*, November 29, 1993.

29. Penelope Leach, *Children First: What Our Society Must Do — and Is Not Doing — for Our Children Today* (New York: Alfred A. Knopf, 1994), see esp. chaps. 6 and 7.

30. Ibid., 198.

31. Cook and Brown, *Summary of Key Issues in the Welfare-Reform Debate*, 6.

32. Cited in Edsall and Edsall, *Chain Reaction*, 236.

33. *USA Today*, November 14, 1994.

34. Cook and Brown, *Summary of Key Issues in the Welfare-Reform Debate*, 4.

35. Sidel, *Keeping Women and Children Last*, 133.

36. Cook and Brown, *Statement on Key Welfare Reform Issues: The Empirical Evidence*, 18.

37. Jacqueline Jones, "American Others," *In These Times*, February 7, 1994, 14.

38. Ibid., 14–16.

39. David C. Korten, *When Corporations Rule the World* (West Hartford, Conn.: Kumarian Press, and San Francisco: Berret-Koehler Publishers, 1995), 12.

40. "All Things Considered," National Public Radio, Wednesday, October 26, 1994.

41. Jeff Browne, "Distortions Feed Our Fears," *Milwaukee Journal*, October 23, 1994.

42. "Reported Crime Falls: Killing by Teens Is Up," *Star Tribune*, May 22, 1995.

43. Browne, "Distortions Feed Our Fears."

44. To find out more about this positive and compelling approach to community

renewal, write to the Center for Urban Affairs and Policy Research, 2040 Sheridan Road, Evanston, IL 60208. The center has a book describing its methods, *Building Communities from the Inside Out.*

45. Molly Ivans, "It's a Mean Nation That Hurts Those Who Are Weakest," *Star Tribune*, February 2, 1995.

46. Jones, "American Others," *In These Times*, 17.

47. Wallis, *The Soul of Politics*, 20–21.

Chapter 17: Market and Nonmarket Values

1. Richard Barnet in *The Global War against the Poor*, a pamphlet published by Servant Leadership Press, 1640 Columbia Road NW, Washington, DC 20009.

2. Cited in David Walsh, *Selling Out America's Children* (Minneapolis: Deaconess Press, 1994), 32.

3. Cited in Alan Durning, *How Much Is Enough?* (New York: W. W. Norton, 1992), 42.

4. Ibid., 43.

5. Ibid., 46.

6. Donald M. Fraser, "HUD's Role in Strengthening Families," November 1, 1994, 1–2. This paper was produced with assistance of the Housing and Urban Development Working Group on Families and Children.

7. Durning, *How Much Is Enough?*, 43.

Chapter 19: Interests

1. Cited in Michael T. Klare and Peter Kornbluh, eds., *Low-Intensity Warfare: Counterinsurgency, Proinsurgency, and Antiterrorism in the Eighties* (New York: Pantheon Books, 1988), 48.

2. The Center for Global Education is a program of Augsburg College in Minneapolis. The center offers semester programs for college students in Mexico, Central America, and Namibia. It also offers travel seminars, usually two weeks in length, to countries throughout the world. My wife and I co-directed the center's House of Studies in Nicaragua from 1984 to 1986. The center's experiential learning programs are among the best offered by any group in the United States.

3. Cited by Penny Lernoux, *People of God* (New York: Viking Press, 1989), 373–74.

4. For a detailed look into the strategy of warfare known as low-intensity conflict, see Jack Nelson-Pallmeyer, *War against the Poor: Low-Intensity Conflict and Christian Faith* (Maryknoll, N.Y.: Orbis Books, 1986).

Chapter 20: Values, Debt, and the Environment

1. Penelope Leach, *Children First: What Our Society Must Do — and Is Not Doing — for Our Children Today* (New York: Alfred A. Knopf, 1994), 4.

2. Richard Barnet in *The Global War against the Poor*, a pamphlet published by Servant Leadership Press, 1640 Columbia Road NW, Washington, DC 20009.
3. James G. Miles, *Five Trillion Dollars and Ever Deeper in Debt* (Carlton Press, 1994), 19.
4. Ibid., 35.
5. *Star Tribune*, January 11, 1995.
6. *Star Tribune*, October 25, 1995.
7. Michael Lind, "To Have and Have Not," *Harper's Magazine*, June 1995, 38.
8. *Star Tribune*, January 10, 1995.
9. David Broder, "GOP Economics at Odds with Family Values," *Des Moines Sunday Register*, September 24, 1995.
10. Bob Woodward, *The Agenda* (New York: Simon & Schuster, 1994), 91, 165.
11. Ricki Thompson, "A Consuming Wilderness," in *Who Is My Neighbor?* a study guide from the editors of *Sojourners* magazine, 60.
12. Ibid.
13. Lester Brown et al., *State of the World 1991* (New York: W. W. Norton, 1991), 171.
14. Ibid.
15. Sandra Postel, "Carrying Capacity: Earth's Bottom Line," in ibid., 4.
16. Hawken, *The Ecology of Commerce*, 6.
17. Ibid., 12.
18. Lester Brown et al., *State of the World 1994* (New York: W. W. Norton, 1994), 19.
19. Brown et al., *State of the World 1991*, 177.
20. Lester Brown et al., *State of the World 1990* (New York: W. W. Norton, 1990), 190.
21. Alan Durning, *How Much Is Enough?* (New York: W. W. Norton, 1992), 22.
22. Hawken, *The Ecology of Commerce*, 73.
23. Ibid., 60.
24. Wendell Berry cited in ibid., 14–15.
25. Durning, *How Much Is Enough?* 23.
26. Brown et al., *State of the World 1994*, 13.
27. Korten, *When Corporations Rule the World*, 18–19.
28. Brown et al., *State of the World 1990*, 16.
29. Hawken, *The Ecology of Commerce*, 161.
30. Korten, *When Corporations Rule the World*, 35–36.

Chapter 21: Values, Prisons, and Poverty

1. Paul Hawken, *The Ecology of Commerce* (New York: Harper Business, 1993), 58.
2. Jack Nelson-Pallmeyer, *Brave New World Order* (Maryknoll, N.Y.: Orbis Books, 1992), 1–17.
3. Pablo Richard, "The 1990s: A Hope for the Third World," in *Total War against the Poor* (New York: New York Circus Publications, 1990), 201.
4. Briefings of this kind were off the record. Therefore I withhold the name of this high-level official.

5. Richard Barnet and John Cavanagh, *Global Dreams: Imperial Corporations and the New World Order* (New York: Simon & Schuster, 1994), 17.

6. Xabier Gorostiaga, "World Has Become a 'Champagne Glass,'" *National Catholic Reporter,* January 27, 1995.

7. Ibid.

8. Ibid., 13.

9. Alan B. Durning, "Ending Poverty," in Lester Brown et al., *State of the World 1990* (New York: W. W. Norton, 1990), 148.

10. Ibid., 136.

11. United Nations Children's Fund (UNICEF), *The State of the World's Children 1993,* 1.

12. Coleman McCarthy, "'War on Crime,' in Operation, Becomes War on Blacks and Poor," *Star Tribune,* February 8, 1994.

13. Bill Nelson, director of Prison Release Programs for the Volunteers of America, in a talk at Holy Trinity Lutheran Church, Minneapolis, March 17, 1991.

14. Daniel D. Polsby, "The False Promise of Gun Control," *Atlantic Monthly,* March 1994, 69.

15. Jonathan Kozol, *Amazing Grace: The Lives of Children and the Conscience of a Nation* (New York: Crown Publishers, 1995), 143.

16. Ibid., 162.

17. Stephen Hartnett, "Cell Block Grants," *In These Times,* April 17, 1995.

18. Sylvia Ann Hewlett, *When the Bough Breaks: The High Cost of Neglecting Our Children* (New York: Harper Perennial, 1991), 337, 339.

19. *Within Our Means: Tough Choices for Government Spending,* from Minnesota Planning, January 1995, 22–23.

20. Leonard Inskip, "State Looks for Ways to Balance Punishment, Prevention," *Star Tribune,* January 30, 1995.

21. *Star Tribune,* January 12, 1995.

22. Noam Chomsky, "Democracy Enhancement I," *Z Magazine,* May 1994.

23. "Contract with America," *Star Tribune,* November 9, 1994.

24. *Bill Moyers' Journal: Campaign Report #3* (1983), 7. This is a transcript of a documentary aired on WNET by the Educational Broadcasting Corporation.

25. Cornel West, lecture presented at the Westminster Town Hall Forum, Minneapolis, October 13, 1994.

Chapter 22: Are You a Good Parent?

1. Arthur Jones, "Haiti, Salvador Links Viewed," *National Catholic Reporter,* November 19, 1993.

2. *National Catholic Reporter,* July 1, 1994.

3. Ibid.

Chapter 23: Toward a Better World for Children

1. Sylvia Ann Hewlett, *When the Bough Breaks: The High Cost of Neglecting Our Children* (New York: Harper Perennial, 1991), 61, 313.
2. For information on membership and policy options contact Families Against Violence Advocacy Network, c/o Parenting for Peace and Justice Network, 4144 Lindell Blvd., # 408, St. Louis, MO 63108; Bread for the World, 1100 Wayne Avenue, Suite 1000, Silver Spring, MD 20910; and Children's Defense Fund, 25 E Street NW, Washington, DC 20001.
3. Penelope Leach, *Children First: What Our Society Must Do — and Is Not Doing — for Our Children Today* (New York: Alfred A. Knopf, 1994), 194.
4. Ibid., 83.
5. Kurt Chandler, "Should Being a Parent Require a License?" *Star Tribune,* December 17, 1994.
6. Donald L. Barlett and James B. Steele, *America: Who Really Pays the Taxes?* (New York: Simon & Schuster, 1994), 72.
7. Ibid., 104.
8. David C. Korten, *When Corporations Rule the World* (West Hartford, Conn.: Kumarian Press, and San Francisco: Berret-Koehler Publishers, 1995), 261–62.
9. Ibid., 91–92.
10. "The U.S.–Russian Conversion Crisis," *In These Times,* July 11, 1994.
11. *Star Tribune,* February 12, 1994.
12. Excerpts from Lawrence Korb's article appeared in the *Star Tribune,* November 6, 1995.
13. Randall Forsberg, "Defense Cuts and Cooperative Security in the Post–Cold War World," *Boston Review* 17, nos. 3–4 (May–July 1992), 5.
14. "Contract with America," *Star Tribune,* November 9, 1994.
15. *Star Tribune,* November 6, 1995.
16. "Asians Rushing to Make Enough Power Rangers for U.S. Children," *Star Tribune,* December 17, 1994.
17. Cited in Alan Durning, *How Much Is Enough?* (New York: W. W. Norton, 1992), 12.

Index

269